AMONG WOMEN

Among Women

Louise Bernikow

HARPER COLOPHON BOOKS
Harper & Row, Publishers
New York, Cambridge, Hagerstown, Philadelphia, San Francisco
London, Mexico City, São Paulo, Sydney

Grateful acknowledgment is made for permission to quote from the following sources:

Selections from "Camp Cataract," by Jane Bowles. In *The Collected Works of Jane Bowles*, Copyright, 1949 by Jane Bowles, renewed © 1976 by Paul Bowles, reprinted by permission of Farrar, Straus and Giroux, Inc., New York. In *Plain Pleasures*, Copyright © 1966, reprinted by permission of Peter Owen Ltd., London.

Selections from *Earthly Paradise: An Autobiography of Colette Drawn from Her Lifetime Writings*, by Robert Phelps. Translated by Herma Briffault, Derek Coltman, and others. Copyright © 1966 by Farrar, Straus and Giroux, Inc. Reprinted by permission of Farrar, Straus and Giroux, Inc., New York.

Selections from *The Other One*, by Colette. Translated by Elizabeth Tait and Roger Senhouse. Copyright © 1960 by Martin Secker & Warburg Ltd. Reprinted by permission of Farrar, Straus and Giroux, Inc., New York, and Martin Secker & Warburg Ltd., London.

Selections from "Cora Unashamed," in *The Ways of White Folks*, by Langston Hughes. Copyright, 1934. Reprinted by permission of Alfred A. Knopf, Inc., New York.

Selections from *The Bluest Eye*, by Toni Morrison. Copyright © 1970. Reprinted by permission of Holt, Rinehart & Winston, New York.

Selections from *Sula*, by Toni Morrison. Copyright © 1973. Reprinted by permission of Alfred A. Knopf, Inc., New York.

Selections from *The Street*, by Ann Petry. Copyright © 1964. Reprinted by permission of Houghton Mifflin Company, Boston.

Selections from *Letters Home*, by Sylvia Plath. Copyright © 1975. Reprinted by permission of Harper & Row, Publishers, Inc., New York.

Selections from the works of Virginia Woolf: *The Death of the Moth and Other Essays*, Copyright, 1942; *A Haunted House and Other Stories*, Copyright, 1944; *Mrs. Dalloway*, Copyright, 1949; *Orlando*, Copyright, 1928; *A Room of One's Own*, Copyright, 1929; *Three Guineas*, Copyright © 1963; *To the Lighthouse*, Copyright, 1949; *The Diary of Virginia Woolf*, edited by Anne Olivier Bell, Copyright © 1977, 1978; *The Letters of Virginia Woolf*, edited by Nigel Nicolson and Joanne Trautmann, Copyright © 1975, 1976, 1979. Reprinted by permission of Harcourt Brace Jovanovich, New York, The Author's Literary Estate and The Hogarth Press Ltd., London.

Selections from *Moments of Being*, by Virginia Woolf. Copyright © 1976. Reprinted by permission of Harcourt Brace Jovanovich, New York, and Sussex University Press, East Sussex, England.

First HARPER COLOPHON edition published 1981.

ISBN: 0-06-090878-5

82 83 84 85 10 9 8 7 6 5 4 3

In memory of Muriel Rukeyser
and for Ilyse, the future

ACKNOWLEDGMENTS

Hopefully, the text of this book evokes the people and the kind of aid generally described by a writer on the "acknowledgments page." My intellectual debts are set down in the bibliographical section at the end of the book. I would only like to underscore here my pleasure in having, as friends and colleagues, Nancy Evans, Honor Moore, Inez Martinez and Ellen McManus, who were able to provide the intellectual and emotional support so crucial to the enterprise at hand and so well articulated by Gertude Stein when she described how, at some point in the work, someone says "yes" to it. I feel fortunate in having had various kinds of "yes" served up with intelligence, sensitivity and generosity by the people involved in the publishing life of this book—Bruce Harris, Manuela Soares and Wendy Weil.

CONTENTS

Introduction

TWO WOMEN ARE ALONE
IN A ROOM

I was sitting at a table on a cloudy day. The table was stacked with books—biographies, diaries, letters, novels, Shakespeare's plays, studies of fairy tales. My mind was running along a certain track, thinking about the books, what was in them, and the life around me, what was in it, simultaneously. I had copied, from *A Room Of One's Own* by Virginia Woolf, the following passage:

> "Chloe liked Olivia," I read. And then it struck me how immense a change was there. Chloe liked Olivia perhaps for the first time in literature. Cleopatra did not like Octavia. And how completely Antony and Cleopatra would have been altered had she done so.... All these relationships between women, I thought, rapidly, are too simple. So much had been left out, unattempted...

and tacked it to the wall above the table as a signpost on the road of my investigation.

I read the rest of the passage, where Woolf observes that women in fiction were, for a long time, "not only seen by the other sex, but seen only in relation to the other sex." To indicate how preposterous this is, she asks the reader to imagine what literature would be like if men were "the lovers of women and were never the friends of men, soldiers, thinkers, dreamers."

I tried to imagine. Nothing came to me, because the literature called to mind, from the most remembered myths to the most current popular culture, was full of the passions and permutations of relations among men: Cain and Abel. Butch Cassidy and the Sundance Kid. The Knights of the Round Table. The Prince and the Pauper. Tom Buchanan and Jay Gatsby. King Henry and Thomas a Becket. God the Father and Adam. Karenin and Vronsky. Batman and Robin.

These are the stories we grew up on. As a result, I thought, following Woolf's implications, when a woman walks out of a room leaving two men behind, she has a good idea of what might happen between them. She can imagine them hunting together, strolling the streets of the world's capitals and shantytowns, boxing, playing baseball or poker, having a meeting, fighting a war, discussing women or praying to God. A man walks out of a room, leaving two women behind. The images on this score, as Woolf said, are simple. The women will argue. Or nothing will happen.

I considered what actually happens in women's lives, in my life and the diminished reflection of that in literature. I considered myself among women: mother, grandmother, aunt, sister-in-law, colleagues, friends, enemies. There were many stories to be told there, much to be understood. I turned to the books on the table, looking for what had been said about such relationships, wondering about what had not been said and why not.

The wind came humid off the water; downstairs in the house, my friend Sharon was at work with the man she lives with. It was his house. From time to time, I wandered to the kitchen, drank coffee, and met Sharon. Together, we spoke a language that was, in tone and content, structure and style, different from the way either of us spoke with men or the way men, we thought, spoke with each other, different in ways that went beyond the length of our friendship. The talk was intimate and nonlinear, moving from books to people, literature to life, nixing domestic with philosophic quickly, with few bridges. There was an interplay of mothering behavior—Do you need more of this or that? Is it going well for you today?—a certain solicitude, and a hint of reassurance. We were personal. And physical—one commented on a shirt, the other said something about a hairstyle. Colette observed that women insist on telling one another about their lovers, their monthly periods and their illnesses. The talk of myself and my friend bore out what Colette said, but was also laced with literature and with thought. Still, it was familiar to us, startling to others in its physicality. Female physical talk like that is often, sub rosa, about survival. Much female conversation is, in fact, about survival—but in code.

The man Sharon lives with entered the room and the tone changed. We spoke of other things. Another language shaped in each throat. We were then three friends together, but the light was different. Then each went back to work.

In a biography of the Russian poet Anna Akhmatova, I came across a description of the meeting between Akhmatova and Russia's other major woman poet, Marina Tsvetaeva. There was something peculiar in the description:

> Tsvetaeva had dedicated poems to Akhmatova years before and the two had corresponded but never met. Victor Ardov recalls letting Tsvetaeva in. He did not have to introduce his guests. They met without the usual politenesses, simply pressing each other's hands. The two poets went into the tiny room where Akhmatova usually stayed when visiting the Ardovs and remained there alone together the best part of the day. Akhmatova never spoke of what they discussed.

The peculiar thing was, I thought, the silence. Not a word about what happened. The story seems to take place on a stage and behind a screen, where shadows gesture, figures lean toward and away from one another, voices rise and fall, but all of it is far away and impenetrable. Neither literature nor history nor biography offers, with any substance or until our time, a record that includes a woman in a house on a cloudy day talking with her friend or a meeting between two major women writers.

"I have heard the mermaids singing each to each," says Prufrock, "I do not think that they will sing to me."

Perhaps Prufrock is the problem. If he cannot hear what the mermaids say or if they do not in fact sing to him, he cannot tell us. In the same way, Nick Carraway, the narrator in *The Great Gatsby,* can observe women talking with one another but offer no report on what they say because he is not part of the conversation. The absence of female intimacy in literature is, partially, the result of the masculine point of view. Many of our stories are told by narrators who have no part in the conversation.

Most female people in masculine literature drift about in the cosmic air, unconnected to anyone, as though they have sprung full blown from the head of Zeus. When connected, the threads go from the woman to a man or to men, as though male people are the sole anchors for gossamer women, as though without heart and mind fixed on father, brother, husband, lover, the woman would become a helium balloon. There was one Eve in the garden with two men. A Madonna with a boy-child. Snow White and Seven Dwarfs.

When women connect with other women, the interaction is hostile. Classical goddesses, the ones whose stories we still know, owe their beginnings to men and act, generally, on behalf of men and against other women. Athena sends Medusa into exile. Odysseus can rely on Athena, but his patiently waiting wife, Penelope, cannot. Artemis keeps the Greek fleet from sailing to Troy until a maiden has been sacrificed to her.

The "business" of engaging or disengaging a man is the woman's purpose in literature. I began to reread the fairy tales of my childhood, noticing that in those stories, the "quest" for females is seduction of the Prince, a task in which the female, usually a young girl, is obstructed by other women. This quest is what female characters have in common. It is the basis of their understanding of each other, their mutual recognition, but not their common enterprise. What they have in common is what keeps them apart.

Men and boys perform great feats while women and girls primp. Whether a female is "pretty" or not is crucial to the story, determining her success or failure at winning the Prince and determining what other women will think and feel about her. In fairy tales and then in more "sophisticated" fiction, being pretty is an aspect of character *and* an activity. Getting your hair right is the female equivalent of slaying the dragon. The distance from a thick waist to a thin one equals all the terrain trodden by knights and heroes in search of whatever they search for. What is possible among women in this kind of world-view revolves around dresses and tresses, how "pretty" one or the other can make herself. The mirror is the primal focus of a woman's relation to herself and to other women.

D. H. Lawrence takes the masculine attitude a step further. What is necessary to life, for Lawrence, is the blood connection between man and man and between woman and man. A connection between women becomes, in his fiction, something poisoned, sick and sullied. At the end of *Lady Chatterley's Lover,* Lawrence describes Connie's relief at having found her Prince and being "free of the dominion of other women":

> Ah! that in itself was a relief, like being given another
> life: to be free of the strange domination and obsession
> of other women. How awful they were, women.

Women appear, at first, to be awful to other women in actual life as well as literature. I turned to biography, to the record of the lives women have lived and I saw that, again, the fragments of information we possess have, until recently, filtered through an interpreting sieve that looks only to male connection. We know Emily Dickinson in relation to Higginson and Colette in relation to Willy and Virginia Woolf in relation to Leonard. Elizabeth Browning and Robert. George Sand and Chopin. Margaret Fuller and Emerson. Edith Wharton and Henry James. We are made aware of Dorothy Wordworth's devotion to her brother William, and of Mary Lamb's to Charles, but what of Dorothy and Mary in relation to each other? We know, interminably, what the men in Bloomsbury said to one another, even what they said to Virginia Woolf and she to them, but what transpired among the women?

I sat there at my table contemplating the blankness. My mind shifted. I was contemplating something as simple as the week that had just passed in my life. Against the blankness, I set:

The good times I have with my friends. Walking to Soho in the rain with June. Barbara painting. Electa composing footnotes in the proper form. Rollicking around town with Blanche, sitting stoned at a Patti Smith concert drinking champagne. Muriel being interviewed. Honor traveling to California for a production of her play. Stephanie in London writing a letter about royalties. The good times I have, but also the dimensions into which these good times reach. I ride with Priscilla in a car discussing female psychological development and then go shopping for silk shirts. I have a lesson in deference from a young woman, a student of mine, who allows me to win effortlessly on the tennis court.

I thought about our common intellectual life. How something Joan said about courtly love triggered a strain of thoughts in me. I remembered how Victoria, about to direct a theatrical evening based on Colette's writing, acquired films of Colette and we sat in the dark, Victoria, Janet, Stockard, Honor and I, as Colette came to life on the screen and how we laughed in the street afterward when, contemplating the subway, we decided not to, for "les filles de Colette," we insisted, deserved a cab ride home.

Ruth noticed that the label of my dress had slipped out, reached over and tucked it back in.

My mother, lonely and depressed, feels rejected by her mother. The volcano of my feelings, ancient, rises up against her.

My niece, five months old, tries to walk.

My grandmother has no documents.

I became an archaeologist, digging for relics of female intimacy, unearthing layers of evidence. The masculine vision was only the first layer. My life and the life around me was another. What remained to be unearthed and examined was the layer of what women have written, and what my spade struck at that moment surprised me. I thought I was back at the masculine vision, for women, I saw, had said similar things. That would not turn out to be the whole story, but it was a frustrating beginning.

Like men, many women writers have told stories in which male characters are hypodermic needles, injecting life into inert women characters who, without a male "fix," have no energy and no existence. We have come to expect, because we read so much of this literature, the kind of restlessness that Elizabeth Bennet is plagued by in Jane Austen's *Pride and Prejudice*:

> Anxious and uneasy, the period which passed in the drawing room, before the gentlemen came, was wearisome and dull to a degree that almost made her uncivil. She looked forward to their entrance, as the point on which all her chance of pleasure for the evening must depend.

Likewise, in Charlotte Brontë's *Jane Eyre:*

> Coffee is handed. The ladies, since the gentlemen
> entered, have become as lively as larks; conversation
> waxes brisk and merry.

And in George Eliot's *Daniel Deronda:*

> In the ladies' dining room it was evident that
> Gwendolyn was not a general favourite with her own
> sex. There were no beginnings of intimacy between
> her and other girls, and in conversation they rather
> noticed what she said than spoke to her in free
> exchange. Perhaps it was that she was not much
> interested in them, and when left alone in their
> company had a sense of empty benches.

In fact, most nineteenth-century fiction is full of ladies in
their lassitude waiting for the door to open. I went deeper.
There were more layers, stories where intimacy was praised, not
denied. These were widely scattered, with great gaps between
them. One is the myth of Demeter, which becomes ghostly in the
context of a culture that sees women in relation to men and set
against one another. Demeter's story is about the separation of
mother and daughter, the quest on the mother's part to heal that
separation. Demeter's grief becomes the world's sterility. The
connection between mother and daughter is the most important
thing in the world. Likewise, the remains of Sappho's poems are
haunting, for they portray a world in which women study, hunt,
make music together, admire one another, have jealous fights,
hurt each other—a complicated picture of female activity and
feeling.

In Emily Dickinson's poems I read that Dickinson imagined
herself going to thank Elizabeth Barrett Browning for the poems

Browning wrote and found her dead. "Ah," Dickinson wrote, "the turning back/'Twas slow." In Browning I found admiration for George Sand and in Sand I found both love and anger toward many, many women. Edith Wharton, I discovered, went several times to visit George Sand's house in Nohant. Once there, she walked around and around, searching for something. Where, Wharton wanted to know, had Sand slept? Janet Flanner, in, *Paris Was Yesterday,* says about Wharton:

> She was regarded as cold. Yet a chord of Bach once recalled to her a moment passed half a century ago with a woman who was ever after to be her fondest companion and to the same woman she wrote, after clipping her gardens' rose in the summer dawn, that the ripe sweetness of the flowers personified and brought their amity endearingly to mind.

Two women are alone in a room. What is possible between them and who will record it? The room, if actual, will fall in time to the wrecker's hand and the room as metaphor, representing an exchange between two women, will pass. The act of writing it down is the first act of acknowledgment: this existed; she meant something to me; I learned something from her; we argued; we had a good time together; our lives were not entirely focused on men. Not everyone has a sense of empty benches when she is alone with another woman.

Around and around. The hand touched the hand. The threads ran through history. You needed a magnifying glass to see them. You needed to be looking for them. And then I came to Virginia Woolf and Colette. I had found two chroniclers of the world of women.

Woolf spoke of the "very fine instinct wireless telepathy nothing to it—in women—the darlings—which fizzles up pretences." Sometimes she spoke of this connection in her own voice, in her diaries and letters, and sometimes she put these thoughts into the minds of her characters, as she does in *Mrs. Dalloway,* where Clarissa Dalloway is thinking about her friend Sally Seton:

> The strange thing, on looking back, was the purity, the integrity of her feeling for Sally. It was not like one's feeling for a man. It was completely disinterested, and besides, it had a quality which could only exist between women just grown up. It was protective, on her side; sprang from a sense of being in league together, a presentiment of something that was bound to part them (they spoke of marriage always as a catastrophe), which led to this chivalry, this protective feeling which was much more on her side than Sally's.

Not like one's feeling for a man. No. We are in a different universe now. It resembles the universe of relations between the sexes, has something in common with the ways men interact with each other, but it is not the same. As I began to understand what I was after, I found in Woolf a guide, an indicator of what needs to be explored. What are the forces at work on two women alone in a room—personally, psychologically, and politically—and how do these show up in literature?

Woolf speaks of "purity," of the "disinterested" quality between women. She is pointing to the political. She imagines that women are natural with each other, that when a man walks into the room, women mask themselves. Her descriptions of how this happens and her analysis of why it does runs through all her work. One's feeling for a man does not exist apart from ways of being in the world, from the necessity that women please men to survive, that they become mirrors who give men a reflection of themselves twice their actual size, as Woolf writes in *Three Guineas,* that they give themselves over to mothering, nurturing and accommodation.

Woolf's idea of women "in league together" is a familiar one. The masculine imagination has fixed on it for centuries, imagining it to be dark and devoted to evil, specifically to the overthrow of the masculine. Masculine authority, feeling threatened, has tried and often succeeded in disrupting the league. Woolf means no evil. Her "league" appears often in diaries, letters and autobiographical writing and first it occurs to her as a description of her relationship with her sister Vanessa. The sisters, as Woolf perceived it, formed a league—she also calls it "a republic"—for support—"protective," says Mrs. Dalloway—against the shared pain of their mother's death followed by the death of their older half sister, against the devouring demands of their father and the manipulation of their half brothers.

Colette called the same thing "alliance." *The Other One* is an extraordinary novel about Farou, a middle-aged, demi-successful playwright; Fanny, his wife; and Jane, hired as live-in secretary, moved to the position of mistress. Fanny becomes conscious of the affair and—this is the resolution of the novel— has a half-confrontation with Jane, but her hurt feelings turn out to be in a minor chord and her bond, she discovers, is with Jane. She imagines the household without Jane in it and realizes how painful it would be, how lonely she actually is with her husband. She knows that this is subversive:

> She was aware that she was denying the remains of a pure religion, whose faithful live solely by waiting for their god, and by the childish ritual of their cult.

but this knowledge cannot stop her feelings. The "help" she needs lies not in her husband, not in marriage, but in

> an alliance, even if it were uncertain and slightly disloyal, from a feminine alliance, constantly broken

by the man and constantly re-established at the man's expense.

Reading Colette is like walking slowly through a museum hung with female portraits. Women are together backstage at the music hall. Women are riding on a train. They are changing their clothes, talking, dancing in a bar, thinking about each other. This is familiar. This resembles what I know in my life and see in the lives around me. This tells me to go on, says I am on the right track.

There is more to be unearthed. Things are missing in what Woolf and Colette have written, or are contradicted elsewhere. Woolf's women, for example, see marriage as catastrophe. Other women, in other kinds of literature, see marriage as salvation. This is the dream that haunts much of working-class literature—the dream of escape from the other women in the spinning room, the desired man who will take them away, make life better. How would it be for two women slaves on the Underground Railroad or two Jewish women on the eve of the uprising in the Warsaw ghetto?

I have changed direction. I am thinking now of differences rather than similarities. What I have found so far occurs between women who are very much alike, but I begin to search for records of interaction between women of different classes or races. Such interaction between men is common in literature and popular culture—from Huck Finn and Nigger Jim through Elvis Presley recording in a studio full of black musicians. Political literature is full of it. The image of "brotherhood" is the hand of the black man clasped in the hand of the white man. On both sides of the question, the literature of antagonism and the literature of overcoming antagonism, the characters are men. Do women engage in this enterprise at all?

In one of Flannery O'Connor's stories, a white woman dies because she has seen a black woman wearing a hat just like hers.

The women never speak to each other. Since white and black women hardly ever inhabit the same room, unless one is telling the other to mop the floor, a scene from Carson McCullers' *The Member of the Wedding* is all the more extraordinary. F. Jasmine, also called Frankie, is a thirteen-year-old white girl and Berenice is a thirty-year-old black woman:

> F. Jasmine rolled her head and rested her face against Berenice's shoulder. She could feel Berenice's soft big ninnas against her back, and her soft wide stomach, her warm solid legs. She had been breathing very fast, but after a minute her breath slowed down so that she breathed in time with Berenice; the two of them were close together as one body, and Berenice's stiffened hands were clasped around F. Jasmine's chest. Their backs were to the window, and before them the kitchen was now almost dark.

The profound passion of this scene is rare in literature. Its evocation of the mother-lover defies our fiercest taboo. There is hardly such intimacy depicted anywhere, between any two women. The scene is full of love and passion, but under controlled circumstances. It comes out of a culture in which black women are paid to love white children. Berenice is employed by F. Jasmine's father. Although Berenice feeds the needs of young, troubled Frankie, attends to her and loves her mightily, the father is always present, by implication, and unloving. Berenice's love is one-sided; theirs is essentially a one-way relationship. Frankie worries most about her own destiny. Her concern about Berenice takes the form of wondering whether or not Berenice will marry her current beau. Women in literature rarely consider taking care of each other, which is what makes the visions of Colette and Virginia Woolf so rare and compelling.

Woolf and Colette represent a province in the world of women, one way of feeling, of looking at things. The terrain is complicated. It has, as other writers have shown and our own experience has told us, rivers of violence and plains of ambivalence. There is delicate sensuality in the sky and hills of fierce, driving passion. It is unknown territory, banked by silence but approachable by the maps of our own lives and the faint clues of the written word.

I rose from my table and paced the room, turning the subject over and over. There were pieces to be put together and silences to be broken. This was an investigation that could be made at this point in time and not before because of the evidence we now have and the lives we are now living. I had on my table some of the evidence: new biographies, republished novels, Woolf's letters and diaries, the result of the wave of intellectual change that has swept us, making women's lives serious subjects in the eyes of men and women. I live at a turning point. There are more books now than before in which women tell the truth. My life has changed; the lives of women around me have changed. We are not mesmerized by father, brother, lover. There are women in our lives.

What happens among women? The cloudy day on which I had first asked the question was long gone. I knew where to look. And I knew I would have to take myself along on this journey, use my experience as a guide. I would become a character in the book and have, within its pages, relationships with other women. It frightened me, exciting though the prospect was, because I knew that the world of women would not be a garden, not entirely telepathy and alliance.

From archaeologist, I became a cartographer, set out to draw a map of the world of women. It would be tentative, the results of what information I possess, open to revision by others who have read other books, traveled other roads. I divided the map into large sections, the kinds of relationships that can be named: mothers and daughters, sisters, friends, lovers, enemies. I would draw on what was useful to describe each relation, show how it played itself out in life and in the imagination. It would not be a linear story. I would draw the shape of each relation, the images that stood for it.

One image appeared, unbidden but appropriate. It was an image of women together and has been with me since childhood. I drew Cinderella, the stepmother, the nasty sisters.

1

Cinderella

SATURDAY AFTERNOON
AT THE MOVIES

No, Cinderella, said the stepmother,
you have no clothes and cannot dance.
That's the way with stepmothers.

Anne Sexton, *"Cinderella"*

Turn and peep, turn and peep,
No blood is in the shoe;
The shoe is not too small for her,
The true bride rides with you.

Grimm's *Cinderella*

I begin with a memory of movies and mother, a dark theatre and a Saturday afternoon. In a miasma of Walt Disney images, Bambi burning and Snow White asleep, the most memorable is "Cinderella." I carry her story with me for the rest of my life. It is a story about women alone together and they are each other's enemies. This is more powerful as a lesson than the ball, the Prince or the glass slipper. The echoes of "Cinderella" in other fairy tales, in myth and literature, are about how awful women are to each other. The girl onscreen, as I squirm in my seat, needs to be saved. A man will come and save her. Some day my Prince will come. Women will not save her; they will thwart her. There is a magical fairy godmother who does help her, but this, for me, has no relation to life, for the fairy is not real and the bad women are. The magical good fairy is a saccharine fluff.

There are two worlds in the Cinderella cartoon, one of women, one of men. The women are close by and hostile, the men distant and glittering. Stepsisters and stepmother are three in one, a female battalion allied against Cinderella. The daughters are just like their mother. All women are alike. Lines of connection, energy fields, attach sisters to mother, leaving Cinderella in exile from the female community at home.

Father is far off. On film, neither he nor the Prince has much character. Father is her only tie, her actual blood tie, but the connection does her no good. Daddy is King in this world; I cannot keep Daddy and King apart in my memory. My own father was as far off, as full of authority, as surrounded by heraldry, the trumpets of fantasy, to me, to my mother. King Daddy.

The Prince is rich and handsome. Rich matters more than handsome. The girl among the cinders, dressed in rags, will escape—I am on her side, I want her to escape, get away from the cinders and the awful women—because the Prince will lift her out. The world of the Prince is the world of the ball, music, fine clothes and good feeling. Were everything to be right at home, were the women to be good to one another and have fun together, it would not be sufficient. The object is the ball, the Prince, the big house, the servants. Class mobility is at stake. Aspiration is being titillated.

To win the Prince, to be saved, requires being pretty. All the women care about this. Being pretty is the ticket and because Cinderella is pretty, the stepmother and stepsisters want to keep her out of the running. There is no other enterprise. Cinderella does not turn up her nose and hide in a corner reading a book. Being pretty, getting to the ball, winning the Prince is the common ground among the women. What we have in common is what keeps us apart.

Cinderella must be lonely. Why, I wonder, doesn't she have a friend? Why doesn't she go to school? Why doesn't her father tell the awful women to stop? A hurt and lonely girl, with only a prince to provide another kind of feeling. Why doesn't she run away? Why can't the situation be changed? It is as though the house they live in is the only world, there is no other landscape. Women are always in the house, being awful to each other.

Magic. Cinderella has a fairy godmother who likes her and wants her to be happy. She gives the girl beautiful clothes. She doesn't have to instruct Cinderella or give her advice about how to waltz or how to lift her skirt or even give her directions to the palace. Only the clothes and the accoutrements—and a prohibition about coming home at midnight. A powerful woman who wants Cinderella to be pretty and successful in the social world. I know, at whatever age it is that I watch this story unfold, that the mother beside me is not the woman on the screen. Her feelings on such matters are, at best, mixed up. She is not so powerful.

I am stirred and confused by the contrast between bad and good women and the way it all seems to revolve around the issue of being pretty. Some women are hostile and thwarting, others enabling and powerful. The stepmother hates Cinderella's prettiness; the fairy godmother adorns it. I look sideways at my mother, trying to decide which kind of woman she is, where she stands on the business of pretty. Often, she braids my hair and settles me into polka dot, parades me before my beaming father. It is good to be pretty. Yet, onscreen, it is bad to be pretty—Cinderella is punished for it. In the enterprise of pretty, other women are your allies and your enemies. They are not disinterested. The heat around the issue of pretty, the urgency and intensity of it, is located among the women, not the men, at whom it is supposedly aimed. Luckily, we move on to the ball and the lost slipper.

This is one of the oldest and most often-told stories, varying significantly from one version to another, one country to another, one period to another. What appears on movie theatre screens or television on Saturday afternoons comes from as far away as China, as long ago as four hundred years. Each teller, each culture along the way, retained some archetypal patterns and transformed others, emphasized some parts of the story, eradicated others. Disney took his version of Cinderella from one written down by a Frenchman named Perrault in the seventeenth century. Perrault's is a "civilized" version, cleaned up, dressed up and given several pointed "lessons" on top of the original material.

Many of the details about fashionability that we now associate with the story come from Perrault. His has the atmosphere of Coco Chanel's dressing rooms, is modern and glamorous. He concocted a froufrou, aimed at an aristocratic audience and airily decorated with things French. He named one of the sisters Charlotte and set the action in a world of full-length looking glasses and inlaid floors. He invented a couturière called Mademoiselle de Poche to create costumes for the ball, linens and ruffles, velvet suits and headdresses. Disney dropped the French touches.

Perrault's story is set in a world of women with their eyes on men. Even before the King's ball is announced, the stepmother and stepsisters are preoccupied with how they look. They are obsessed with their mirrors, straining to see what men would see. Once the ball is on the horizon, they starve themselves for days so that their shapes shall be, when laced into Mademoiselle de Poche's creations, as extremely slender as those in our own fashion magazines. The ball—and the prospects it implies—intensifies the hostility toward Cinderella. They have been envious. Now, they must keep the pretty girl out of competition. Most of the action of Perrault's story is taken up with the business of the ball.

Cinderella is a sniveling, self-pitying girl. Forbidden to go to the ball, she does not object but, instead, dutifully helps her stepsisters adorn themselves. She has no will, initiates no action.

Then, magically, the fairy godmother appears. She comes from nowhere, summoned, we suppose, by Cinderella's wishes. Unlike the fairy godmother in other versions of the story, Perrault's and Disney's character has no connection to anything real, has no meaning, except to enable Cinderella to overcome the opposition of the women in her home, wear beautiful clothes and get to the ball. Cinderella stammers, unable to say what she wants—for she is passive, suffering and good, which comes across as relatively unconscious. The fairy divines Cinderella's desire and equips her with pumpkin/coach, mice/horses, rats/coachmen, lizards/footmen, clothes and dancing shoes. She adds the famous prohibition that Cinderella return by midnight or everything will be undone.

These details of the fairy godmother's magic—the pumpkin, image of All Hallows' Eve; midnight, the witching hour; mice, rats and lizards originated with Perrault. They are specific reminders of an actual and ancient female magic, witchcraft. Since Perrault wrote his story in the seventeenth century, it is not surprising to find echoes of this magic, which was enormously real to Perrault's audience.

Thousands had been burned at the stake for practicing witchcraft, most of them women. A witch was a woman with enormous power, a woman who might change the natural world. She was "uncivilized" and in opposition to the world of the King, the court, polite society. She had to be controlled. Perrault's story attempts to control the elements of witchcraft just as various kings' governments had, in the not too recent past, controlled what they believed to be an epidemic of witchcraft. Perrault controls female power by trivializing it. The witchcraft in this story is innocent, ridiculous, silly and playful. It is meant to entertain children.

The prohibition that Cinderella return by midnight is also related to witchcraft. She must avoid the witching hour, with its overtones of sexual abandon. The fairy godmother acts in this capacity in a way that is familiar to mothers and daughters—she controls the girl, warns her against darkness, uses her authority to enforce restraint, prevent excess, particularly excess associated with the ball, the world of men, sexuality.

Cinderella's dancing shoes are glass slippers. Perrault mistranslated the fur slipper in the version that came to him, substituting *verre* for *vire* and coming up glass. No pedant came along to correct the mistake, for the glass slipper is immensely appropriate to the story in its modern form and the values it embodies. Call it dainty or fragile, the slipper is quintessentially the stereotype of femininity. I wonder how Cinderella danced in it.

The rags-to-riches moment holds people's imaginations long after the details of the story have disappeared. It appeals to everyone's desire for magic, for change that comes without effort, for speedy escape from a bad place—bad feelings. We all want to go to the ball, want life to be full of good feeling and feeling good. But Cinderella's transformation points to a particular and limited kind of good feeling—from ugly to beautiful, raggedy to glamorous. The object of her transformation is not actually pleasure (she does not then walk around her house feeling better) but transportation to the ball with all the right equipment for captivating the Prince.

Transformed, Cinderella goes to the ball, which is the larger world, the kingdom ruled by kings and fathers. The stepmother has no power in that world and does not even appear. This part of the story focuses on men, who are good to Cinderella as forcefully as women have been bad to her. Perrault embellishes Cinderella's appearance in a way that would have been congenial to the French court. In fact, she seems to have gone to the French court. The story is suffused with perfume and "fashionability." The Prince is taken with Cinderella and gives her some candy—"citrons and oranges," according to the text. How French. She, forever good, shares the candy with her stepsisters, who do not, of course, know who she is.

Cinderella has a wonderful time. As readers, hearers,

watchers, we have a wonderful time along with her. More than the music and the dancing, the aura of sensual pleasure, everyone's good time comes from the idea that Cinderella is a "knockout." This is exciting. Perrault's word for what happens is that the people are *étonnés,* which means stunned. Cinderella is a showstopper, so "dazzling" that "the King himself, old as he was, could not help watching her." He remarks on this to his Queen, whose reactions we are not told. Being "stunning" is being powerful. This is the way women have impact, the story tells us. This is female power in the world outside the home, in contrast to her former powerlessness, which was within the home, which was another country. This tells me why women spend so much time trying to turn themselves into knockouts— because, in Cinderella and in other stories, it *works.*

Presumably, Cinderella's giddiness over her own triumph at the ball makes her forget her godmother's command and almost miss her midnight deadline. Lest we lose the idea that all men adore Cinderella, Perrault adds a courtier at the end of the story, as the search for the missing Cinderella is carried out, and has him, too, say how attractive Cinderella is. She fulfills, then, the masculine idea of what is beautiful in a woman. She is the woman men want women to be.

Cinderella flees at midnight and loses her shoe. Perrault plays this part down, but Disney has a visual festival with the glinting glass slipper on the staircase and the trumpet-accompanied quest to find its owner. Perrault's Prince sends a messenger to find the shoe's owner, which puts the action at some distance, but Disney gives us a prince in all his splendor.

Cinderella is a heroine and in the world of fairy tales what the heroine wins is marriage to the Prince. Like any classic romance, wafted by perfume and fancy clothes, the young girl is lifted from a lowly powerless situation (from loneliness and depression, too) by a powerful man. He has no character, not even a handsome face, but simply represents the things that princes represent, the power of the kingdom.

Opposition to achieving this triumph comes from the women in the house; help comes from daydream and fantasy. The only proper activity for women to engage in is primping. What is expected of them is that they wait "in the right way" to be discovered. Cinderella obeys the rules. Her reward is to be claimed by the Prince. The lesson of Cinderella in these versions is that a girl who knows and keeps her place will be rewarded with male favor.

Like a saint, she shows neither anger nor resentment toward the women who treated her so badly. In fact, she takes her stepsisters along to the castle, where she marries each off to a nobleman. Now everyone will be happy. Now there will be no conflict, no envy, no degradation. If each woman has a prince or nobleman, she will be content and the soft humming of satisfaction will fill the air. Women otherwise cannot be alone together.

This is the sort of story that poisoned Madame Bovary's imagination. In Flaubert's novel, a woman married to a country doctor, with aspirations for a larger life, goes to a ball where a princely character pays her some attention. The ball and the Prince, seen by Emma Bovary as possibilities for changing everyday life, haunted her uneasy sleep. The ball was over. Wait as she might for its return, for a second invitation, all she got was a false prince—a lover who did not lift her from the ordinariness of her life—and then despair.

The romance depends on aspiration. The Prince must be able to give the heroine something she cannot get for herself or from other women. He must represent a valuable and scarce commodity, for the women must believe there is only one, not enough to go around, and must set themselves to keeping other women from getting it. In "Cinderella," like other fairy tales and other romances, the world of the Prince represents both actual and psychological riches.

Perrault's Cinderella is the daughter of a gentleman, turned into a peasant within the household. She has been declassed by female interlopers, reduced to the status of servant, for she belongs to her father's class only precariously. One of the ways women exercise their power, the story tells us, is by degrading other women. Cinderella will be saved from her female-inflicted degradation first by another female, the fairy godmother, who puts her on the road to her ultimate salvation. At the end of the story, she is restored to her class position, or, better, raised to an even higher position by the Prince.

Her fall from class is represented not only by her tattered clothes, but by the work she is forced to do. She is the household "drudge" and housework is the image of her degradation. Her work has no value in the story; it is the invisible, repetitious labor that keeps things going and makes it possible for the sisters and stepmother to devote themselves to *their* work, which is indolence on the one hand and trying to be beautiful for men on the other. Historically, indolence has been revered as the mark of a lady. What is "feminine" and "ladylike" is far removed from the world of work. Or the world of self-satisfying work. A man prides himself on having a wife who does not work; it increases his value in the eyes of other men; it means he provides well; it enforces conventional bourgeois "masculinity." A lady has long fingernails; neither the typewriter nor the kitchen floor has cracked them. She has porcelain skin; neither the rough outdoors nor perspiration has cracked that. Out of the same set of values comes the famous glass slipper.

The stepmother's class position is as precarious as Cinderella's is. The story does not tell, but we can imagine that whether she was married before to a poorer man or one equally a gentleman, her status and security are now tied to the man she has married and the ones she can arrange for her daughters. History, experience, and literature are full of landless property-less women trying to secure marriage to stand as a bulwark against poverty, displacement and exile, both actual and psychological. The actual situation bears emphasis. The economic reality behind the fairy tale and the competition among the women for the favor of the Prince is a world in which women have no financial lives of their own. They cannot own businesses or inherit property. The kingdom is not theirs. In order to survive, a woman must have a husband. It is in the interests of her daughters' future—and her own—that the stepmother works to prevent competition from Cinderella. She is not evil. Within the confines of her world and the value systems of that world, she is quite nice to her own daughters, only cruel to Cinderella.

Still, the stepmother is an archetypal figure in fairy tales, always a thwarter, often a destroyer of children. Psychologists, and Bruno Bettelheim in particular, have a psychological explanation for this. The "bad" stepmother, Bettelheim points out, usually coexists with the "good" mother, representing two aspects of a real mother as experienced by a child. The stepmother is shaped by the child's unacceptable anger against her own mother. But there are real facts of life at work in these stepmother stories, too, especially as they describe what can happen among women at home. To a man's second wife, the daughter of the first marriage is a constant reminder of the first wife. The second wife is continually confronted with that memory and with the understanding that wives are replaceable, as they frequently and actually *were* in a world where women died young in childbirth, and men remarried, moved on.

A woman marries a man who has a daughter and comes to his household, where the daughter's strongest connection is to her father; the stepmother's strongest connection is to the husband. The Eternal Triangle appears, husband/father at the center, mediating the relationship, stepmother and daughter as antagonists, competing for the husband/father's attention and whatever he may represent. Anxious, each in her own way and equally displaced, they face each other with enmity. The masculine imagination takes prideful pleasure in the story, placing, as it does, husband/father at center stage, making him King, arbiter of a world of women.

In the nineteenth century the Grimm brothers recorded a version of "Cinderella" that was, in fact, a very old folktale, full of the "barbaric" elements that characterized such tales. It is a more frightening story with a very different emphasis. The lesson in this version is not that a girl who knows and keeps her place will be rewarded with male favor. Instead, the actual and original and far more interesting conflict of the story stands at the center: a conflict between two female forces, one represented by the stepmother, the other by the fairy godmother, who, in this and other versions, is an incarnation of Cinderella's real mother. The connection between mother and daughter was buried by Perrault, by Disney. This connection balances the idea that women are always each other's enemies. It provides a glimpse of something else.

As told by the brothers Grimm, the tale is closer to folk sources, denser with ritual and symbolic action, far from the perfumed courts of the French King. This version retains archetypal elements obliterated by the "civilizing" hand of Perrault. It does not show the mind of a censor who deems certain things "unfit" for children and is, therefore, like primitive tales, violent, bestial and grotesque.

The tale is divided, classically, into a brief prologue, three parts of action and an epilogue. Cinderella's real mother is present in the prologue—she is shown dying, telling her daughter to be good—and present throughout the story, so that the magical force that transforms Cinderella belongs less to the world of make-believe and more to the psychologically and spiritually actual. The first "act" shows life among the women at home—Cinderella, stepmother, stepsisters together and the father far off. In fact, father leaves on a journey. The second "act" is about the ball, here called a "festival." The third is the climax, the "test" of the shoe and the moment of recognition. The epilogue tells how the stepsisters get their retribution. It is very unlike Perrault's resolved, conciliatory finale.

Throughout the Grimm version, Cinderella has a counter-life. She has one kind of existence indoors, dominated and degraded by her stepmother, another kind outdoors, beside her mother's grave. There she is active, plants a tree, nourishes it with her tears and encounters a white bird, which flies out of the tree, representing her mother's spirit and changing her life. The two mothers take on another kind of meaning. The relationship of Cinderella's original mother to the girl is enhancing. The second mother, present because of the father's actions and therefore tied to him, dramatically, is the woman who degrades the girl.

The presence of the first mother changes the story and suggests other ways of reading it. Not only do we have a good and bad mother, but two different ways of seeing connections between women, particularly between mothers and daughters. The first mother—the "real" one or the "good" one—embodies matriarchal values. She cherishes her daughter. She values the feminine. She is allied with the natural world, either as Nature's representative or as a force in sympathy with nature. These are elements of the myth of Demeter, who searched for her daughter, Persephone, also called Kore. Demeter caused the grain to cease growing in sympathy with her grief and her loss. The power of the matriarchal mother would allow her to perform the kind of "magic" that more conventional versions of "Cinderella" show the fairy godmother performing. She can rearrange the world. The patriarchal mother or the mother in a patriarchal world is herself degraded, robbed of her power. Like the stepmother in this story, her energies are directed to patriarchal institutions, to becoming skillful at manipulating within them (the court, the ball, the festival or the world of fashion) and the power she exerts can only be over other women.

Cinderella is not passive. She acts and her action is ritual action. She plants the twig on her mother's grave. Nourished by her tears of lamentation, it grows into a tree out of which comes the white bird that is her mother's spirit. Her tears are not only cathartic, but productive. Unlike the sniveling of Perrault's Cinderella, the Grimm story shows Cinderella engaged in meaningful action—profound mourning leading to regeneration. Three times a day, the story says, Cinderella goes to her mother's grave. Three times, she approaches the tree and is given the means with which to go to the ball and three times, in the denouement, the slipper is tried on a foot, once on each step-sister, then on Cinderella. Only on the third try is the "problem" resolved and the "quest" fulfilled.

In language and imagery, as well as action, the story evokes ancient sources. Cinderella is assigned the task of picking lentils from the cinders of the hearth. This separation of the grain connects her again to the myth of Demeter, emphasizing the mother-daughter relation. Cinderella stands for all the daughters; in terms of the Demeter myth, she is the "Kore," the maiden or virgin. The white bird is a conventional representation of the Spirit, in this case, her mother's spirit. The action is set around the hearth, with all its symbolic resonance.

Throughout its history, "Cinderella" has been associated with the hearth. The ash girl is not only dirtied by the hearth, but, far more profoundly, derives her identity from it. The hearth was the center of homelife and, as such, it, too, represents Cinderella's mother and, beyond her, the matriarchal principle. By staying close to the hearth, Cinderella enacts her attachment to her mother and her ritual mourning for her death. The hearth is the antithesis of the stepmother's world, the world of women with their eyes on men. Far from being a symbol of degradation, the hearth is, or would have been in its original meaning in the story, a place of honor.

The matriarchal hearth reappears often in literature and has particular meaning for girls and women. The journey of Odysseus may have been to see the smoke in his own chimney again, but it was Penelope's task to keep the smoke going, to tend the hearth. The world of *Little Women* is a world centered around the hearth; the extent to which the patriarchal world intrudes on it, pulls women away from it is the drama of that novel. The tension between staying and leaving the hearth is one way of seeing the tension in women's lives.

Two women are alone in a room. One is content to sit near the hearth, stirring the evening's meal. Perhaps she is not really content, only appears so. It is her assigned task to stir the evening's meal. The second woman is restless. She wants to do something else, go elsewhere, take up a bow and prowl the woods, ride a horse. What will happen depends on how closely each woman feels compelled to translate her own preferences into proscription to say *all* women should stay near the hearth, or *all* women should reject the hearth. Do these women grant or withhold approval for differences? Will one chain the other to the hearth?

The honor of the hearth is derived from classical myth where the goddess Hestia, refusing the courtship of Poseidon and Apollo, chose to remain a virgin. Zeus took this to mean that Hestia preserved peace on Olympus and rewarded the goddess by placing her at the center of the house, where, sitting, she received offerings. "Hestia," means "hearth." The Romans called Hestia Vesta and her altar was tended, in religious ceremony, by Vestal Virgins. Cinderella is guardian of the hearth; she is a Vestal Virgin.

"Virginity" in the ancient world meant belonging to oneself. Ovid said that a virgin "neither gives nor takes seeds, and she loves companions in her virginity." From a female point of view, this "virginity" is valuable because it points to a woman's primary relation being with herself, as opposed to lover, husband or children.

The value accorded female virginity in most cultures does not stem from so benevolent a source, nor is its intention pure nor its presence in our lives so helpful. The Christian cult of the Virgin gives us Virgin as mother in spite of Ovid; the Virgin Mary gives seeds anyway and does not love female companions in her virginity, surrounded, as she is, by father and son. Virginity is a good thing for girls in Western culture for other reasons, having little to do with a woman's self-development and much to do with the patriarchal structure of the world. It has always been economically and politically important for men to know that they are the fathers of their children. The passing on of property and title depended upon paternity. How was a man to know? Once the connection between copulation and issue was established, it became an urgent matter of state to ensure that the seed in the woman's womb was her husband's. Virginity meant some naïve kind of assurance. If you "get" a woman for your wife who is virgin and enforce chastity in your married life, you, the patriarch, might have a chance at keeping social order, developing laws of inheritance and imagining that you have got some aspect of human life and history under control.

So Cinderella dwells beside the hearth in the world her stepmother rules. This part of her life appears to be an empty shell. Her stepmother's house is where her body lives, but not her soul, her spirit or her consciousness, all of which thrive in another place, beside her mother's grave, in the world of the tree and the spirit/bird. Cinderella's transformation, in this version, comes because of her own action. She addresses this other part of her life, asks the tree to provide for her. From her mother's spirit, then, she gets what she needs to journey into the outer world. The tree delivers the ability to cope; the clothing needed to make her way. This is a serious transformation, not the simple silliness of being fashionably garbed. Three times, Cinderella asks. Three times, she is transformed and goes to the ball. Each step in her transformation is an echo of another ancient magic— she is given silk and silver, then gold, a progression that is the basis of the art of alchemy, where base metals were transmuted into higher ones. The source of this magic, the spirit of Cinderella's mother, is as powerful as Merlin the Magician was.

At the ball, Cinderella is taken up by the Prince, who says "This is my partner," much the way the Song of Solomon says "this is my lover and my friend." Each time, Cinderella decides to leave before nightfall. She *decides* to leave; no fairy godmother controls her. And nightfall, not midnight. She wants to avoid whatever is constellated by festivity, dancing, men and darkness.

Since we know that Cinderella is a virgin, it is clearly fear of a male sexual advance that causes her to leave. There are many versions of the story earlier than this one in which Cinderella's primary antagonist is male. In some parts of Europe, the story is known as "Brother and Sister" and she flees her home because she refuses her brother's sexual proposals. In others, the daughter's antagonist is her father and his sexual desire for her.

In conformity with conventional psychoanalytic theory, the tension that causes her to flee belongs to the daughter. What is represented in the story, for an orthodox Freudian interpreter like Bruno Bettelheim, is the daughter's desire for her father. Freud, of course, in one of his most familiar interpretations— cited by Bettelheim at exactly this point in his discussion—did the same thing. The good doctor mused on his female patients' report of rape by their fathers and decided that what they were really telling him, these troubled and repressed women, were their most unconscious fantasies.

Not one to discount the unconscious, nor fantasy nor Oedipal craving, I am still troubled by the avoidance of certain facts of life in the thinking of both good doctors and troubled in a way that relates to Cinderella. In the actual world, now, in Freud's time, and before that, there is a great deal of aggression on the part of men toward little girls. Freud's patients might well have been reporting the emotional content of something that happened and happened frequently—not rape, but sexual aggression. I remember the pinches and pats of my father, grandfather and other male relatives, gestures never bestowed in the same way on my brother. Given the sexually proprietary nature of the way men touch women and the terrifying modern statistics of incest rape among fathers and daughters, the reality of that male sexual aggression does not seem farfetched.

Suppose that the original Cinderella stories in which the antagonist is male and the antagonism sexual actually reflect something of how it was in the world out of which the stories came. Why, then, would female hostility replace male? Why would Cinderella's antagonists become stepmother and step-sisters rather than father and brother? It must have to do with what is congenial to the mind that tells the story. This is not a scientific matter—transformations do not proceed in a linear fashion; there is no single moment in time when it occurs, but simply a pattern and a possibility. The intensity of female hostility toward women might, in the hands of male creator, mask male hostility. It is certainly more congenial to a masculine world view.

The presence of earlier masculine antagonists and the incest theme go a long way toward illuminating one of the more bizarre details in the Grimm story. The father, virtually absent from Perrault, appears in this tale just once before Cinderella goes to the ball. Then he leaves on a trip, asking the girls left at home what they would like him to bring them. The stepsisters ask for pearls and Cinderella requests the twig of the first tree that touches his hat on his return journey. The twig becomes the tree on her mother's grave. This is a helpful gesture on the father's part, "fertilizing" Cinderella's connection to her mother. Cinderella goes to the ball three times and decides each time to leave. The Prince follows, but she disappears, first into a dovecote or pigeon house, the second time into a pear tree. Her father appears, asks for an ax, and chops down the pigeon house, then the pear tree. Each time, Cinderella escapes. Such violent phallic behavior is not peculiar in terms of the story's history. The echo of earlier Oedipal stories points toward the father's action as a symbolic representation of rape.

The third time Cinderella escapes, the Prince has laid a trap—cobbler's pitch on the staircase—and he retains her shoe. So we come back to the shoe, the best-known image in the story.

The motif of Cinderella's shoe appears first at the moment of her degradation. Cinderella is forced to wear wooden clogs, which are peasant shoes, sturdy, unyielding, meant to be labored in. If the foot on the ground is our relation to the earth, the wooden clog fixes that relation, keeps it rigid. When Cinderella asks her stepmother for permission to attend the feast, she is told that she has no clothes and cannot dance—she is a girl of wooden clogs. The stepmother seeks to tie her down, her mother seeks to free her. Her mother's spirit "transforms" Cinderella and sets her free: silk and satin slippers replace the clogs, then golden slippers.

I am writing an essay about Cinderella, spending mornings at the typewriter, afternoons in libraries, interpreting information on index cards of various colors and sheets of yellow paper.

I discover something bizarre woven in the story as we now know it: that the story took root in ancient China. The remnants of that culture, especially of the ancient practice of footbinding, are in the story, in the value of the small foot, in the use of the shoe to represent the potential bride. I see, then, the historical truth behind the terrible moment at the end of "Cinderella."

The Prince brings the slipper to the house of Cinderella's father. First one stepsister, then the other attempts to slip her foot into it, but each foot is too large. The first stepsister's toe is too large. The stepmother hands her daughter a knife and says, "Cut off the toe. When you are Queen you won't have to walk anymore." The second stepsister's heel is too large and her mother repeats the gesture and the advice.

Mutilation. Blood in the shoe, blood on the knife, blood on the floor and unbearable pain, borne, covered, masked by the smile. It is too familiar, frightening in its familiarity. The mother tells the daughter to mutilate herself in the interests of winning the Prince. She will not have to walk. Again, indolence enshrined. As mothers, in fact, did in China until the twentieth century—among the upper classes as unquestioned custom and among peasants as great sacrifice and gamble.

It began when the girl was between five and seven years old. The bandages were so tight, the girl might scream. Her mother pulled them tighter and might have tried to soothe her. Tighter. At night, in agony, the girl loosens them. She is punished, her hands tied to a post to prevent unlacing. The bones crack. The pain is constant. Tighter. She cannot walk. Tighter. By her adolescence, the girl has learned to bind her feet herself and the pain has lessened. She has, as a reward, special shoes, embroidered and decorated, for her tiny feet.

I translate the actual foot-binding, the ritual interaction of mother and daughter, to metaphor. A black mother straightens her daughter's hair with a hot iron, singeing the scalp, pulling and tugging. The daughter screams. My mother buys me a girdle when I am fifteen years old because she doesn't like the jiggle. She slaps my face when I begin to menstruate, telling me later that it is an ancient Russian custom and she does not know its origin. I sleep with buttons taped to my cheeks to make dimples and with hard metallic curlers in my hair. Tighter. I hold myself tighter, as my mother has taught me to do.

Is the impulse to cripple a girl peculiar to China between the eleventh and twentieth centuries? The lotus foot was the size of a doll's and the woman could not walk without support. Her foot was four inches long and two inches wide. A doll. A girl-child. Crippled, indolent and bound. This is what it meant to be beautiful. And desired. This women did and do to each other.

Pain in the foot is pain in every part of the body. A mother is about to bind her daughter's feet. She knows the pain in her own memory. She says: "A daughter's pretty legs are achieved through the shedding of tears."

This women did to each other.
This women do.
Or refuse to do.

What began in a movie theatre ends in an apartment. Our drama is still played indoors. It is thirty years later and I have come to share my work with Nancy and to see hers. We do this now every other week. This time, I bring notes and ideas about Cinderella, the making of this essay. Nancy's friend Ann is in town for a fellowship interview. Ann understands that Nancy and I need to do our work and withdraws into her nervousness. Unstated but very present is the enormous respect we three have for each other.

Later—I am not sure how it happens—in sympathy for

Ann's nervousness, having come to a stopping point in our work or understanding that what happens to Ann at her interview involves us, Nancy and I turn our attention to her. Nancy has done much of this the night before—rehearsing Ann, imagining the questions, helping her present herself and her work in their most effective way. Now it becomes a three-way enterprise. We look over the wardrobe, choose a lavender blouse and skirt, a jacket lent by Nancy. I suppose we have agreed on the "strategy" of looking conventionally feminine at these things. Ann is urged to eat and manages an English muffin. She likes having our help, but neither demands it nor overwhelms us with her need for it.

We share what we know about the lurking interview and speculate whether there is an unstated quota for women. Our fates, Nancy's, mine and Ann's overlap in specific ways. What happens to the project Ann has in mind, whether she gets the money that will enable her to do it or not, is something we will draw a lesson from. We are neither saints nor martyrs. We know it to be in our own best interests to support Ann's progress in the world.

We are not the terrible stepsisters.
What we have in common is not what keeps us apart.
Cinderella goes to the ball and wins the fellowship.
This is a happy ending.
Somehow, we have come to this.

2

Mothers and Daughters

BLOOD, BLOOD AND LOVE

"Mother, what should I do when some man tells me he wants me?" I asked her once.

Her large grey eyes smiled at me as she whispered, "Babe, if a man wants you and you want him, just take him.... Don't be afraid of life and love and nature. Anything you want to do is all right with me. Men can't do you any harm. Nobody can hurt you but yourself. Every experience you have makes you all the more fit for life. Men are wonderful. When you get tired of them, or they of you, leave them without bitterness or regret. No matter what happens to you, I'll stand by you."

Sister of the Road: The Autobiography of Box-Car Bertha

1940. It is slow, coming to consciousness. The drug is like eiderdown, gentle and muffling. She swims upward, as she has, in fact, done for so many years, late afternoons in the ocean and now in a hospital bed, the muscles of her forearms contract, release as though—and because—she is, in fact, swimming. Breaking the surface, she sees her husband and, behind him, the blur of the nurse in white. A girl. A healthy girl. A girl with all ten fingers and ten toes—that was where she had fixed her worry, on deformity. A healthy breathing girl whom she comes to name after her dead father—Louise for the defunct Louis.

She intends to have nine children, all perfect. Against the constant hum of her own imperfection: the immigrant experience, the fear and shame of her "difference" and her strange language in an alien country; the sickliness, from scarlet fever and the humiliating loss of hair to the tubercular hip and nearly a

year's immobilization in a hospital; the confusion and awkward-
ness about boys and men, the recoil from sex, feeling that life
was too much for her, overwhelming and coming at her, something like the erection of a man in heat; the imperfection of her
own body, with its embarrassing bleeding (there had been rags
soaking in disinfectant in the home that she shared with her
mother and sister, in the bathroom, under the sink, hidden) and
the breasts that grew too large, exposing her to taunts, making it
difficult to find clothes that fit right, the imperfection of a body
that broke down and blew up and needed tending and was
"wrong" in comparison to the beautiful older sister's sleek shape
and natural charm. The nine perfect imagined children would
stand against her loneliness.

She was a bookish girl with few friends, afraid of the world
outside the family, which meant the mother and sister because
the father was away at war, then ill, then dead. A husband came
along to be savior and companion and then, he, too, although she
would never say so out loud, became irritatingly and disappoint-
ingly absent, a man who worked hard, fourteen hours a day in
The Store, for actual reasons upon which her life now depended.
She would never say out loud how awful, how empty, how
lonely, how frightening. Instead she would have children, beginning with the girl baby sleeping on another floor of the hospital. She is my mother. I am sleeping on another floor. Our life
begins in this separation.

Hamlet turns to Horatio at the end and bids him carry on
the name and the fame, bids him tell the story. We do not ask this
of each other, much less bid it. For centuries, we have shrunk
under two kinds of hopelessness that prevent us from being
Hamlets and Horatios to each other: an internal and external
hopelessness and the rebound between them.

Internally, let my grandmother stand as example. Hers is a
life story full of interminable variations of heroism—a struggle

for survival worthy of Sisyphus. She knew how to make a stew for seven from a lonely potato. She was as wily as any con man in life or literature, as resourceful, as imaginative, but honest. Her journey, like any pilgrim's progress, was from oppression, degradation, danger and terror to a freedom laden with responsibility. And she persisted in the face of odds as great as any that faced Odysseus. Her education in the ways of the world was as interesting and more profound than all the "young man from the provinces" novels I have read. She does not think her story worth telling. She could not—and I, for many years could not—imagine that it would be the stuff of literature, of chronicle, of history. It is, after all, *only* a woman's story, *only* about food, cooking, shelter and families—and about women. Horatio would scoff.

The external forces preventing such stories from being written down (they are often told aloud, but that is considered a "secondary" form and does not survive beyond the teller and the rememberer, nor does it extend outside the family) are the collective scoffing of Horatios through centuries. Posterity has not been the country of women. What chance has the female storyteller had, making her way through closed gates to an alien city to an inhospitable audience in the town square of the patriarchy? She might have an audience if she spoke about men—about a male god or about a band of marauders who attacked and raped her in the desert outside the city, about the man whose love eludes and obsesses her, forces her to travel from one square to the next in search of him. If she wanted to speak of her mother...

Before the resurrections in our lives and literature of the past decade—and aside from the occasional Jane Austen or Louisa May Alcott—there is absence, invisibility and silence about mothers and daughters. Mothers had sons—like Oedipus or Hamlet—and daughters had fathers—like Athena, who was born from the head of Zeus (masculine usurpation of parturition —the kind that had Eve made from Adam's rib), and the daughters of King Lear with their curiously unmentioned mother. There were daughters and there were mothers, but they did not inhabit the same world.

The father tells the story, bringing to his description of mother and daughter what he can see, literally and figuratively, what he has had access to, what his consciousness can take in. In literature, the world of the father is not the world of the family, not in any central way. Father is in the library or on the battlefront, on a chain gang or running the store; he is traveling to America to make a new life for his family; he is contemplating his existential angst or his boss or the empty canvas on which he desires to prove himself an artist. He is shooting lions in Africa or holding up subway booths or drinking himself silly on the 5:05 to Darien.

Mother and daughter sit beside the hearth. In spite of the fact that mother, too, may be at work, on the assembly line or in her own office, most of what has been recorded in the past, shaped our experience, become cultural ideology shows mother and daughter beside the hearth. Father is back from the wars or the office and stands on the threshold, gazing at wife and daughter, knowing himself a stranger to their intimacy. His identity as stranger, their identity as intimates—this must have begun at the child's birth, perhaps before, the father not being part of the "mystical" (to him) mother-child event. A girl-baby, announced to the world, in ancient times, at various moments, might have been murdered, but let us assume that these times are modern and the girl thrives. The identity between herself and her mother is assumed by everyone. The matching outfits. The girl is a "little mother," with her dolls and her maternal imitations. She grows. Mother buys the girl her clothes. Mother conducts the initiations—the first bra, menstruation, those "facts of life" conversations. Mother irons the white blouse in the morning.

Father the stranger, loser of that share of mothering he had from "his woman" before there was a child between them, is the alienated outsider and yet somehow, he keeps reminding himself, proprietor of all this. Bestirred by angers and jealousies he cannot understand, he closes his eyes. He has, for so long, been the teller of the story.

"But if I turn to my mother," Virginia Woolf wrote, "how difficult it is to single her out as she really was; to imagine what she was thinking, to put a single sentence into her mouth." If we turn to the mothers to tell us stories about themselves and their daughters, we are confounded by silence. Not a sentence in their mouths. For so many centuries, not a syllable. The great silence results, in part, from female silence, certainly female silence in art or the suppression of female artistic voices, so that we perceive silence where, in fact, there is a muffler. Beyond that is the specific denigration of female experience by women themselves, the cultural taboos against speaking of childbirth, of mothering—along with several other subjects—in truthful, nonsentimental ways, in ways that disturb patriarchal myths. So yes, there is that subliterature of female sentimentality, all the sweet and loving mothers, all the dutiful daughters, a literature that exults the passive, pastoral world of mothers and daughters and that comes packaged in a peculiar vagueness that we have yet to penetrate.

Many of the women writers whose work we have come to know had no children: Emily Dickinson, the Brontes, Jane Austen, Gertrude Stein, Virginia Woolf. The mothers have not on the whole left us a literary legacy because they were the ones risking death in childbirth, they were the ones mothering instead of becoming educated, they were the ones trained for marriage and domestic life, not for the solitude of pen on paper or brush on canvas.

When the mothers do speak, their voices are filled with guilt. Sylvia Plath's mother edited her daughter's letters and published them with introductory comments, prefatory remarks. The collection, *Letters Home,* cannot be thought of as an accurate document, not the whole story, for there are many elisions in crucial places. Still, we have the sound of the mother's voice, the guilt, the self-justification, the defense against an unheard attacker:

> Both my babies were rocked, cuddled, sung to, recited to, and picked up when they cried.
>
> At the end of my first year of marriage, I realized that if I wanted a peaceful home—and I did—I would simply have to become more submissive, although it was not my nature to do so.
>
> The children would never recognize their father, I felt, so I did not take them to the funeral, but placed them in the kind, understanding care of Marion Freeman for that afternoon. What I intended as an exercise in courage for the sake of my children was interpreted years later by my daughter as indifference.

So, too, the voice of Liv Ullmann in *Changing:*

> I was to give a child security and tenderness, but didn't feel I received enough of this myself. In the loneliness on the island I was often a nervous and short-tempered mother.... My disappointments at times worked themselves out on her. There were days with guilt feelings when I became the doormat for both of them. He who sat in his study and wanted to own me alone. And she who could barely walk, and cried for me from the other end of the house. I rushed from one to the other, always with a bad conscience.

A masterpiece, in this and many other ways, is the title story of Tillie Olsen's short story collection, *I Stand Here Ironing,* a monologue in the mind of a mother who has been asked by her daughter's high school teacher to come to school for a talk because the daughter "needs help." The mother's mind moves like her iron. The family is poor. The mother, abandoned by her husband, has struggled. Everyone is cornered. "Good enough" is a crowded day nursery for the second child so that the mother can work. The pain of the daughter as she grows into adolescence, which the mother can share but not banish. The daughter's gift for comedy, inexplicable. Back and forth, like the iron, the mother's mind moves, love and despair, blame and resignation. There is nothing else like it in literature. The iron stops:

> Let her be. So all that is in her will not bloom—but in
> how many does it? There is still enough left to live by.
> Only help her to know—help make it so there is cause
> for her to know—that she is more than this dress on
> the ironing board, helpless before the iron.

My mother says that the eyes in the photograph on the jacket of my first published book haunt her. They follow her around the room. She has turned the photograph to the wall.

What does she dream about me?

The daughter comes to tell the story.

The daughters have taken it upon themselves to tell the story of mothers and daughters, partly to break the silence of the mothers and partly to stand against the primacy of the father in our lives, in culture and in history. In becoming archaeologists of the world of our mothers, we are trying to retrieve the female past and to invent a future.

I the daughter am aware, as I write this, of the voices of

other daughters. I can hear Virginia Woolf describe, several times over, the floral pattern on Julia Stephen's dress. I can hear Colette re-creating Sido's voice, her antic, courageous speech. The deep, deep love of Carson McCullers and the profound respect of Alice Walker. I can hear Wendy talking about her yearly fishing trip with her mother—two women alone in nature, the sound of rushing water in their voices.

I long for a similar voice. Instead, I find:

A rage still raw and riotous, embarrassing in its power. Not simply never loved enough and lonely in that lack but, more specifically, hampered, poisoned, crippled by a frightening example. The woman was a sick child, remained a sick child. Yes, the outer eye sees the patriarchal encouragement, sees it in the world and in the actual personal father, the encouragement to be a sickly child, to lean, always, on the arm. Yes, the outer eye sees and the inner eye still fills with tears. This heritage passed on, becomes the coinage of all female relations in the family: Who now is the most sick child? My grandmother in her eighties and my mother in her sixties in terrible struggle, today, of who takes care, who is cared for, as though it is one or the other in some horrible final way, never reciprocal. And between myself and my mother, the same. This is our bond. This is the way we understand each other and, more horrible still, love each other.

The other day, I saw a daughter running. It was the end of the New York City marathon and she came, enervated and pleased, toward the finish line. Some yards before she reached it, another woman, older, stepped from the crowd. This woman, who looked like my mother, was not wearing athletic clothes, but she stepped into the path of the marathon, grasped the younger woman's hand, and they held those clenched hands aloft running slowly toward the end. They were clearly mother and daughter and their hands were raised together in a gesture of victory. They ran. They were full of pride. They ran in a way that makes the dark side of this subject, the violence between mother and daughter, bearable. They ran as though someone had made a crack in the universe and mother and daughter were rushing toward it.

1956. A suburb in Queens, as far from Manhattan as Peoria, Illinois, was. In the kitchen, where so many mother-daughter dramas unroll. Everywhere, in the lighted windows of two-story, red brick houses, women stand over their sinks, finishing washing the dishes of the evening meal. The fathers have sunk into armchairs in front of television sets. The brothers are out toting the garbage or dashing to basketball practice. I, a daughter of sixteen, and my mother of forty-three are having a discussion that begins quietly, full of tension. The situation is simple: I have been invited by my boyfriend to Fall Weekend at Cornell. This means a great deal in the world of adolescence. As I must, I am asking my mother's permission and my mother is refusing.

Foot-binder.

Mothers are the ones who stamp out the flowers.

Corset. Straitjacket.

"Let me out to the night." As Anna Wickham cried in a poem, "Let me go, let me go."

The mother has been charged with control of these things. She wants her daughter to "behave" because a badly behaved daughter means, in the mother's world, a failed mother. Sex is in question. It rises like the Loch Ness monster in the mother's mind. She imagines beer brawls and orgies—this is what is in the popular mind about such events as fall weekends at Cornell. (She knows the boy; she likes the boy; she cannot match the boy with orgies, but she sets that aside.) Sex troubles her in her own life; it troubles her in relation to her daughter in ways she cannot begin to think of.

Mother as Tree of Life.

Mother the protector, caretaker, nurturer.

To keep the child from harm. To protect her, even at the risk of her own life. To sense danger, as an animal does, and shield the young.

The mother says you cannot go and the daughter says why not and the mother falls back to parent language to say because I said so and the daughter presses and the mother says because and the daughter, more agitated, more provocative, insists WHY and the mother says that thing about "nice girls don't" and the daughter wants to be nice because her mother will love her if she is nice but wants to see Cornell and be with Robert and tell her friends she has been at a college weekend...

All the time, the mother is bending over the kitchen sink, washing the dishes. On the wall above her is a magnetic knife rack and five gleaming blades.

There is blood swirling between them. The daughter goes blind and out of her senses. Her hand is tight around the handle of the knife and her arm is raised—all very quickly—over her mother's bent head and shoulders. She grazes the bone at the top of her mother's spine.

1796. A thirty-two-year-old woman is sewing. The place is London and the time is a time of ferment, including a particular kind of ferment about women. The words "liberty," "equality," "fraternity" are in the air. Edmund Burke has proclaimed those words and they have been trumpeted throughout the American colonies. The idea of "freedom" is being acted on in all quarters and Mary Wollstonecraft has produced a passionate tract ap-

plying this idea to women—*Vindication of the Rights of Woman.*
Another Mary, Lady Mary Wortley Montague, had stood as
example of intellectual freedom. Her friendship/feud with Al-
exander Pope made her one among many women in the literary
limelight. A woman sewing would have known that there were
women writing, arguing; the sewer would have been stirred by
such examples.

All over London, there are salons and literary women,
while Mary Lamb sews in her cottage and her brother, Charles,
is an apprentice at the East India House, on the road toward a
profession and engaged in making a name for himself. It was
conventional for a young man to bring home acquaintanceship
with the ways of the world instead of income. In the evenings,
Charles carouses with his friends, men like himself who are
becoming serious writers.

In the century of great talk, the sewing is silent.

Charles has become friendly with Coleridge who, at the
moment, for nefarious and domestic reasons having to do with
marrying one woman and jilting another, has retired to the
country. Coleridge wishes, in the isolation of his country
domesticity, for the whiff and energy of literary London. He
invites Charles for a visit and begs Charles to bring his sister,
whom everyone finds intelligent and literate. Although she sews
while Charles scribbles and carouses, Mary Lamb holds her own
in literary company. She also supports the family. Sewing brings
the pounds to feed, clothe and house an invalid mother and a
senile father and to provide in various ways for Charles.

Charles Lamb heeds Coleridge's call from the country, but
demurs on behalf of his sister, explaining that Mary cannot come
because "my mother has grown so entirely helpless, not having
any use of her limbs, that Mary is necessarily confined from ever
sleeping out, she being her bedfellow." It is not unusual. None of
it is unusual. The labor of the daughter—always domestic, ill-
paid, piecemeal labor supporting the family—is common. The

care of the parents, especially the mother, is consigned to the daughter who is mother's "bedfellow." The unquestioning support for the brother and his aspirations, providing the labor that makes such aspirations possible—this, too, is common. The illness of the mother is not unusual either.

Mary Lamb's mother is crippled, confined to a wheelchair, probably with severe arthritis. Having no evidence to the contrary, one can only attribute to her the general attitudes of the time, the attitudes about women and about daughters, the sense that it was "natural" for Charles to do what he did, for Mary to care, sew and support. Elizabeth Lamb was poor and uneducated and she lived in a world that did not question the "naturalness" of her own family arrangements. Had Charles stayed home to sew and Mary gone out to make her way, the world would have fallen apart and everyone would have starved to death.

September 22. Mary Lamb is not alone at her sewing. She has an apprentice working beside her. A young woman, naturally. An argument breaks out between them. There is no record (*naturally*) of the cause of the argument—the way a garment was cut, perhaps, the color of a thread, woman's lot, the price of flour. No one told the tale. From her wheelchair—this much is told—the mother interferes and, it seems, takes the part of the apprentice. There is a knife on the table, part of the paraphernalia of Mary Lamb's trade.

The daughter has a knife in her hand.

Blood flows.

The blade went straight into Elizabeth Lamb's heart. She died immediately.

What would make the world safe for mothers and daughters?

—

The story does not end there. It moves both backward and forward. The apprentice fled. No one knows her name nor what happened to her afterward nor what effect what she witnessed had on her. Three women alone in a room: one dead, one fleeing, one with a knife in her hand. The father rushed in and cradled the dead wife. There was another character, present, reactions unrecorded—Mary Lamb's Aunt Sarah, Elizabeth Lamb's sister. Family records indicate that the sisters were enemies. What preceded the murder were three decades of life in a family where women were at each other's throats, sister against sister, seamstress against apprentice and, on the outskirts, the father in his senility, his withdrawal, and the brother in his ambition, another kind of withdrawal. What followed was quite different.

Charles returned for dinner. His mother was dead, his father sobbing, his sister had a knife in her hand, and there was blood. He took control, managed everything very well, found, quite quickly, remarkably human and progressive doctors who treated Mary as though she were ill and not a criminal. She was declared insane at the coroner's inquest and taken to a mental hospital. For the fifty-two remaining years of her life, she goes in and out of mental hospitals. She lives in the dark and in the light.

An odd thing happens. A rather frightening thing happens. Mary's life improves tremendously. Charles is a caring and devoted brother and in his scrimping to pay for Mary's medical care, he engages Mary, when she is feeling well, in various literary enterprises, among which is the *Tales from Shakespeare* that many of us read as children. Mary finds a friend named Sarah Stoddart, about whom one biographer says: "All that she was to achieve for herself independently in the way of fame and fortune she owed to Sarah Stoddart." Sarah, described as a woman with "boyish freedom," a woman of "considerable reading and vigorous understanding," liked to wear her hair short and drink brandy. In the latter enterprise, Mary often joined her. As she began to write, the poems were sent to Sarah. In uncanny irony,

Sarah Stoddart, who knew literary people and inspired Mary
Lamb, who had seen a bit of the world, retired, in 1805, to the
town of Winterslow to nurse her invalid mother.

In *Sanity, Madness and the Family,* R. D. Laing and A. Esterton
tell the story of Maya, who was sent to a mental hospital for at-
tacking her mother:

> According to her mother, Maya attacked her for no
> reason. It was the result of her illness coming on again.
> Maya said she could not remember anything about it.
> Her mother continually prompted Maya to try to
> remember.
>   Maya once said, however, that she could remem-
> ber the occasion quite clearly. She was dicing some
> meat. Her mother was standing behind her, telling her
> how to do things right, and that she was doing things
> wrong as usual. She felt something was going to snap
> inside unless she acted. She turned round and bran-
> dished the knife at her mother, and then threw it on
> the floor. She did not know why she felt like that. She
> was not sorry for what had happened, but she wanted
> to understand it. She said she had felt quite well at the
> time: she did not feel that it had to do with her
> "illness." She was responsible for it.
>   Our construction is that the whole episode might
> have passed unnoticed in many households as an ex-
> pression of ordinary exasperation between daughter
> and mother.

1979. My friend Leeny has a memory of something in her
adolescence, which she recounts now with great pain. When she
was seventeen and had dropped out of her first semester at New

York University, she "really needed help" and her parents were pressuring her to go back to school. She says: "I was talking to my mother, brushing my hair and I blacked out. I came to, beating her with a hairbrush. I freaked out. Crashed my hands through a chandelier. My hands were cut. I was whirling around, blood flying. A white carpet. I remember blood on a white carpet. The stain. I don't know what it means, but I had recently lost my virginity. I knew something important had happened. I went up to my room shaky but somehow cleared. It was horrible but important. My father calls this time in my life the 'calf age.'"

Toni Morrison's novel *Sula* is, like so much of her work, a labyrinth of female relations, their content understood and not understood by the characters, the force of the emotions among them—grandmother, mother, daughter, friend—a hurricane and none of it acceptable in polite society. Mistah Kurtz saw nothing ("the horror," he said at the end of *Heart of Darkness*) compared to what Toni Morrison saw and readers see in *Sula*.

Eva is the grandmother, one-legged, getting about in a wagon. She is in her bedroom looking for a comb, looks out the window and sees Hannah, her daughter, lighting a small fire in the yard. Eva finds the comb:

> Then she trundled back to the window to catch a breeze, if one took a mind to come by, while she combed her hair. She rolled up to the window and it was then she saw Hannah burning. The flames from the yard fire were licking the blue cotton dress, making her dance. Eva knew there was time for nothing in this world other than the time it took to get there and cover her daughter's body with her own. She lifted her heavy frame up on her good leg, and with fists and arms smashed the windowpane. Using her

stump as a support on the windowsill, her good leg as a lever, she threw herself out the window. Cut and bleeding, she clawed the air trying to aim her body toward the flaming, dancing figure.

She fails. Hannah dies ("the women who washed the body and dressed it for death wept for her burned hair and wrinkled breasts as though they themselves had been her lovers") and Eva nearly dies, too, left alone and unattended at the hospital. A male orderly saves her. Later, Eva remembers that she had seen Sula, her granddaughter, Hannah's daughter, standing on the back porch of the house watching Hannah burn:

> When Eva, who was never one to hide the faults of her children, mentioned what she thought she'd seen to a few friends, they said it was natural. Sula was probably struck dumb, as anybody would be who saw her own mamma burn up. Eva said yes, but inside she disagreed and remained convinced that Sula had watched Hannah burn not because she was paralyzed, but because she was interested.

This is not a novel about the viciousness of women. It is, instead, about not knowing, about the ways women deny their love for one another, within the family and between friends— "the eyes not seeing what the heart cannot hold," as one of Morrison's characters says. It is about a world in which women are all the same and Sula becomes "different." The ranks close against her and Sula is then "the most magnificent hatred they had ever known." The female community in its most conservative aspects is a larger version of the tensions between mother and daughter. Neither can allow the other's "difference." The force of respectability sets women against each other. Nel, Sula's girlhood friend, behaves as respectable women do; she joins the ranks of the rejectors.

This, then, is what begins to appear when daughters tell their stories. It is one part of what appears. There is more to come, but my eyes are fixed for the moment on what the heart cannot hold: the pain of this violence.

I return to myself in 1956 with a knife in my hand, raising it over my mother, who is washing the dishes.

I became unmanageable as a daughter when aspiration took over and what had smoldered burst through, bringing fear, confusion, and terrible anxiety. To be a daughter, up to that point, to be my mother's daughter, does not seem, looking backward, to have been a difficult task. Certain kinds of compliance were required, which wore thin. I was an adequate enough doll to be displayed and then I wasn't. It was my mother's job to manage this.

Now why was it to have been my mother's job? By whom was she assigned this task and in what ways equipped to carry it out; for whose good did the task exist at all? To "socialize" a rambunctious (I remember that word, it was applied to me often), tense, intellectual, turbulent daughter—this was the task, to tame, train her to be "woman" at the same time retaining love between them and looking good in the eyes of the world. A link in the chain of women binding each other's feet. The corset. The straitjacket.

Sula is "different"; she wants a larger life. One can only begin to imagine Mary Lamb's despair. In his study, Laing says that "schizophrenic" behavior is socially intelligible, that it makes sense in the context of each particular family. In Maya's case, every attempt at "individuation" was interpreted as "crazy" within the family. Against these aspirations, these struggles, these gaspings for air, stand the mothers. Or stands something that we take to be the mothers. "Aspirations," in this context, means much more, applies in many different ways, than the girl who wants to grow up to be Virginia Woolf. (Or Tolstoy.) It means the desire to live.

A twenty-one-year-old migrant farm worker is pursued by the crew leader. She refuses him and is known in the community as "uppity" and "strange." The crew leader comes to talk with her mother who is evasive. The young woman, listening behind a door, has heard, is angry. As Robert and Jane Coles report what happens next:

> She charged out of the bedroom, crying and shouting at her mother. Why was she so quiet, so acquiescent? ... She told her daughter that there would never be a chance that she would speak back to the crew leader, speak up to him, let him know what she felt. She told the daughter that it was foolish for them to argue, they both knew the truth—and were turning on each other for a lack of an opportunity to go after their real enemy. The daughter was impressed, but still quite suspicious: "I can't even believe my own mother, I realize that now. She is so tired and scared.... My mother has lost track of herself; she thinks of herself as someone's echo. It is too bad for her. And she is the one who tells me I can't afford to be like that. I can't afford *not* to be like that!"

Personal pathology begins to cross centuries, to appear in our literature, to point not only to psychology but to politics. The motif of repression comes up again and again, with mother as the agent. It is expected, of course, that rebellion be natural in a growing person, that one needs to push against in order to establish what one is. The rebellion of girls against mothers focuses on sexuality, just as "adventure" for girls is usually sexual. For every man who climbs a mountain or becomes President of the United States, there is a woman who sleeps with someone her mother would not "approve" of.

In the 1930s, Nancy Cunard, a British poet, journalist and editor, published a pamphlet called "Black Man and White Ladyship," which was a vicious attack on her mother, particularly her upper-class mother's attitude toward race. Cunard had been "romantically involved" with black men, politically involved with black literature. She had been "seen" in London with what she calls "a great Negro friend" and her mother had objected most forcefully, with certain economic force behind her objections. Cunard's pamphlet purports to ridicule her mother—whose yearly clothing budget, among other things, was printed in a London newspaper, causing great envy among its readers. In fact, it attacks the politics of her mother's class, with Lady Cunard as an example of it. Sir Thomas Beecham and George Moore are quoted as making some especially critical and repressive remarks to Nancy Cunard—on her mother's behalf. The diatribe ends with these words: "How come, white man, is the rest of the world to be reformed in your dreary and decadent image?"

A woman of extraordinary political consciousness, Nancy Cunard seems, here, to have failed to make the kinds of connections she is able to make in so many other contexts. To confuse and accuse her mother for the attitudes of the white man, especially the British ruling class, is to conform to the consciousness of a mother-blaming culture. The facts of the accusation are certainly true. Had Cunard read Virginia Woolf's *Three Guineas,* she might have gone further in her thought and feeling on the matter. She might have asked how it came to be that Lady Cunard aligned herself with the Lords of the Empire.

"A very common termination of despair is murder." An eighteenth-century doctor wrote that, a friend of the man who treated Mary Lamb in her madness. Although it is true that Mary Lamb's life "improved" in many ways after she killed her mother, it is also true that Mary Lamb suffered endlessly. Virginia Woolf wrote eloquently about the need to kill "the Angel in the House," that woman who represents everything men want women to be:

> She was intensely sympathetic. She was immensely charming. She was utterly unselfish. She excelled in the difficult arts of family life. She sacrificed herself daily. . . . She was so constituted that she never had a mind or a wish of her own, but preferred to sympathize always with the minds and wishes of others.

Yet the Angel does not die, even in these extreme and bizarre circumstances. Mary Lamb was haunted by her mother's presence the remainder of her life, hallucinated her frequently. Guilt, certainly, shaped those hallucinations but so too did the need for a mother. "Until I was in the forties," Virginia Woolf wrote, "the presence of my mother obsessed me. I could hear her voice, see her, imagine what she would do or say as I went about my day's doings." Mary Wollstonecraft had two daughters. One became Mary Shelley and wrote *Frankenstein;* in giving birth to Mary the mother contracted purpureal fever and died. The other daughter, Fanny, was three and a half years old at the time. When Fanny was twenty-two, she killed herself with laudanum and was found wearing corset stays marked with her mother's initials. The corset stays gleam in the darkness, emblems of the twin themes of mothers and daughters: the passionate anger and the passionate need for reconciliation.

It is easier to write about anger than love, and easier still to write about love than need. From generation to generation, the idea of heritage appears and reappears as a hall of mirrors, daughter reflecting mother, mother reflecting grandmother. A woman on a bus this morning told me that she has found herself collecting small scraps of rags. When her husband asked her what they were for, she said—to make a braided rug with. Her mother had always done it. In fact, though, the last person in the family to actually make a braided rug was her grandmother. Out went the rags. Some of these rags of ours belong in the trash; others become braided rugs.

Something that looks like love runs through Sylvia Plath's published correspondence with her mother, beginning with Plath's arrival at Smith College in 1950 and ending a week before her suicide.

Aurelia Plath was a bookish girl, she says, always reading, hiding books under the mattresses of the beds she was meant to be making, sneaking the books in between domestic chores, much as Dorothy Wordsworth crammed the *Iliad* before making breakfast. Aurelia Plath had a genuine passion for literature— along with and different from her passion for her daughter's "success." This literary passion was, in her own life, transformed to service. She did not see herself—not consciously, or she won't say so or she was aware of history and limitations and put it aside—as a writer, as a maker of literature but, instead: "My evergrowing wish became to open to other young people this wonder of multiple living through vicarious experience—to teach."

Although she claims to have lived in a matriarchy, the facts of Aurelia Plath's life (in fact, the facts of *life*) deny it. "It never occurred to me," she writes, "to question my father's decision as to the type of education I should receive." She was trained for "business," became a high school English teacher, and sent herself back to school for a master's degree in German and English literature, met and married one of her professors, Otto Plath: "I yielded to my husband's wish that I become a full-time housemaker." He was engaged in "important" work. She helped. His books lined the dining room table and Aurelia Plath managed to have friends for dinner the one night a week Otto was out teaching an evening course. "During the first year of our married life, all had to be given up for THE BOOK," she writes. "After Sylvia was born, it was THE CHAPTER." She helped: "My husband outlined the sections, listing authors and their texts to be used as reference and I did the reading and note-taking along the lines he indicated, writing the first draft. After that he took over, rewriting and adding his own notes. Then he handed the manuscript to me to put into final form for the printer."

There is only the faint hint of complaint in this, always balanced by a "but"—the brilliance of her husband and, later, the brilliance of her daughter. Her own mother, says Aurelia Plath, "was sympathetic. And when I was in college read my literature books too, saying cheerily, 'More than one person can get a college education on one tuition.'" The same, of course, occurs between Aurelia Plath and her daughter.

Together, through most of the letters, Sylvia and Aurelia Plath seem to be braiding an elaborate literary rug. The daughter sends the mother reading lists, discusses her courses, professors, ambitions, triumphs. Drafts of poems pass through the mail. Early successes and crushing disappointments. Impassioned ambition. The mother sends the daughter notices of writing contests, copies of reviews, articles, suggestions, comments. She suggests sending a short story to *Woman's Day* instead of *The New Yorker,* offers to teach her daughter shorthand. It is, like everything, a mixed bag, this rug they weave, and it unravels often, but both mother and daughter pretend that it doesn't.

"All the schoolboys I know here think of me as a second Virginia Woolf," wrote Sylvia Plath. What did the girls think?

Sylvia and Aurelia Plath are bound together in a frenzy for male approval. Although Sylvia's letters from her college years are full of the discovery of other women, her classmates, and the various relationships she makes there, it is the men who have the glitter, who hold the key to the success she is bent on. Although her first major success in the world was at *Mademoiselle* where she worked with women, she sets her sights "higher," which meant aiming at acceptance by the men who ran *The Atlantic* and *The New Yorker, London Magazine,* the Fulbright Commission, and the BBC. The poets she admires are men. There is a short note about meeting Adrienne Rich at lunch, but nothing happens between them; Sylvia writes to her mother about the male poets present. After her marriage to Ted Hughes and her exhilaration at having found the only man there could be for her, her delirium about the writing they will do together, after the honeymoon come the two babies. Sylvia assumes the role in Ted's life that her mother played in her father's: she minds the children, cooks the meals, types his manuscripts and writes to everyone asking about a teaching job for him in America. Ted edits an anthology with his "poet-twin," as she calls him, Thom Gunn, and generally, with the success of his book *Lupercal,* he moves not so much into the limelight—which must have presented a different set of problems—but into an enormous support network of poets and editors, award dinners and a pint at the "local."

There has been speculation about Plath's suicide and the forces bearing down on her in the winter of 1963: the exhausting care of the children and struggle for money, the bitter winter, the desertion by Hughes and jealousy about his "other woman," the quirky events that lead some people to think that she did not intend to die but to be found and that she miscalculated. I would add to these forces the special nature of her isolation from other women. There is not a note in her letters about reading Virginia Woolf, although schoolboys thought of her as a reincarnation. No Colette or Stein. No Sexton or Rich or Levertov or Rukeyser. Just before she died, she expressed an interest in meeting the British woman poet Stevie Smith. Plath refused, continually, her mother's offers of assistance, asking, instead, that her brother's wife come to be with her. She had always been a daughter and she seems to have been trying to free herself.

She had always been a daughter. And to more than one woman. The novelist Olive Higgins Prouty, who had made a fortune and great popular success with *Stella Dallas,* sponsored the scholarship that enabled Sylvia Plath to go to Smith College and Mrs. Prouty became, as Aurelia Plath said, "her literary mother." Plath was "saved" continually by women as she pursued the accolades of men. This is not to blame her. She was in this way quite conventional. She needed other women to "mother" her—as her culture told her women would and could do. A college classmate told, years later, of Sylvia's desperate and coercive need. She found Plath one morning screaming with "recrimination and pain":

> "My head is flying off," she shrieked. "I can't stand the pain. Do something; I'm dying."

The friend found a doctor, then discovered:

Sylvia's reasoning was simple: I could not possibly leave to take an exam when she needed me there, allied with her against the fear and pain.

I could not escape the feeling that she was asking me to Play God. . . . I could not promise to keep her going like some intricate, erratic timepiece and I could not face the guilt that would result if I failed to try. So I drew back instinctively, allowing some distance to come between us like an invisible barrier.

This is a daughter remaining a daughter in relation to her mother and to other women. Plath could not find in her culture or in herself a force to set against daughterness. The information in her letters and the comments of people who knew her show

Aurelia and Sylvia Plath complying in carrying on the father's definition of this relation: that mother be selfless and sacrificing; that daughter behave like father and son, expecting nurturance and selflessness as her due, as her mother's job, denigrating its value. Plath dedicated her first book to her "literary mother," Olive Prouty. While Aurelia Plath typed Sylvia's work, submitted her poems to magazines, requested application forms for her, Sylvia was helped and suffocated at the same time. Every once in a while, she encouraged her mother to do her own writing, suggesting small "tidbits" Aurelia Plath might write up for local magazines.

They are both playing by the rules. Sylvia becomes wife and mother, finds selflessness expected of *her*. No one can change the rules. No one can see the rules. Sylvia dies.

Mother as muse. It is not infrequent to find, in literary women, the inspiring mother, feeder and enabler. It is not very different, either, from the Stage Mother. What is different is the way one looks at the content of these relationships. They are of course ambivalent—on both sides. A daughter living out a mother's thwarted ambition is a cause of fulfillment and envy to the mother, has a sense of the "mission" of her heritage and a terrible feeling of pressure. Such daughters have never felt free to fail. The darker sides of this shadowy terrain receive the most emphasis—it is the clash and not the bond that makes, conventionally, the stuff of drama. Acknowledging the tension, distance, and conflict, where is a map of the nurturance, the connection, the ways in which the torch is passed from mother to daughter or from daughter to mother?

In Colette.

Colette is the poet of passion between mother and daughter. Colette paints the portrait of mother as the Tree of Life. *Sido* and *My Mother's House* are profoundly romantic, resonating courageously against the mother-hatred of our culture—born of the fear and denial of the sons, the need to master and to distance, caught with terrible contagion in the daughters. Colette stands, too, at the other end of the scale or the other side of the coin, against the sickly idealization of mother-love:

> I did not learn from her that between mothers and offspring there exists a strict and perfect love called sacred, which cannot be broken except at great cost and great scandal. On the contrary, with an imperious hand she waved away the fruits of these teachings that I had acquired at school or in my books.

What she learned from Sido on this score, she says, is that it was "written" that she should leave her mother. She describes Sido in wrath about a neighbor who cannot let her own daughters go:

> "Madame Thomazeau is a harpy, a bad mother, an old horror, a dangerous fool, a fake, a criminal.... At a distance, Madame Thomazeau is cleverly poisoning the life of her daughters and son-in-law, she's carrying out an abominable blackmail to get back her daughter!"

"Throughout her prose and poetry, Sylvia fused parts of my life with hers," wrote Aurelia Plath. That peculiar combination of semblance and difference, or "the problem of merging" as psychologists call it, that so plagues mothers and daughters seems to have been spared Colette and Sido. "I never thought of our resemblance," Colette says, "but she knew I was her own daughter and that, child though I was, I was already seeking for that sense of shock, the quickened heartbeat, and the sudden stoppage of the breath." Colette writes of Sido's "native lucidity," her "wild gaiety, a contempt for the whole world, a lighthearted disdain" and her intermittent "urge to escape from everyone and everything, to soar to some high place" and her "love of combat."

Miracle or myth? The uniqueness of Colette's vision of her mother makes it important to probe the context in which it came to pass or in which it took shape in the writer's imagination. What Colette so loved in Sido was a special kind of female strength. She loved what her mother knew about the world—which way the wind was blowing, where it was raining. Sido was close to nature and alert to portents. She made barometers out of oats and could tell whether it would be a cold winter or not based on the number of skins an onion had. These are ancient female arts, the talents of shamans and witches, and they were practiced in a culture that neither demeaned nor tamed them.

Sido does not seem to have lived in the patriarchy. Or Colette did not see her in that way. Both mother and daughter had a shared distance from and benign contempt for male authority, in fact for what Virginia Woolf called "the male sphere." For example:

> If the newspapers foretold a thaw, my mother would shrug her shoulders and laugh scornfully. "A thaw? Those Paris meteorologists can't teach me anything about that. Look at the cat's paws." Feeling chilly, the cat had indeed folded her paws out of sight beneath her, and shut her eyes tight. "When there's only going to be a short spell of cold," went on Sido, "the cat rolls herself into a turban with her nose against the root of her tail. But when it's going to be really bitter, she tucks in the pads of her front paws and rolls them up like a muff."

Sido is "irreverent." She holds herself "aloof" from "Catholic trivialities and pageantries." In this aloof space, mother and daughter can meet, the air can be clear between them. Colette describes herself curled up at her mother's feet, her head at Sido's knees:

> No half-grown males anywhere, no sign of a man. . . . The deep peace of a harem, under the nests of May, and the wisteria shot with sunlight . . . and the hands of my mother at the back of my neck, deftly braiding my hair.

The sunlight is clear. It does not hold the shadow for Colette that it did for Virginia Woolf, whose memory of her mother was that she was always surrounded by men. Woolf said that every time she imagined her mother's deathbed, she thought she saw a man sitting on the bed's edge. There was, in reality, none, but there were, in other ways, many.

Shall we discount our own mythmaking?

A daughter looking at her mother's life is looking at her own, shaping and fitting one life to suit the needs of another. Some have shaped monsters and some angels. Most who make angels see their mother as the sources of art, the tree of creative life. We need to do this. We have always needed to do this. Margaret Fuller founded a group of women in Boston in the nineteenth century with whom she could discuss serious questions of the day. Alice Walker sees in her mother's garden the mirror of her own activity as a poet; so does Colette. We need to find or make more women like ourselves. We need to find or make foremothers. And mothers.

1926. Colette is fifty-three years old. She has married M. Willy and written several racy "Claudine" novels, published under Willy's name, and made a sensation. She has left Willy, become a music hall performer, written *La Vagabonde*, become part of the lesbian life of Paris, lived with her woman lover for four years, become a journalist, married her editor at *Le Matin*, had a daughter, survived Sido's death and a world war, achieved serious recognition as a writer called "Colette Willy." She is working on a book called *Break of Day* and has decided to name herself now only "Colette." In *Break of Day,* she names herself in another way:

> I am the daughter of a woman who, in a mean, close-fisted, confined little place, opened her village home to stray cats, tramps and pregnant servant girls. I am the daughter of a woman who many a time, when she was in despair at not having enough money for others, ran through the wind-whipped snow to cry from door to door, at the houses of the rich, that a child had just been born to a poverty-stricken home to parents whose feeble, empty hands had no swaddling clothes for it. Let me not forget that I am the daughter of a woman who bent her head, trembling, between the blades of a cactus, her wrinkled face full of ecstasy over the promise of a flower, a woman who herself never ceased to flower, untiringly, during three quarters of a century.

1978. I am standing in a large room in New York City at night, part of a circle of women. We have just seen a theatre piece at Womanrite Theatre about mothers and daughters. This is the closing ritual:

> "I am Honor, daughter of Jennie, daughter of Margarett, daughter of Jane, daughter of Isabel."

> "I am Helene, daughter of Rosemary, daughter of a woman from Hungary..."

Some of us have the same names in our pasts. Some can only name two generations before us; others go further.

I am Louise, daughter of Rita, daughter of Pauline.

Against the flatness of the cultural stereotype, the multiplicity of experience, stands the specificity of time, place, class, race, the setting, the context. Which mother–daughter relationship? The one between the mother at one end of the cotton mill, working, and the nine-year-old daughter at the other end, also working, both awake since the whistle blast at five in the morning? Or the one between the lady of the house who sits near her fire in the morning room doing her correspondence and the daughter being fitted for a dress for the debutante ball?

I want to leap, pretending to have a confidence none of us has, into a place in our imaginations where our mothers stand on firm ground, along with our sisters, daughters, friends, lovers, grandmothers, aunts, nieces, to a place where we become the mythmakers and these female connections are the stuff of our myths and we consider these to be the *primary* stories, the *Odyssey,* the *Iliad,* Greek drama, Shakespeare, Tolstoy. To work of this stature we bring all we know. Imagine: a woman is wandering in the countryside; at the foot of a gnarled tree or at a crossroads she encounters another woman making a journey. . . .

Imagine that we conjure up a world that is safe for mothers and daughters. A great celebration takes place at the birth of a daughter. The mother is honored; the girl-child is honored. Imagine the attention paid to her development, attention to her strength, her courage. Will she be taught to use a microscope, cut down a tree, invent a new art form? Imagine the mother thinking as Oriana Fallaci thought, considering the child then unborn who was in fact never born:

> Will you be a man or a woman? I'd like you to be a woman.
>
> I'd like you for one day to go through what I'm going through. I don't at all agree with my mother, who thinks it's a misfortune to be born a woman. . . . It's an adventure that takes such courage, a challenge that's never boring. You'll have so many things to engage you if you're born a woman. To begin with, you'll have to struggle to maintain that if God exists he might even be an old woman with white hair or a beautiful girl. Then you'll have to struggle to explain that it wasn't sin that was born on the day when Eve picked an apple: what was born that day was a splendid virtue called disobedience. Finally, you'll have to struggle to demonstrate that inside your smooth shapely body there's an intelligence crying out to be heard. To be a mother is not a trade. It's not even a duty. It's only one right among many. What an effort it will be for you to convince others of this fact. You'll rarely be able to.

Imagine that when the mother of the American novelist Zora Neale Hurston told her to jump at the sky she was simply reflecting the norms of the culture, the enterprise to which she had set her own heart.

Someday my mother and I will ride out to Ellis Island and stand on the spot where the ship came in, the ship that bore the technician who put a rusty needle into her arm, intending inoculation, carelessly causing disease and shaping her first years in the New World. Someday I will see where my grandmother

laid down the eiderdown, all she had brought, to answer
questions, turning, I imagine, to watch over each of her young
daughters as she answered or invented. Someday the silence that
dampens the female side of my family history will be broken and
the eiderdown will replace the diamond that Izzy brought in his
shoe or the two women grandfather had, one in Warsaw, one in
America, that are told to the children as marks of heroism.

3

Sisters

SOMETIMES I FEEL
LIKE A SISTERLESS CHILD

You know full as well as I do the value of sisters' affections to each other; there is nothing like it in this world.

Charlotte Brontë

I am very much interested in your life, which I think of writing another novel about. It's fatal staying with you—you start so many new ideas.

Virginia Woolf to Vanessa Bell

My sister four years older simply existed for me because I had to sleep in the same room with her. Besides, it is natural not to care about a sister, certainly not when she is four years older and grinds her teeth at night.

Gertrude Stein

Sometimes I feel like a motherless child.
Sometimes I feel like a sisterless child.
Sometimes I think Louisa May Alcott's novel *Little Women* ruined my life. It presented me, in my childhood, an image of what I did not have. I never forgot it. *Little Women* was to middle-class white girls what the Hardy Boys books were to our brothers. The adventure of female domestic activity was our equivalent of adventure in the world. I was mesmerized by the fun girls had together, the warmth of the hearth, the love and the intimacy. This is what a girl takes away from that novel.

The presence of sisters seemed to me a wonderful thing,

standing for companionship, physical intimacy, all varieties of warmth and some vague sense of a circle of female protection. Against the "otherness" of father and brother, I dreamed up many mother/friends, caring females, playmates. My phantom sister was always younger than I, somewhat of a follower, somewhat of a fan, somewhat more a child than myself. I would be, like Jo in *Little Women,* the writer/sister. My one or several phantom sisters would draw or play the piano. I was dreaming up sisterhood.

I held to this idea in spite of the tension between my actual mother and her own sister in which I was often the pawn. My aunt could cause my mother shame by dousing me with love—it was easier; she was not my mother; I was not her responsibility, her daily life. I kept this idea in spite of seeing that they had made or accepted a conventional sibling division, my mother and my aunt, one becoming the serious, intellectual, "smart" sister, the other outgoing, sociable, the "pretty" sister. I held to this imaginary sisterhood in spite of the bickering, the mockery, the competition of my grandmother and her sisters, the guilt that bound them to one another, the rivalry over who had the cleanest house, cooked the best meals, had daughters who made the best marriages, husbands who earned the highest income. I clung, still, to my desire for a phantom sister when my best friend, in adolescence, bonded with me against her own sister, used me, in a way, as a reproach—see, my friend is a better friend to me than *you* are—and I shared with her the youthful sadistic pleasure of excluding the sister. If I knew, in spite of what I saw around me, that there were other ways for women to treat each other, better things that we could be to and for each other, it was because of what I made and retained from my reading of *Little Women*.

I bought the myth of devotion. Whatever its actual undercurrents, *Little Women* exudes, more in memory than in reading, an atmosphere of female fidelity, sensitivity and support. In part, like most myths, the myth of devotion is true, for life with a sister, especially youth with a sister, is one place where it is all right to love another woman, to have mutual care and solidarity. Boys will be boys. They will fight with each other and with their sisters. Everyone expects it. But girls will be sugar and spice, everything nice, little mothers, sweetness and light. Conflict will be banished and bottled. It will seep out of the edges in conventionally "feminine" ways, as jealousy and envy.

In spite of the myth of devotion, most of our intellectual inheritance shows sisters deep in antagonism, as most women are shown deep in antagonism. The particular conflict of female siblings is more marked by the blood they have in common and is almost always the specific conflict over men. Mothers are hardly mentioned. A man stands between sisters. What he does or thinks determines what happens between them. Rachel and Leah in the Old Testament are married to the same man, competing to have his child. Jesus stands between Mary and Martha. Although "Cinderella" is not actually about three sisters, it echoes the motif of stories that are, which are many, and which all include, in one guise or another, a virtually offstage prince who, as symbol, motivates the women at home.

Shakespeare's *King Lear* is one such story. In *Lear,* the action begins when King Father assembles his daughters, asking them to pay obeisance to him, his law, his language, his property. Cordelia, the youngest daughter, refuses, alone among the sisters. Cordelia stands in loving revolt against patriarchal authority in its outward forms, but no one stands with her.

Chekhov's *Three Sisters* is another. In both, the focus of the action is the attempt by sisters to get hold of a man's property: in *Lear,* the father's kingdom, for Chekhov, the brother's house. This sets in motion a Cinderella-like configuration among the sisters. The older sisters are evil and the young one is good, virtuous, virginal. The youngest usually wins whatever there is to be won. From Cinderella through Cordelia to the latest pulp novel, the youngest daughter is the best daughter, for she is daddy's favorite girl. The youngest child is the family baby; the youngest daughter is doubly infantilized. Pliant child-women devoted to daddy are consistent literary heroines.

They do each other no good, these female siblings, if the stories are to be believed. One would be better off without them. In this masculine vision, all women would be better off without other women, for the woman alone—motherless, sisterless, friendless—can fix her eyes solely on father, brother, lover, and therefore peace will reign in the universe. Or masculine power will have its way.

Remove the man from the room. Say that King Lear is not the initiator of the action. Say that there is, for the moment, no kingdom to inherit, that what the King Father can bring, do or give is not the heart of the matter. Other things exist, rise to the foreground, beat the way blood does in the body.

When women write about sisters, the myth of devotion returns. Mrs. Gaskell, the first biographer of Charlotte Brontë, gives us mid-nineteenth-century England, the Yorkshire moors, a woven cloth of devoted sisterhood:

> It was the household custom among these girls to sew till nine o'clock at night. At that hour, Miss Branwell generally went to bed, and her nieces' duties for the day were accounted done. They put away their work, and began to pace the room backwards and forwards, up and down—as often with the candles extinguished for economy's sake, as not—their figures glancing into the fire-light, and out into the shadow, perpetually. At this time, they talked over past cares, and troubles; they planned for the future, and consulted each other as to their plans. In after years, this was the time for

discussing together the plots of their novels. And again, still later, this was the time for the last surviving sister to walk alone, from old accustomed habit, round and round the desolate room, thinking sadly upon the days that were no more.

But each of these sisters was human, complex. Each was subject to her own kind of tension, her own aspect of the pull of one sister against another, little of it having to do with the father's property. Look to dreams, to Charlotte Brontë's dreaming, for something between sisters less easily said in waking life. At the time of one recorded dream, Charlotte's two older sisters have died, two younger sisters are very much in her care. Charlotte told her friend Mary Taylor that she had been dreaming about the dead sisters, but resisted telling what she had dreamed, stopped, claimed there was no more. Mary urged her to "go on! *Make it out!* I know you can."

Charlotte forced herself to go on. She had dreamed, she said, a change in her sisters. She saw them fashionably dressed and critical, while, in reality, their lives had been homespun and innocent. They were alienated from Charlotte and turned against her. "They had forgotten what they used to care for," she said to Mary Taylor, meaning, presumably, not only the simplicity of their values, but their love for Charlotte. The dream shows the underside of the myth of devotion, touching, as it does, something Charlotte would resist telling. It appears to be about the pain and anger, on Charlotte's part, of rejection. There is some aspect of betrayal here, some of the pressure Charlotte must have felt as she assumed the role of mother to her younger sisters, some anxiety she must have had about her ability to care for the still living sisters. The oldest sister takes on aspects of mother and, too, shows the way to the younger ones. Charlotte dreamed her failure at these tasks. You left me. You hurt me. I have failed by not providing for you, by not keeping you alive. Have you turned on me now?

Charlotte's dream language is the countercurrent to the myth of devotion, to the picture of unity and solidarity presented to the world by the Brontë sisters and enshrined by Mrs. Gaskell in her biography of Charlotte. Gaskell was Charlotte's good friend and in writing about her made her more saintly than anyone could have been, less ambivalent about caring for her sisters. Some aspects of the Brontë myth of devotion were a matter of style and some of it was need, for a sister was all Charlotte, Emily or Anne actually *had* in the world. It was not the style of the time to air private tensions, but dreams disobey style.

In imagining myself the older sister with a phantom younger one, I have overlooked Charlotte Brontë's fear and guilt. I have not walked through her dreams.

Several historical realities burn in the fireplace Mrs. Gaskell describes, casting shadows as insistent as the shapes of three sisters pacing. They were born into limited possibility. Women whose families were not rich and who did not make "good" marriages lived with the constant press of poverty, constant thwarting of ambition, slow and painful depletion. The Brontë sisters were daughters of a country curate. Their mother died when they were all quite young and for them the only economic possibility was that they become governesses, which each did in turn and for various lengths of time. They were allowed to see the world through the shutters of other people's houses, generally despised and degraded (the boys who were being educated got male tutors when their education became "serious") and the object, often, the vulnerable prey, of the sexual attention of the master of the house. Harriet Martineau, who knew what she saw around her, said that governesses comprised the largest segment of the population of madhouses.

Family hopes rested on the shoulders of the brothers. It was Branwell in the case of the Brontës, as it had been Charles in Mary Lamb's life, William in Dorothy Wordsworth's. It was Branwell for whom the women of the house sewed clothes and

saved and sent off to London to make his fortune. Where Charles
Lamb and William Wordsworth succeeded, dooming their sisters
to servitude and shadow, Branwell failed.

Branwell failed dramatically and ended crushed by brandy,
opium, debts and thwarted hopes of union with the lady of a
house in which he had been a tutor. His shoulders caved in. In
1845, three years before his death but with the dissolution well
along, Charlotte "found" her sister Emily's poems and their lives
turned around. Charlotte was twenty-nine, Branwell twenty-
eight, Emily twenty-seven and Anne twenty-five. They had
behind them, all four, a childhood history of shared writing—
Charlotte and Branwell's *Angria,* Emily and Anne's *Gondal,*
fantasy epics begun at a very young age, taken up and dropped
for years. Their mother had been a graceful letterwriter; the
Reverend Brontë had published a novel and some poems—it was
in the air, along with the repression, disease, isolation, and
despair of Haworth parsonage.

For most of their lives, Charlotte was the oldest child in the
family. She tested the waters of the world. She went out as a
governess first. She fell passionately in love with a married man
who, from her point of view, invited her attention, then refused
to answer her letters. She suffered and conquered most visibly,
whether she shared confidences with her sisters or not. They
watched. Charlotte's initial bonding was with Branwell and
with her father; she linked her literary ambition and desire for
growth to the men around her, later to men in the world. But it
was an ambivalent linking and it left her sisters behind. As eldest
daughter, she tended her father and was mother to the younger
children, taking charge of their education and, eventually,
managing their lives—or attempting to. With such power and
control went guilt and responsibility. Were it not for Charlotte,
most likely, we would not now know the Brontë name.

Emily was the middle sister, Anne the baby. Emily shuttled back and forth, going as little sister on Charlotte's expeditions, the most important one being a year's journey to Belgium, where Charlotte developed a passion for a married man. These forays into the world made Emily ill and each time she demurred and returned home. Each illness was real, each had the effect of an act of defiance, for between Charlotte and Emily there obviously existed, covered, severe and ordinary kinds of conflict. Between Emily and Anne, the air was calmer and others observed the younger sisters to be "almost like twins," although they were not. Still, like a middle child, Emily shuttled and moored nowhere. As Margaret Drabble once shrewdly saw, Charlotte and Anne were preoccupied with and wrote about loneliness, while Emily's subject was solitude. She made great peace with certain aspects of the world, those aspects that were not the objects of both Charlotte's and Anne's ambition. In many ways, she was not interested in what her sisters and society would have called "The World." Setting herself apart from it and from them, she found solitude.

It has to do with the shape of family relations, as well as with character, that Emily Brontë could arrive at that place which so resembles the solitude and inner life of her spirit-sister in America, Emily Dickinson, and out of that create *Wuthering Heights*. It is not simply a feeling for nature that Emily Brontë had, but a feeling for the single self alone in the world.

This is what Jungian analyst Marie-Louise von Franz points to as a great problem for women, given the ways we live in the world. Von Franz is interpreting a fairy tale, considering the point in the narrative where the female character is banished to the forest:

> Most women, since they depend so much on relationship and long for it, have great difficulty in admitting to themselves how lonely they are and in

accepting that as a given situation. To retire into the forest would be to accept the loneliness consciously, and not to try to make relationships with good will, (for that is not the real thing.) According to my experience, it is very painful, but very important, for women to realize and accept their loneliness. The virgin soil would be that part of the psyche where there was no impact of collective human activities, and to retire to that would be to retire not only from all animus opinions and views of life, but from any kind of impulse to do what life seems to demand of one. The forest would be the place of unconventional inner life, in the deepest sense of the word. Living in the forest would mean sinking into one's innermost nature and finding out what it feels like.

In these terms, all of the Brontës were fortunate, for their lives were played out at a greater distance than most from "collective human activities." Haworth parsonage was, in that sense, a given forest. Loneliness resolved is solitude. Emily's embracing of it cut her off from Anne, for it was not a shareable thing. They were not twins. The pairing of Emily and Anne was in Charlotte's eyes, and it was a measure of her feeling of isolation from the two and the ways in which she was haunted by it.

The conversation among sisters proceeds subliminally. They speak to each other in dreams, implant one another in their novels, make gestures whose meaning is buried to the outside eye. One such gesture occurred when Charlotte found, accidentally, as she said, her sister Emily's poems. The ease of that finding is interesting, for Emily was capable of secreting what she wanted to keep secret. The poems must have been set where they might be found. How simple an avoidance of the direct action: Emily need not subject herself to Charlotte's authority, need not submit, need not be apparent in her need for Charlotte's approval. She needs simply leave the poems to be found.

When Charlotte found Emily's poems, she was astonished, which shows the great distance between them—in spite of the knot of sisters sharing their work that Mrs. Gaskell described, she was surprised by the quality of the poems. She thought them "masculine" in their force, which shows something about Charlotte's thinking. She took the opportunity that her sister's poems provided, the key that they were to what she was seeking. She intensified the role she had played in her sisters' lives all along, but gave it a dramatic turn. She had always been Mother, now she became Rescuer. A great deal of frenzied and persistent activity on Charlotte's part followed and within a year the first published work of the Brontës appeared, Emily's poems surrounded by those of Charlotte and Anne.

To dress the literature of women in male trousers was, as the sisters knew, a necessary nineteenth-century strategy, and so the sisters Brontë became the brothers Bell (Acton, Currer and Ellis) and ended up with a book in their hands. That it sold only two copies is less important than what it seems to have set off in their lives—they began immediately to write novels. It was, biographers say, an idea Charlotte picked up from Branwell, who had begun and abandoned a novel years earlier, but pick it up she did—and carry it forward. Again, we have this part of the story through Charlotte's eyes—her version, as told to her biographer, carries the greatest weight, but it does seem true that the force behind the novel writing, the sending out and resending, the agent in charge of a common enterprise was the oldest sister.

Emily provided the key, but it was Charlotte's hand that turned it in the lock. The older sister's energy and determination had carried the sisters to where Charlotte, surely, and the other sisters, more ambivalently, wanted to be—in print, in the public eye. Emily's ambivalence on this score is surmised from slight evidence, but seems consistent with her character. There was a journey under way. Charlotte was at the helm. Would Emily be a passenger? She stiffened against Charlotte's control. She refused to accompany her sisters when, later, Charlotte and Anne went in defiant triumph to unmask themselves as women before the eyes of their London publishers.

Charlotte Brontë rescued her sisters from oblivion, that is easy enough to see, but she rescued them also, or together they rescued each other, from the patriarchy. The Brontë sisters established a relatively closed world in which female people were of value in ways that went beyond tending father and doing the ironing; they redefined, together, the enterprise of their lives.

We know little of the Sister Rescuer because we entertain such paltry notions of female strength, of what women can do for one another, ways in which we can give or lend each other strength. The sister in history represents comfort and nurture— this is what we have called nuns and nurses—someone to be leaned on, not someone to take charge.

The Sister Rescuer emerges in the figure of Charlotte Brontë and is there again, to look to America in the same period, in the story of Angelina and Sarah Grimké, major figures in the abolition movement. The Grimké sisters were expected, on a plantation in South Carolina, to grow into ladies, be decorous and modest, oversee luncheons and the whipping of slaves. They defied these expectations and escaped them because one sister rescued another. The Sister Rescuer will show herself in the dark Victorian drawing room of the Stephen family, half a century later, as Virginia Woolf and Vanessa Bell.

Sarah Grimké confided a dream to her diary. She is standing

at a wharf looking at a ship ready to sail for Charleston. The ship beckons. It is a journey she wants to take. Her sister, Angelina, is on another part of the wharf, holding her child, wanting the journey as much as Sarah does. Sarah attempts to reach the ship, but falls in the mud. Angelina comes toward her, but she, too, falls, although the child does not. The sisters are defeated. Sarah dreams her return to the wharf, the helping hand of a man extended to her and his mild comment: "I advised thee not to go."

There is a journey to be taken. Sometimes, sisters have the same journey in their hearts. One may help the other or betray her. Will they cross over? Will the ship sail without them? If the man advises one or the other not to go, will a sister go alone and will other sisters follow?

Sarah Grimké, like Charlotte Brontë, had as her first close childhood companion the brother of the house and likely for similar reasons, for it was the brother who had access to the world and to education. These early brother bonds seem to be formed out of need for access to a certain kind of permitted energy and in avoidance of a certain kind of female suppression. Sarah's first rebellion consisted of teaching a slave girl to read, for which she was, according to the law of the land and the family, punished. In the same year, Angelina was born and Sarah was named the child's godmother.

If a passion for justice and the courage of rebellion cannot be genetically inherited, it can certainly pass among members of a family or a society as example and here it passed from sister to sister. Gerda Lerner, biographer of the Grimké sisters, tells a story out of the younger sister's childhood:

> Returning from meeting one morning she saw a
> colored woman in much distress pleading with two

white boys, one about eighteen, the other fifteen. Angelina suspected that they were leading her to the workhouse. She wanted nothing more than to avoid her, but could not help hearing the younger boy say: "I will have you tied up."

Angelina felt ill, her worst fears confirmed. Now the woman appealed to her. "Missis!" But Angelina could not utter a sound, it took all her strength to hurry past the pitiful creature. The woman's cry for help pursued her; that she had been helpless to answer it made her feel obsessed with guilt.

A woman asked to rescue another woman, inhibited from doing so, intimidated by male power. How often it happens. Angelina could not utter a sound. The example of Sarah, punished for teaching a slave girl to read, is a powerful example. We watch each other's punishments as we watch each other's triumphs—here the punishment looms stronger than the triumph, for Sarah's triumph had not yet come, nor that of Angelina, who first followed in her footsteps. Angelina's helplessness exists in the face of two young white boys and the legal, social, psychological power that stands behind what they are doing. She hurries away.

"It is dangerous for a woman to defy the Gods," wrote a poet called Anne Spencer in her "Letter to My Sister." Together, the Grimké sisters did that, each with the example of the other, with the support of the other. The course of their alliance brought them before huge audiences all over the country, speaking against slavery, and made them among the earliest women in America to break the taboo of public life for women; the measure of their effectiveness in the antislavery movement has still to be given its due.

Sister Rescuer and the escape from patriarchy, resistance to it or collusion with it—I am concentrating for the moment on those triumphs that stand out in history, for much literature is devoted to the failures. The sisters in "Cinderella," *Lear* or

Chekhov's *Three Sisters* cannot help each other. Life is full of this
kind of failure, the retreat of a woman who cannot come to
another's aid because to do so would mean taking on masculine
power and that power appears, perhaps temporarily, overwhelming. Virginia Woolf must have felt it one evening on a
London street when Leonard encountered a prostitute being
harassed by several men and it was Leonard who stepped in to
put an end to it. It occurs in all our relations with women, tells
what we can or cannot expect of each other, limits our dreams
and is the source of extraordinary pain.

She was not my sister. She was Lena, sister of Minnie and
Penny, daughter of Rachel. My father's mother; my grandmother. We had between us that bond that so often appears
between grandmother and granddaughter, a bond that skirts or
allies itself against the mother-in-the-middle, that frees us. I was
Lena's physical likeness, from the shape of my cheekbones to the
color of my skin and hair. Between sisters, this is problematic;
between us, or for my part, it was inspirational. I never
understood other women's worry about aging because Lena
grew more beautiful as she grew older, the skin tighter and
shinier across those cheekbones, the hair quite black. (She might
have dyed it; I never imagined that.) What impressed me about
my grandmother was not only her beauty, but her perfume,
cigarettes, coffee, cardplaying, jewelry and incessant social life,
all of which caused her to be considered a "bad" mother in the
family and all of which stood, to me, against the gray dumpiness
of the "good" mothers. Lena was glamorous and she shared that
glamour with me, taking me with her, when I was a child, to
luncheons, to shows, to the big town and the smell of perfume
and people having fun.

I loved her more than I've loved anyone.

She was dying. She had been dying of breast cancer for
quite some time, the putrefaction spread throughout her body.

She had grown thin and gray and not my grandmother, and the life had certainly gone out of her, but something resembling synthetic life was kept going, for reasons that had nothing to do with Lena and everything to do with the guilt of her children. I saw her in a nursing home and watched her wither, watched the pain become more and more difficult to conceal, saw the degradation of the place, the impersonality. My grandmother was dying horribly, surrounded by people who had made themselves immune. She had asked little of me and then she asked the smallest favor, the greatest gift—that I bring her something to end the misery, terminate the charade.

I loved her more than I've loved anyone.

I have no intellectual argument against euthanasia.

I was afraid of my father.

I let her down. It took months before she died and I could not return to see her, having so betrayed her.

The intimidated woman. The dying woman. The act of love stifled by fear of paternal authority, anger while one wastes to eighty pounds, then seventy, then less and the woman, myself, freezes in impotent guilt.

Fear of father, Daddy King, the State, the Rector, the General runs through the literature of the daughters. In this, sometimes, sisters are bound. This is a common ground in Katherine Mansfield's brilliant short story "The Daughters of the Late Colonel," where sisters confront life after the death of father, haunted by father. Constantina and Josephine are described as "they" from the first: "The week father died was one of the busiest weeks of their lives. Even when they went to bed it was only their bodies that lay down and rested...." At tea, "their cold lips quivered at the greenish brims." And eventually: "Father would never forgive them. This was what they felt more than ever when, two mornings later, they went into his room to go through his things." They cannot. The sisters flee from the cold empty room in terror, their father's arms imagined in bureau drawers, in the wardrobe, his intimidating self everywhere. United in fear and obedience, the sisters seem to live and act in extraordinary concord. Only when Mansfield gives us glimpses of their inner lives do we see them as separate and separated from each other. Neither has married; each is somewhat bewildered by the world outside her dutiful daughter existence; but there is a great deal of longing. We get to see Constantina's longing at the end, in the drawing room:

> She remembered the times she had come in here, crept out of bed in her nightgown when the moon was full, and lain on the floor with her arms outstretched, as though she was crucified. Why? The big, pale moon had made her do it. The horrible dancing figures on the carved screen had leered at her and she hadn't minded. She remembered too how, whenever they were at the seaside, she had gone off by herself and got as close to the sea as she could, and sung something, something she had made up, while she gazed all over the restless water.

The moon and the sea. If there are archetypes in the consciousness of women, these are surely the most primal. The moon, its tides, controller of menstrual cycles and the sea, the source—these have always been associated, by men and women, with women. The longing they represent in Mansfield's story is for bodily life, female, sensual, that it be let out of the closet of her father's house. This Constantina would have in common with her sister, but this is precisely what she cannot share. She says to Josephine:

"Don't you think perhaps——"

But Josephine interrupts her. "'I was wondering if now—' she murmured. They stopped; they waited for each other."

Nothing happens. Each waits for the other; a cloud comes by; they forget what they were going to say.

The silence here and elsewhere speaks as loudly as the clamor between sisters. Silence on the subject of sensuality, silence about those longings, so much like the silence between mothers and daughters. But there is silence, too, on those matters that would remove one sister from the other, the throwing off of repression being but one form that longing can take. Abandonment lurks behind the realization of these female longings—in the eyes of the sister.

"Camp Cataract" is a story by Jane Bowles in which there are three sisters—Evelyn is married and lives with her husband in an apartment, shared by Sadie and Harriet. Sadie has made the apartment, what it represents, her lifework and Harriet has gone off for a cure to Camp Cataract, to be away from her family. Bowles unravels the skeins of ties that bond too tightly. Both Sadie and Harriet have longings. Sadie is afraid, rightly, that Harriet will act on them:

> I fear nomads. I am afraid of them and afraid for them too. I don't know what I would do if any of my dear ones were seized with the wanderlust. We are meant to cherish those who through God's will are given into our hands. First of all come the members of the family, and for this it is better to live as close as possible.... When you are gone, I get afraid about you. I think that you might be seized with the wanderlust and you are not remembering the apartment very much.... Remember, the apartment is not just a row of rooms. It is the material proof that our spirits are so wedded that we have but one blessed roof over our heads.

That is Sadie's letter to Harriet, who, in her mind, with great trepidation, has begun to move away, out of the apartment,

out of the weddedness. Harriet has a friend to whom she can tell
these things, as sisters always seem to have friends who take up
the slack, with whom certain silences can be broken. Harriet
tells her friend:

> As I remove myself gradually from within my family
> circle and establish myself more and more solidly into
> Camp Cataract, then from here at some later date I
> can start making my sallies into the outside world
> almost unnoticed.

The common ground among all three sisters is madness.
Each is afraid the other will go mad; each tyrannizes the other
with the possibility. Harriet has gone off to the camp for a cure.
Madness means, here as elsewhere, the unconventional life.
Harriet and Sadie long for the world, are afraid of their
longings, and each makes the other the enemy of that longing.
They cannot tell each other the truth, do not know it, so they
speak about madness. Sadie violates the "rules" and goes to see
her sister. Harriet recoils. In a scene that appears to be a
hallucination only in hindsight, Sadie comes to consciousness:

> "Let's not go back to the apartment," Sadie said,
> hearing her own words as if they issued not from her
> mouth but from a pit in the ground. "Let's not go back
> there . . . let's you and me go out in the world . . . just
> the two of us." A second before covering her face to
> hide her shame Sadie glimpsed Harriet's eyes, impos-
> sibly close to her own, their pupils pointed with a
> hatred such as she had never seen before.

This happens in Sadie's mind, not in fact. What actually
happens is far more horrible. Sadie, like Cinderella, like the
Vestal Virgins, is trapped in ideology and her own fear. She is
meant to be and has taken on herself the role of guardian of the

hearth, but it is no longer a sacred role and it carries neither inner nor outer satisfaction. No one values what she does. Her blood rises against it. Her psyche does what her waking life cannot do—let's go out in the world, she can say to her sister. She asks to join hands and is, in her imagination, rebuffed. In the actual life of the story, she cannot act at all. The conversations between sisters turn subterranean.

One was a painter; one a writer. One was a mother; one not. Virginia Woolf and Vanessa Bell, originally Virginia and Vanessa Stephen, three years apart in age, fifty-nine years of relationship, sisters, intimates, antagonists, shadows. For sheer impact on the life of Virginia Woolf, we have looked to Leonard, thought of Leonard, read and remembered Leonard, yet the force of Vanessa as it touched or withdrew from Virginia was enormous, accountable and illuminating.

Where to look for the shape of relationships? In the lives of sisters, perhaps in the lives of women, the turning points, the junctures where things are joined or violently ruptured, come at the primal moments of life—the moments of birth, marriage and death. They do not come in the countinghouse or on the battlefield. Significant exchanges do not occur in the locker room or the playing fields of Eton. The social organization of life has shaped the terrain, laid out the chessboard on which certain moves can be made. Our dramas have been domestic. They take place in rooms. Someone is dying and a woman is attending; someone is giving birth and a woman is attending; a marriage is taking place.

The childhoods of Virginia and Vanessa Stephen, the ways they saw each other, what one came to mean to the other, were fiercely marked by the deaths of two women. When Vanessa was sixteen and Virginia thirteen, their mother, Julia Stephen, died. Two years later, Stella Duckworth, the Stephens' half sister, who had taken on the role and duties of mother, died. The impact of each of those women, the response to their deaths, were the shaping events in the sisters' lives.

Virginia Woolf described, as she remembered her childhood, the distance between herself and her mother, a distance that stood beside and was equal to the warmth she remembered, the tenderness and the beauty. It was a particular kind of distance:

> Can I remember ever being alone with her for more than a few minutes? Someone was always interrupting. When I think of her spontaneously she is always in a room full of people; Stella, George and Gerald are there; my father, sitting reading. . . . There are visitors, young men like Jack Hills who is in love with Stella; many young men, Cambridge friends of George's and Gerald's; old men, sitting round the tea table talking— father's friends, Henry James, Symonds.

As she remembered her mother dying, Woolf said, she always saw a man in the scene who had not actually been there and had no particular shape, a man sitting bent on the edge of the bed.

Similarly, she remembered Stella Duckworth:

> There were many young men, it seemed when one dashed in for a second, sitting round her.

Between herself and Vanessa, there was often, in those years, no such intrusion. Vanessa was her first intimacy and when she described how, in that "republic" that the Stephen family was, she and Vanessa formed a "conspiracy," that they were "in league together," she is describing the alliance of feminine forces against separating distances as well as against masculine authority:

In that world of many men, coming and going, we formed our private nucleus. . . . The staple day would be a day spent together. And therefore we made together a small world inside the big world. We had an alliance that was so knit together that everything (with the exception of Jack perhaps) was seen from the same angle; and took its shape from our own vantage point. Very soon after Stella's death we saw life as a struggle to get some kind of standing place for ourselves.

How to develop a vantage point of one's own? How to defy the gods? In Woolf's family, in the society in which she lived, the gods were those same masculine gods who had always hounded women. From father to State, the gods laid down laws about women's lives. Virginia Woolf experienced all of this directly— from the father demanding care by women, replacing his wife with his stepdaughter in the role of angel of the house, as Woolf said, to the half brothers requiring girls who could be made fashionable and taken out into society, to the brothers sent off to Oxford for education and exposure to the life of the mind. Against these gods, establishing a vantage point of her own, Vanessa Stephen was the first to revolt and her younger sister watched.

Vanessa's rebellion was active. Virginia's was, at least in part, a retreat into madness. Vanessa struggled with her father, refused his demands, withstood his anger and the approbation of the family. Vanessa defied convention by becoming involved with Jack Hills, who had been married to Stella Duckworth. She was the first to refuse to be "done up" by her Duckworth half brother, who wanted to drag her to dances; Virginia was more ambivalent about the whole business. Vanessa painted, quite seriously, took lessons with Sargent, worked at her painting. Virginia's early letters are filled with that mixture of admiration and self-deprecation so characteristic of younger sisters. She writes to everyone about what Vanessa is doing. "I like Nessa very much," she says when she is twenty, "but she gets so bored with me (tho' she's very fond of me too)." And in a petulant mood—"I don't get any attention now. Nessa gets it all. She has so many intimates."

"Let's you and me go out in the world."

The line from Jane Bowles's story, the buried desire of one sister toward another, the dream of common adventure, is echoed and enacted by Vanessa Stephen's gestures in the early part of the sisters' lives. The death of Leslie Stephen in 1904 released his daughters into a life of their own, but Virginia fell into madness while Vanessa made arrangements:

> While I had lain in bed at the Dickinson's house at Welwyn thinking that the birds were singing Greek choruses and that King Edward was using the foulest possible language among Ozzie Dickinson's azaleas, Vanessa had wound up Hyde Park Gate [where the family had lived] once and for all. She had sold; she had burnt; she had sorted, she had torn up. . . . And Vanessa—looking at a map of London and seeing how far apart they were—had decided that we should leave Kensington and start life afresh in Bloomsbury.

Imagine a stage set on which this first prolonged act of the Stephen sisters had been played out—"Victorian" in every sense of the word: cumbersome furniture, draperies, everything overstuffed, and then imagine the second act set again in a house, but in extreme contrast. As Virginia Woolf settled into Gordon Square with Vanessa and her brothers Adrian and Thoby Stephen, one has a sense of the drape torn down, sunlight flooding the place, white walls. It is not quite accurate, but it will do.

In Bloomsbury, Vanessa and Virginia were what Virginia

called "free women," which meant, to slip several years and rather uneven events into a single sentence, that they began to know the men their brothers had met at Cambridge, that they developed what in the eighteenth century was called a "salon," that they stayed up until all hours, talked about sex with rebellious openness, and engaged several philosophic and artistic ideas, all of which would later go by the name of the district, "Bloomsbury."

The conspiracy went forward but, like most, it had a darker side. The alliance appeared to hold, set in a new "republic" that replaced the family scene with a drawing room full of Cambridge men and, later, when Virginia took a more active part, a drawing room full of various kinds of women. Still, the conversation between the sisters was in part subterranean, the alliance resting on several things that were only half-spoken, that were to emerge more clearly as Virginia Woolf got older and could look back with more clarity.

First was the passion of her love. It stood beside and probably replaced, in Woolf's heart, the thwarted love for her mother. Its driving need was intense and romantic. Vanessa was her Sister-Lover. Virginia experienced herself as the yearner, the longing and fearful suitor and the dependent child. Between sisters, often, the child's cry never dies down. "Never leave me," it says; "do not abandon me."

Also unspoken in their conspiracy was an agreement about certain kinds of divisions between them. These held throughout their lives, although the promise not to abandon did not, could not. Vanessa was the painter; Virginia was the writer. A sibling fears to tread on another's turf. So all their lives the sisters said one way or another—this is yours, that is mine. A necessary part of the process of individuation, such marking out, but one that seems to require eternal vigilance—I shall not overstep the line. So Virginia Woolf seems careful not to know much about painting, careful to distinguish the capacity for words from the capacity for color and form. In 1930, in a foreword to a catalogue of a painting show by Vanessa Bell, she says:

> No stories are told; no insinuations are made. The hillside is bare; the group of women is silent; the little boy stands in the sea saying nothing. If portraits they are, they are pictures of flesh which happens from its texture or its modelling to be aesthetically on an equality with the China pot or the chrysanthemum.

Most of this essay is taken up with a firm delineation of the differences between the writer, whose expressiveness lies in words, in revelations of what lies under and what is the meaning of the "china pot or the chrysanthemum," and the world of the painter/sister where "psychology is held at bay and there are no words."

In Virginia's letters and diaries, Vanessa stands as the one with a sense of visual beauty, the one to recommend furnishings, the one to paint a table. Virginia extends this definition to mean the one who lives in the world of the senses, which is another agreement made between them. Virginia saw Vanessa as beautiful, herself as distinctly not. This distinction had extremely painful kinds of resonance. Vanessa was beautiful, like their mother, and to Virginia, whose childhood was full of such comparison, this was a source of profound admiration and profound anxiety. (On her deathbed, Virginia said, Julia Stephen told her, "Stand up straight, little goat.") It is difficult to look at photographs of Virginia Woolf without wincing at the memory of this endless and destructive image of herself. Setting aside for the moment the damage done by the insistence on physical attractiveness in women, which belongs to all women and all cultures, accepting for the moment those unacceptable terms— Virginia Woolf was, to my eye, a most beautiful woman. I would have been drawn to her in any room. She is the embodiment of that Renaissance idea that the soul resides in the eyes, for it is the eyes that attract, the mystery of what they have seen, the portrait of a life deeply felt. What she thought frumpy, I think elegant. I would like to avoid "delicacy" in describing what I see when I look at her, for it makes women into small birds in patronizing and disabling ways, yet surely "delicacy" is a word that applies. She seems to embody, in this way, Henry James' dictum to those who would be writers: "Be one of those on whom nothing is lost" and that is part of what would have drawn me.

Vanessa was, in her sister's eyes, Aphrodite, the favored goddess on Mount Olympus, the romantic, the sensualist. She was also the Earth Mother; fecund, mothering, nurturing; powerful in her ability to draw people to her, especially men. If there were profound female friendships in Vanessa Bell's life, they have gone unrecorded. Virginia saw Vanessa, as opposed to herself, as a Real Woman. She was the woman men want women to be. And Virginia was not.

No one has escaped this tyranny of beauty, the devastation it causes in the lives of individual women and in our relations with one another. Charlotte Brontë, like Virginia Woolf, saw herself as not beautiful—as, indeed, the men who knew her saw her as not beautiful—and this vision had enormous force in her life, her work and her relationship to her sisters. Her biographer reports a conversation among the Brontës in which they discussed beauty in terms of the heroines of their novels. Charlotte insisted that a heroine need not be beautiful—was insisting, perhaps, on her own behalf—and carries her insistence into *Jane Eyre* who, we are told over and over again, is "plain." Jane's "plainness" is meant, in the novel, to strip away a mask, forcing the reader—and Mr. Rochester—to *look* at her, to *see* her.

Hardly a woman exists to whom the question of masculine definitions of beauty are not central and hardly a woman writer exists who has not considered the question in the creation of her characters, for it affects a woman's life far more than it does a man's. Hardly a relationship between women exists in which beauty is irrelevant and this seems especially true among sisters, for the issue of beauty is transmitted from the social world to the girl through the family and it is in the family that girls first receive approval and love for their attractiveness. Mother fusses with her daughter's hair, and tells her to stand up straight. In the lifelong course of her relationships with other women, confined, for centuries, to the women of the family, we have had beauty given us as a focus for drives that have little to do with it. This has been our only permissible area of activity.

What gets funneled into the "beauty" question is a turbulent set of drives, problems, desires, needs that have little to do with beauty. Survival is one—how shall a woman survive if she cannot win a man or win what a man can bring? But there is another question, far more pressing in human development, that women work out with one another around the issue of beauty and that is what's called identity—to find the self as it is, to ride the waves of fusion and separation with other people, especially other women, and to emerge from that ride with a sense of both likeness and difference. It occurs with our mothers. Competition seems to be the language we use for the process of separation, seems to be the kind of activity we throw up against the desire to merge. To separate oneself from the woman who mothered us is, as so much brilliant recent work has shown, a far easier process for boy-children, for such separation is fostered by the social structure. Boys are encouraged to leave mother, punished for not doing so; girls are encouraged to stay with mother, punished for leaving. When these forces turn lateral, the process is played out among sisters.

To Virginia, then, Vanessa was beautiful and she was not; Vanessa was a Real Woman and she was not. Virginia's passionate attachment was bound to be broken, her fear of abandonment realized, around these distinctions. Vanessa married. It was a breaking point, a trial, in the relationship of the Stephen sisters as it has been in the relationship of others. In *Little Women,* Jo thinks that she would like to marry Meg, to keep her in the family, to prevent her from marrying the boy Laurie and, thus, leaving. Angelina Grimké, writing to Theodore Weld, who had proposed marriage, wondered why the love of her sister and her friends was not sufficient, what this different love had that set it apart. Her older sister wondered too, more fretfully, and when the marriage was about to take place, an event that coincided with the fulfillment of their common dream, the appearance of the Grimké sisters speaking on abolition before a public session of the legislature of the state of Massachusetts, Sarah fell ill and could not go on. Such anger. Such loss. For Virginia Woolf, Vanessa's marriage to Clive Bell was an event against whose effects she struggled with the kind of courage that one associates with forthcoming amputation.

When she saw it coming, she wrote: "I look at him [Clive Bell] and think how one day I shall look him in the eye and say you're not good enough—and then he will kiss me, and Nessa will wipe a great tear, and say we shall always have a room for you." Close to the date of the marriage, she imagined: "I don't think marriage will make any difference, because the best of us survives though it is d——d painful to cut away the inferior parts," but then acknowledged, "I did not see Nessa alone, but I realize that that is all over, and I shall never see her alone any more; and Clive is a new part of her, which I must learn to accept." At the very same time, though, Virginia felt compelled to say that she thought Clive lacked inspiration of any kind and that "old Nessa is no genius."

Vanessa Stephen and Clive Bell married in February 1907 and Virginia came to understand that it did make a difference in her life. It always does. Marriage has consistently, throughout history, disrupted the life of a woman far more than it does the life of a man—she changes her name, her rhythm, often her country to "follow" her husband, his life, his work. Charlotte Brontë said it was "a perilous thing for a woman to become a wife." Female relations reshuffle when a woman marries. Angelina Grimké's mother, who had long opposed everything her daughter did, began to send knitted socks and approval. Sylvia Plath's mother sent magazines and recipes. And the sisters? And the friends? The intimacy of sisters is lost or transformed when one marries. The shape of their lives comes to resemble parallel tracks, a great divergence, followed by a return to the parallel, for women, and sisters especially, spend the beginning and end of their lives together.

We have died in each other's arms far more than the romantic novel or cinema would lead us to believe. We are perpetual, historical attendants at the deathbed. The female Brontës, for example, died in one another's arms (while Branwell spent his last breath alone with his father) and had gone ceremoniously all their lives to attend the deaths of other women. Martha Taylor, sister of Mary Taylor, Charlotte Brontë's friends, died of cholera and on the following Sunday, Emily and Mary made a long funereal walk, six miles to the cemetery on the outskirts of Brussels. Six years later, Charlotte and Anne watched Emily die, a prolonged, resolute death. Emily refused the care of a doctor, spurned the aid of her sisters. Hers was death that resembles suicide, willful and possibly angry, as though Emily might have muttered to Charlotte: "You have controlled everything else, but you will not control this." Charlotte wrote to her friend Ellen Nussey:

Yes; there is no Emily in time or on earth now. Yesterday, we put her poor, wasted, mortal frame quietly under the church pavement.... Could you

come to us for a few days? . . . I never so much needed
the consolation of a friend's presence.

Anne moved into Emily's chair near the fire, grew ill and
weak. With Ellen Nussey, the sisters traveled to the sea, as Anne
wished, and there, in a boardinghouse, they watched Anne die.

Vanessa Bell did not see Virginia Woolf die, but she did
have a suicide note addressed to her. Long before death—to
return to the Stephen sisters—there was a birth and it had an
enormous impact on their relationship. A year after her marriage
to Clive Bell, Vanessa gave birth to a son and Clive and Virginia
became enbroiled in a peculiar flirtation. It is not peculiar on
Clive's part, for men seem consistently to seek out other women
when their wives are about to give birth, particularly the first
time, confessing to the difficulties they have in giving up the
romantic "wife" for the less romantic and less attractive
"mother" in the house.

This predilection for the sister of one's beloved is also a
mark of masculine romantic history. Reasons of convenience
have something to do with it. So, probably, do rather frightening
assumptions about likeness—that one sister will resemble
another. Emily Dickinson's brother could not make up his mind
between two sisters; his choice of Sue Gilbert was described, by
him, as something resembling the toss of a coin.

In a very early work by Jane Austen called *The Three Sisters*,
a suitor bounces from one to the other like a basketball. "If I
refuse him," says one of the sisters, "he as good as told me that
he should offer himself to Sophia and if she refused him to
Georgianna, & I could not bear to have either of them married
before me." There is a pernicious possibility here, too, related to
the role of men in all kinds of female relationships and that is the
desire to break a bond, to disrupt an intimacy. The man-in-the-
middle is a powerful figure, the apex of the triangle, the focus of
attention for two females, the barrier between them, the
possessor of inordinate power.

Whatever moved Clive Bell to flirt with his sister-in-law, Virginia Woolf's motives are murkier, more complicated, related to her relationship with Vanessa. Her letters to Clive are teasing, affectionate, constantly urging him to "kiss my old Tawny [Vanessa] on all her private places—kiss her eyes, and her neck socket" or "whisper into your wife's ear that I love her," and she dreams that Vanessa has been killed in an accident. In one of the most remarkable voices of subterfuge, she writes to him: "Why don't you come to lunch with me on Thursday, 1:30? That seems the only time. Will you and your wife also dine with us on Thursday?" Theirs is a relationship built around Vanessa, some common intimacy with her and some common resentment.

You are that kind of woman; I am not.

Was Virginia testing herself, trying out Vanessa's turf, attempting to reclaim what she had ceded, to become sensual in the way she had decided Vanessa was? I see in this flirtation with Clive the erotic longing for her sister realized in a conventional way—i.e., through a man. I kiss him; he kisses her. I see also a sister off-balance as the other becomes a mother, the questions it raises in herself about her "femaleness" not directly addressed, but enacted. And hostility. Or competition. Or resentment.

When the woman who has a sister is a writer, she leaves us a special kind of legacy, for the sister-figure is so often present in writing, not, most likely, as she was, but as the writer felt her to be. She represents a specific interaction between female Self and female Other and the conversation that a writer has with her sister in writing is often one that she could not have in her life.

Virginia was writing *The Voyage Out* all this time. She thought of it as a novel about Vanessa, based the character of Helen Ambrose on her sister, made Helen Ambrose the aunt of the protagonist, Rachel Vinrace, who is clearly herself. She began the novel right after her sister's marriage and the only person with whom she shared its progress was Clive Bell. "Of

Helen I cannot trust myself to speak," he wrote, "but I suppose you will make Vanessa believe in herself. Rachel is, of course, mysterious & remote, some strange wild creature who has come to give up half her secret."

The flirtation ended, but the shadow of the sister in the writing did not. *Night and Day,* her second novel, is dedicated to Vanessa, who is present in the paintings that Lily Briscoe does in *To the Lighthouse* and in the character of Mrs. Ramsey, where Vanessa amalgamates, as she so often did for Virginia, with the character of their mother, Julia Stephen. Vanessa responded to the autobiography in Virginia Woolf's writing more than she did to the art, sometimes seeing a truth about their lives when Virginia did not. The absence of Vanessa's voice in their correspondence is frustrating; we know what Vanessa said because of Virginia's responses. Like Charlotte Brontë, whose vision of her relationship with her sisters is one on record, Virginia Woolf's voice speaks to us about sisters, Vanessa's is a sharp whisper in the background.

Charlotte Brontë's writing is full of feelings of isolation and guilt about sisters. *Jane Eyre* is built on a configuration of three sisters—two very intimate, one not belonging. The "outsider" is Jane, her alienation represented by the fact that she is not an actual sister, not a blood relation. Her progress through the novel, her development, is built on her relations with women, although everyone remembers Rochester. Jane's relations with women are her education in life and in self, the turning points in a particularly female pilgrim's progress. She moves from standing outside the warmth of sister-love to being taken into it. The grief over the deaths of all her sisters appears over and over in Charlotte Brontë's writing—in the stark death scene of Jane Eyre's school friend, whose death in the novel resembles the death of Charlotte's older sister of typhoid contracted at school. The long death-walk that actually happened in Brussels, she and

Emily accompanying Mary Taylor to her own sister's grave, appears in Charlotte's first novel, *The Professor.* In her third novel, *Shirley,* the main character is, as Charlotte said, Emily, as she might have been if she had wealth and health, Emily transformed, Emily, by then dead, given life by her sister.

At the border of family and friends stands my sister-in-law, Marlene. We do not share a mother, do not worry about the pull of likeness and the need for separation. Much of the conflict and tension between sisters is missing for us. Still, as sister-in-law, it is possible that she might be my sister in spirit. The things that arise between us are things that arise between other women, touched by our family affiliation.

Marlene pulled her coat from the closet and Ilyse, my two-year-old niece, began to scream, squirm in the baby-sitter's arms. Teen-ager and baby followed us to the elevator door. The sound of the crying child followed us several stories down. I wanted to push Marlene's mother-guilt away. She said it never got any better, the guilt or the crying.

We waited in the cold, lit cigarettes, put them out as the bus appeared. We talked about the baby and how she missed Bob, my brother, away on business for a week. Marlene was actually talking about herself. In Chinatown, she chose the restaurant.

It begins. I am walking along a white wall with doors cut into it. I open one. Thick brick behind it. I go on, try another, catch a glimpse of Marlene, smiling, then disappearing. Some doors do not open. I do this calmly. I see the heel of her boot as she walks away. Marlene is doing the same, walking along her own white wall, opening doors in her own manner, peering in, looking for me.

Her mother opposes Marlene working, frets about the baby,

is accusatory. My mother opposes Marlene's working, pretends to hide the criticism, radiates disapproval loud and clear. We have certain things about our mothers in common.

The door opens. A wedge. And closes. Marlene is a mother; I am not. The mothers who oppose my working are less vehement and less conscious of their reasons.

My brother appeared in our conversation. We circled around him. His two phone calls from Mexico. Finicky about food, so she does not eat this kind of meal with him. He is sitting on the table between us and I knock him off. His food habits are annoying and controlling, but they are not part of my daily life.

We ate quickly, the doors drifting open, slamming shut, random, the way conversation is. All the while we were both investigating, searching, and talking the way women do, at least on first acquaintance, looking for what we have in common, for the points of identification between us.

It has been a difficult week for her, a job, a baby and being alone for the first time. I am alone nearly all the time. She did not ask me about that. One door does not open.

We were not dressed warmly enough, but walked anyway, shivering, through Chinatown and up Mulberry Street. I stopped to show her a mural painted on the wall of one of Little Italy's bars and we pressed against the window until the men inside stared out at us and we grew uncomfortable at the same moment, turned and walked away. I wish we had linked arms.

Café Roma was empty. Cappuccino and then the discussion about dessert, the most familiar kind of discussion. She pulled at what she called the "roll" around her waist. We talked about diets. We ordered one cannoli between us and in that moment I felt I had known her all my life, that she was in fact my sister, that we had read the same fashion magazines lying on our beds with our hair in curlers and had been equally tyrannized, equally intimidated by the covert messages that go by the name of "socialization." We must be beautiful. We must be thin. We must hide our bodies in girdles, strap them in. We must not jiggle. We must be vigilant. Marlene and I still looked upon the act of ordering a cannoli as an act of rebellion. We had become co-conspirators.

Bob reappeared. This time, we were looking at him together, laughing slyly at men's foibles, about how he will not buy decent clothes for himself, needs a woman to do it. Marlene is his wife. She does it. We ate the cannoli, dropping confectioners sugar all over ourselves, laughing. She wore a white wool hat close to her head and her blonde hair slipped out all around. Her eyes were very bright in spite of her fatigue (they were quite made up, too) and she looked immensely beautiful. I understood why my brother loved her and then, as though it were too dangerous a thought, asked for the bill.

Outside, it was colder and we were searching for a cab, walking past parked, dark trucks. Street fear. Two women alone late at night on a deserted street. Neither admitted the fear, but we walked faster, arrived where a police car sat vigilant. I could feel her relief as well as my own, but still neither of us said anything about it. We loitered near the police car until a bus came along, rode it to just in front of her building, and she walked with me to the subway station.

Marlene said it aloud: "This is the first time we have been alone, ever."

"Well," she added, with a shake of her head, "you're such a *busy* lady."

"Well," I said, with the same kind of shake, defensive, "you're such a *wife*."

And we laughed.

Later, Marlene came to my house for dinner. My brother came, and my niece. My brother had, for several weeks, been living through a crisis in his professional life, being the object of several offers for new jobs, all offers that would take him, as he saw it, upward, but he was unsure which to accept. We talked about that a great deal, he, Marlene and I. It was the subject of the evening—him, his choices, his problem—and he did not tyrannize us into giving him our total attention, we gave it automatically. The fortunes of his family appeared to rest on the outcome of his choice. It was a very important matter.

At the same time, Marlene had a critical problem, which she mentioned only once. Her work life depends on childcare. The baby-sitter had resigned that day. It was as severe a crisis to Marlene as my brother's problem was to him, yet we, all three, gave it little attention. I did not notice until afterward.

The baby ran around the apartment, pulling things off tables, smearing food across the table, laughing, having a good time, requiring constant attention. It was difficult to have a conversation. I managed to tell my brother that I shared his anxiety, but was also envious. He was being praised in all quarters: whatever would come of it, it was likely to be better than what had gone before. He smiled at what I said—we have understood, at last, our rivalry, acknowledged it and maneuvered around it. But Marlene said she, too, was jealous.

It was the first time she and I made contact all evening long. The look that passed between us was one of rueful understanding, sympathy and identification. Each of us, of course, knew exactly what the other meant, but my brother did not. He was surprised and, I think, hurt. Whatever happened to him happened to her. She was as much a part of the good fortune as he.

"But," she said, "I'd like to have done it myself."

She is struggling to be Wife, Mother and Marlene, to balance work of her own, her home, her family, to be all of the women she can be—to grow, to participate in life, to not be slave to the sandbox. And her baby-sitter had resigned. The women in the family are against her. I understood. She understood that I understood.

In this mutual resentment and struggle, we touched, and the

touching passed. They bundled the baby, along with the myriad comforts with which she must travel, into the carriage. I walked down the stairs with them, kissed each good-night and returned to the dinner dishes.

Phantom sister, I thought.

4

Friends

PERPENDICULARITY

Before they were mothers

Leto and Niobe
had been the most
devoted of friends

Sappho

So closely interwoven have been our lives, our purposes and
experiences that, separated, we have a feeling of
incompleteness—united, such strength of self-assertion that no
ordinary obstacles, difficulties or dangers ever appear to us as
insurmountable.

Elizabeth Cady Stanton to Susan B. Anthony

I thought you had finally despatched me to cruel callous
Coventry without a wave of your lily-white hand.

Katherine Mansfield to Virginia Woolf

"All that time, all that time, I thought I was missing Jude."
And the loss pressed down on her chest and came up into her
throat. "We was girls together," she said as though explaining
something. "O Lord, Sula," she cried, "girl, girl, girlgirlgirl."

Toni Morrison, *Sula*

Fresh air. To move from family to friends is like throwing the
window open on the first true day of spring. The word "bond"

comes to take on a different meaning, one that emphasizes its positive side, the connectedness, and submerges the negative, the bondage. Choice breezes in. One can take and leave a friend with more ease than one can embrace mother, sister, sister-in-law, aunt, niece, grandmother. At the same time, the anchor lifts, for family is at the same time security, rootedness, belonging, and one begins to move in a world of friends with greater risk, less assurance.

A woman who writes, like the woman who is writing this, knows, by acts of choice not entirely visible, other women engaged in similar pursuits. So the threads of my daily life are, in part, the threads of the lives of women artists in this metropolis where I sit at my typewriter and do my daily grocery shopping close to the end of the twentieth century. I am not alone, as Eve or the Virgin Mary were alone; I am less alone than Emily Dickinson or Sylvia Plath. What this does for art remains to be seen, is changeable and variable, but what it does for a life can be described.

The flow of other people's lives passes through my mailbox, the telephone, across a coffee cup or dinner plate, on a street corner, at a meeting. Blanche is in South Carolina, writing a novel and jumping out of airplanes for a magazine story and for her own pleasure. The spirit of Honor's report on Blanche is good. Honor is worried about the progress of her manuscript through the dark caves of the publishing world; she needs information, confirmation, reassurance. Rachel sends an essay on the myth of Psyche and one on the poet H.D., which I read with astonished exhilaration, recognizing common concerns between us, and with trepidation, the unease and distance of unacceptable competitive demons nibbling at me as I read Rachel's pages. One Ann has written about film; another Ann, in another city, has been unable to finish a book, choked at the last words, unable to let go. Leeny, an actress, is trying to create a theatre piece about concentration camps. The daughter of survivors, she faces personal ghosts to write them large, intending tribute and exorcism. She now lives in a gas oven; it is unbearable; I cannot listen.

Nancy is out of town. I have grown so accustomed to our sharing and supporting each other's work—mine is the writing of this book—that I feel her absence strongly. I try to become Nancy when I am stuck in the work, hear her voice, watch her read the pages. I miss her. Marilyn is agitated, moving from one city to another, trying to sell a house, anxious, unable to be a friend. Letty says she is afraid to know about other women's friendships, the way we avoid knowing about love, convinced she will discover that everyone else does it better.

There is a shared sense of risk about our individual lives, as though we were in fact women on the edge of time. We are what sociologists call a "transitional" generation. Our mothers' lives, which so many of us have resisted, stood in opposition against, are actually not possible for us. We know whether we live with men or not, that there is no arm to lean on—the figures of the national economy tell us so. So we all worry about money and we do it together, the worry, the money, the risk as an undercurrent of daily conversation. Will there be a teaching job next year? Will the manuscript be published? Can one take a taxi late at night? How much is the wine? What does a ream of typing paper cost? Shall I call after eleven, when the telephone rates are down? If I bake bread, will you bring a salad?

For most of history, we have, as women, been far from these concerns, at least from their overt manifestations, for we have been busy worrying about whether a man would choose us and how, without marriage, we might endure. Without autonomy and these specific kinds of risk, we have not had the enterprise of our own lives as the plots of our stories. When we did, we were victims, girls of the streets, typists in the typing pool, displaced persons, calling forth pity. There has been in literature until now little suggestion of the excitement of it all, the joy and energy, the common enterprise.

In our various incarnations as characters in other people's stories we have had little to give aside from our bodies and an occasional act of devotion. In fact, we have been given. The remnants in today's marriage ceremony—the handing over of the daughter to the husband by the father—is the trace left of the custom whereby women were the objects of transaction between men, the giving of women being the ways in which men established their relations with one another.

When woman is giver, what can she give? When a woman establishes her relationship with another woman by the giving of gifts, the gifts become metaphors, describe transactions, are in themselves the language of relations. I think of the gifts among myself and the women in my life. The sweater knitted for me by my mother, ill-proportioned, misunderstood in terms of current style, but, still, precious. At Christmas this year, Nancy gave me a scarf that her sister made and I gave her various body lotions. Leeny made a drawing. I baked bread. Rosemary sent running socks, Vicki a photograph of myself with Honor. There was a poem from one of us to another, a pair of hair combs, a soft purse. Simone de Beauvior describes, in *Memoirs of a Dutiful Daughter,* making a purse for her friend Zaza, the embarrassment it caused among the families of the two girls, unaccustomed to such gestures, having no formal gesture with which to contain the gift of girl to girl and probably sensing the sexual content of the gift itself, here, too, a soft purse.

What are these things but a laying on of hands? We touch each other through the things we choose to give. We stroke, decorate, adorn and caress one another, both in body and mind. The glorious gift from Honor sits on my mantle—a leather-bound copy of my last book, marbled paper front and back, deep red covers. In this language, we offer each other double kinds of support—the body and the mind, the woman and the work, each part as valuable as the other. A hand touches a hand. A mind reaches out for another mind. Something connects.

The nobility of friendship is an idea that runs through all of ancient literature and philosophy. It is, on the whole, the most epic of attachments and forms the theme of the oldest literature that Western culture has preserved. Friendship, in a literary sense, involves character in ways that love does not. Friendship rests on honor, among other things, and loyalty. It is freely chosen and spiritual, literally Platonic long before Plato—the being of one person in amiable relation with the being of another, two wholes in concert, an attachment of ideas. It is in actuality an epic emotion, the propelling force of the *Iliad* and all its descendants, through Shakespeare's plays to *Man's Fate* and the novels of Norman Mailer and James Jones. It is an essential theme in popular culture as well, manifested in relations among cowboys on the range and soldiers on the battlefield. The betrayal of friendship is the material for tragedy. This is the legacy of masculine literature, for literary friendships were, for centuries, masculine as the dominant literature was masculine. Our synonyms for friendship are "comradeship," "fellowship" and "fraternity." "Sisterhood" and "sorority," until women came to redefine them, meant something less noble, less strong, less whole, less universal.

Masculine friendship is associated with and elicited by war. It needs an enemy to stand against. The capacity to be a friend to another man is the essential capacity of the ancient hero—not, we ought to note in passing, the capacity to love a woman, not the talent to feel, but the talent to act.

The sources of ideas about friendship are older than the civilizations of Greece and Rome, but it is from the literature and philosophy of those cultures—where women were not citizens—that we get many of our ideas about what friendship is, what needs it serves, how it ought to be. Friendship, to collapse several centuries and several kinds of literary expression into a compact vision, is a matter of ethics and public life. It has its ceremonies. It relates to the welfare of the State, the way men are meant to be among one another. It is public. It involves "citizens"—no one speaks, for example, of friendship among slaves. Friendship is the relation between Achilles and Patroclus in the *Iliad,* Caesar and Brutus, Augustus and Agrippa. It involves "value"—one man valuing another, a relation of equals, based on respect. It is a public emotion enhanced by public ceremony— the funeral oration, the campaign speech, the triumphal parade after victory on the battlefield.

When, in the sixteenth century, Sir Francis Bacon wrote an essay "On Friendship," he looked to ancient sources, quoting the Roman definition—*participes curarum,* partners in care—citing the ceremony whereby the "whole Senate dedicated an altar to Friendship, as to a goddess," and finding, in the masculine friendships of the classical world, this meaning:

> They found their own felicity . . . but as an half piece, except they might have a friend to make it entire; and yet, which is more, they were princes that had wives, sons, nephews; and yet all these could not supply the comfort of friendship.

A half not whole without a friend. Plato's parable of the androgyne, the one sex not whole without its other half, becomes, for Bacon, an entirely masculine operation. Plato's text, ordinarily appropriated by romantic lovers as a true description of the longing of self for other, of masculine for feminine, is, for Bacon, exclusively masculine. Only men, in this vision, are whole and real. Women do not exist. Perpetuation of masculine camaraderie involves the exclusion of women.

Bacon says, too, that a friend can provide "peace in the affections and support of the judgement." Although the first "fruit" of friendship, in Bacon's words, has been taken over by women in more modern times—for women provide far more peace to men in literature after the Renaissance than men provide to each other—the second remains a masculine domain.

"Support of the judgement" is what we would call "validation." This is what Othello assumes Iago to be giving him. This is what passes from man to man, Horatio to Hamlet, John the Baptist to Jesus, Tom Sawyer to Huck Finn, this validation, this agreeable support that announces you are real, you are right, this is in fact the world you think it is, your values are true, you exist, you are.

Being a worldy man, Bacon sees "the help of good counsel" as "that which setteth business straight." Which business? Masculine business, of course, from which women, in life and literature, for centuries, are excluded. Guinevere cannot give good counsel to King Arthur on the subject of battles. Cleopatra cannot give counsel to Antony on military matters that would carry the weight of Caesar's counsel.

When Emerson wrote about friendship, he wrote about struggle, action, competition, and although he said "we shall grasp heroic hands in heroic hands," his thoughts on the subject have the same martial ring that is heard over and over when the masculine voice attempts to talk about affection:

> He who offers himself as a candidate for that covenant comes up, like an Olympian, to the great games where the first-born of the world are the competitors. He proposes himself for contest where Time, Want, Danger are in the lists, and he alone is victor.

Throughout masculine writing on the subject and throughout the living out of friendship and attempts at intimacy in most men's lives, those heroic hands grasp and ungrasp quite spasmodically. Men speak stirringly of their love for one another. The root of their literature on the subject is homosexual, the Greek way involved an older man and a younger man and the intercourse of their friendly feelings was literal. The heritage of that literature retained the rhetoric and buried the touch. A man slaps another man on the back. He throws a friendly punch. The ideology of masculinity reflected in our literature is a straitjacket on the heart, the body, and the hand. Football and war have been the recorded cultural forms of masculine intimacy. Men can care for each other in foxholes and locker rooms. The heroic hand shirks touching another man under other circumstances.

Female friendships are so different in style from masculine ones because female life has evolved along different lines, the process of socialization has worn a different costume. Nothing can be said about nature, but something can be said about gesture. We have been brought up to be relational people and to embody feeling, to develop the affective parts of ourselves. Whether or not we are more at ease with feeling, we have learned to speak that language.

"How are you?" my friend says. "What are you going through?" she implies. We do not have to work toward this intimacy, it arrives. Venable and Douglas, on the other hand, sit down to dinner and one asks the other how he is, but a lot of abstract information passes across the table, some posturing, some accounts of progress at work—and the one tells the other the thing most on his mind.

The baseball game. Men in groups. Men friends are having a good time together. They down their beers and shout at the players on the field. Camaraderie. Their eyes are forward, like the eyes of men marching to war, fixed not on each other but on what is out there. They are shoulder to shoulder. Female friends are more often eye to eye. It is the creation of "us" that is important, we *two*—and in this very different arrangement lie the great depths and the great raptures of our friendship.

The literary history of female friendships begins in Greece, but not in the *Iliad*. It begins with a poet who wrote about mother-love and the extension of that love to other females, a poet who was proud of the women she knew, delighted in their accomplishments and their beauty. The first to mark out female friendships was Sappho, who is always reported on as though her poetry and her life have been set to music by Wagner when, in fact, the atmosphere is more rightly Mozart. "Lyric" is indeed descriptive. But thinking—or talking and writing—about Sappho is done with great limitations, for most of the texts have disappeared. Much of what we think we know of Sappho comes from fragments and the endless amplifications of her "story" by contemporaries and latter-borns. What is most interesting in this context is that Sappho wrote little about physical encounters between women, yet the word "Sapphic" persists, clothed with such connotations, accompanied by Wagnerian music. She did write, and there do remain shards, glints of good feeling among females, in many kinds of relations, with many shades of emotions. In this respect, Sappho did create a "world of women," but it is hardly removed from men, is neither the cloister nor the hotbed it has become by reputation.

Whether or not she actually had a daughter, Sappho wrote some poems in the persona of a mother; she allows us to imagine what might have been expressed had Demeter been real. Hers is one of the few voices in world literature to sing the love of mother for daughter:

> *I have a small*
> *daughter called*
> *Cleis, who is*
>
> *like a golden*
> *flower*
>   *I wouldn't*
> *take all Croesus'*
> *kingdom with love*
> *thrown in, for her*

Mother-love extends to others. Three images remain as Sappho's slim book is put aside—flowers, music and a kind of empty no-color space that stands for the hurt of separation. Among the girls whom Sappho immortalizes—and she makes it clear that they are girls—life seems athletic, with the sound track of a single lyre running through it, and the decorative gestures of twining one's hair, a friend's hair, or one's neck, with garlands of flowers. The aura of good feeling suffusing Sappho's poems is carried, in part, by the scent of roses, dill, crocus, clover, quince apple and hyacinth, by the purple ribbons, headbands, the delicate, adorning gesture. These exist beside poems of separation, of distance and pain. Far more insistent than anger or rejection, which are hardly mentioned, is the pain caused by a woman going away, often to a man, with a man.

As early as Sappho, the hint of man is there, offstage, like a lurker. Between the sixth and seventh centuries B.C. and Restoration England, for all that time, through all the varieties of national literatures as they developed, in the lyric, epic and drama, there is not—the fact still astonishes—a single female voice speaking of her own experience, of her relations with women or with men, with the cosmos or with her own mind, not a voice that has survived as strongly as Sappho's.

Katherine Philips was called "The English Sappho" because a comparison must have seemed necessary—a woman poet in a tradition where there had been no other. It was meant, in the mid-seventeenth century, as a great compliment, tribute to the skill of the woman who took the classical name of "Orinda" to be known by. By Orinda's time, a fierce defensiveness had set in to women's writing—necessitated by history, by the denigration that had kept women from following the footsteps of the singer/poet Sappho. Like Sappho, Orinda was part of a community, a male and female "Society of Friendship," which she constructed. Unlike Sappho, Orinda had to rely on male authority to ensure publication and reception of her work—the poems, when published, were preceded by the voices of male patrons, attesting to the value of her work, defending and promoting her.

Orinda picks up where Sappho left off, but with a defensive edge. Friendship is an important theme in Renaissance literature, nearly as important as it was to the ancient world. There was a great deal of talk in Orinda's time about whether women were capable of thinking or behaving in a way that men would admire—whether women could be rational or loyal or good. The question came up in a treatise dedicated to Orinda herself, Jeremy Taylor's "Discourse of Friendship," where the author is most generous:

> You may see how much I differ from the morosity of those cynics who would not admit your sex into the communities of noble friendship.

He agrees that women might be admitted, might be friends—but friends to *men*. A woman friend is not, according to Taylor, quite as good to a man as a male friend, but she has her uses. His image for the difference is worth noting:

> I cannot say that women are capable of all those excellencies by which men can oblige the world and therefore a female friend in some cases is not so good a counsellor as a wise man and cannot so well defend my honour . . . though a knife cannot enter as far as a sword, yet a knife may be more useful to some purposes. . . . A man is the best friend in trouble, but a woman may be equal to him in the days of joy.

Aside from the relentless phallicism of Taylor's way of experiencing the world, this gentle perceiver of knives and swords has overlooked Orinda's actual theme, which is friendship among women. The bulk of her poems are in praise of other women, most notably Lucasia, the name taken by Mrs. Anne

Owen, and women called Ardelia and Rosania. The flowers and scents of Sappho are missing in Orinda's portraits of friendships, replaced, in accord with literary convention in her period, by Platonic images. "Luster" is the word most frequently used to describe a women friend. The word means for Orinda much what it did for Dante in relation to Beatrice—the woman friend is idealized. The language of courtly love, with its Platonism and Christianity overlaid, becomes Orinda's language of friendship. We see and hear less of the actual women than we do in Sappho's poems, but we get a great deal about the meaning of friendship. We get, in fact, an anatomy of Orinda's thinking about friendship—that it is noble, that it involves honor and loyalty, that it is based on admiration—the "luster"—and that it is at the same time like and unlike love.

Friendship, for Orinda, is union, the two become one. It is the forging of an "us" and not, like masculine friendships, the force set against an enemy. It is, as so many women have perceived friendship to be, an eye-to-eye, face-to-face enterprise, but it exists in a world of its own, apart from the activities of the rest of the world. In this way, Orinda takes her place in the female tradition, whatever she may share with the conventions of her time. Her friendships resemble marriages and the winning of a friend is a courtship. On the darker side of emotional life, friendship, like love, involves pain. On this subject, Orinda is as intense as Sappho, for there are many poems of loss, injury and separation. Orinda variously calls friendship a religion or a science, but the difference between friendship and love is described this way:

> *Friendship's an abstract of this nobler flame*
> *'Tis Love refin'd and purg'd from all its dross*

The "dross" is the body. Orinda's world, unlike Sappho's is de-physicalized. Her friends neither weave garlands for one another nor sing songs nor dance around in nature. These friendships have no setting except in the world of ideas and of the soul. One aspect of the "real world" disrupts friendships, intrudes on the intimacy of Orinda's circle: marriage. She says, in a poem addressed to a man courting one of her friends:

> *To others, courtship may appear,*
> *'Tis sacrilege to her.*

Haughtily, she asks the man if he would turn her friend into "a petty household god" and chastizes him for trying "to strive to fix her beams which are/ More bright and large than this."

This is not literary convention or, if so, only in part, for Orinda's letters have survived and in them she complains that "there are few Friendships in the world marriage-proof" and calls "the marriage of friends the funeral of friendship." This is not only a general attitude, but a reaction to a specific occurrence, for Lucasia, as she was called, married in the course of their friendship and Orinda describes herself:

> I alone of all the company was out of humour; nay I was vex'd to that degree, that I could not disguise my concern, which many of them were surprised to see and spoke to me of it, but my grief was too deeply rooted to be cured with words.

Afterward, Orinda observes the "despotic" behavior of the husband, the "sovereignty" with which he treats his wife—and then the matter is dropped, the friendship fallen away, the "flame" diminished and the luster dimmed. Although she never says so, Orinda obviously admires autonomy in women and experiences, at least in one case, the crushing of that autonomy by marriage.

Where do we meet? The geography of our friendships, the topography of the course of the relation, the spots, the fiery mountainous excitement and valleys, the silences—a steady humming when it is simply there, neither high nor low, not remarked on—all this needs a school of cartographers. Consider the point of origin, the meeting. Ancient legend recounts time after time the meeting of men somewhere in the world of nature. At a crossroads, men meet. They go forward together or they go on alone, marked by the meeting. On the battlefield. In their travels, their movement, men meet other men, but never meet women unless the women are locked in towers, because women themselves are rarely the itinerant travelers.

In actual life the encounter of woman with woman occurs in domestic setting more often than not, along lines dictated by blood kinship and physical proximity. The ancient talk of women at the village well returns in ghostly traces in the talk of women at a quilting bee. These are not women who "make" history; neither their activities nor talk falls on the record, historical or literary. We can imagine, not know. For that reason, it is not until well into what we think of as the modern world that a mark is made on the subject of female friendships, a mark larger than the smidgen of Sappho or Orinda.

These markings, reflections of encounters between women, have much to do with the history of education. The establishment of schools for girls allowed a place outside the family for a girl to come face-to-face with another female person whom one might like or not, have affinity or antagonism with, meet at a crossroads and go on together or alone. There were convents and courts before, meeting places, arenas for the establishment of intimacy and then there were, first, schools, then colleges, so that such meetings and such establishments might happen among girls becoming women, people with intellectual interests, women capable of leaving tracks behind them.

The origin. The meeting. It is important to know how it

comes about, what mutterings presage the meeting, what one knows about the other, what the context is, how much has been defined and arranged before anything happens. Take, for example, literary England, during the First World War. Lady Ottoline Morrell has cut quite a figure, aristocratic patron of the arts, quirky and rich, who liked to people her country place with the best minds of her generation. Her porcelain teacups were rattled by radicals while Ottoline looked on with pleasure. Her country garden was strewn with the talk of the moment. Lady Morrell, like the Bluestockings before her, collected intellectuals and entertained them. By this she meant, enacted, exactly what the Bluestockings had done—she collected men. The brilliance of the talk, the aura of celebrity at Garsington was most masculine: Bertrand Russell, Clive Bell, Leonard Woolf, Lytton Strachey, D. H. Lawrence. There were women present always, beautiful and sociable women, but they were wifely or decorative, not the peers of the men, not intellectuals of equal standing—with exceptions: Virginia Woolf and Katherine Mansfield. Lytton Strachey met Mansfield at Garsington and recommended her to Woolf.

This is a story known in literary circles, relished, often, as an example of how women cannot get along with each other. This is a story told for its cattiness, for the moments when Woolf thought of Mansfield as a civet cat, when Mansfield called a novel by Woolf a lie in the soul, when Woolf refused to read Mansfield. As a story of abrasion and competitiveness, it is hailed and smirked over for the antagonism it seems to celebrate and vindicate. But the story is not truly told. Instead, it is a complex patch of terrain of female friendships and it has jealousy and antagonism aplenty, but shadows of other things too. The excitement of artistic camaraderie. Affinity in more ways than can be counted—affinity of situation, temperament, and experience, sometimes acknowledged, sometimes not, alongside affinities of consciousness. Pathos. Tragedy—parts of one another not seen, screened out, aspects misunderstood. The failure of friendship is an intriguing mirror, reflecting the forces at work in a woman's life, the ground on which she stands, the chorus of observers as it all goes on. Woolf said, when Mansfield was dead, that she had allowed "odious gossip" to cause her to sacrifice her friendship. In the privacy of her journal, she wrote that with Mansfield dead there was no one to write for.

In 1917, Virginia Woolf was thirty-five years old, Katherine Mansfield was twenty-nine. When Mansfield and John Middleton Murry, the man she lived with and married, but not exactly conventionally, came to dinner at the home of Virginia and Leonard Woolf, a great ground was being crossed. An apparently great ground. Virginia had lived through two "breakdowns," published her first novel, *The Voyage Out,* only began to keep a journal, just started the Hogarth Press. Mansfield and Middleton Murry were less "respectable" than the Woolfs, eking out marginal incomes in the literary world. Mansfield was a "colonial," born in New Zealand, quite consistently publishing short stories in small reviews, a "libertine" with one marriage, at least one abortion and a complex series of relationships with women behind her. Her adolescence had been full of crushes on girls and passion for girls and an obsession in her mind with the image and the writing of Oscar Wilde. "I was," she wrote in 1909, "constantly subject to exactly the same fits of madness as those which caused his ruin and his mental decay.... This is my secret from the world...it has been going on now since I was 18." She had come to London and immediately forged a relationship with a sister-student, Ida Baker, an intense relationship that went on until Mansfield died, one that Mansfield's mother tried to break up.

By the time she met Virginia Woolf, Mansfield had been through several stages of relationship with Baker, for it was a violent and erratic connection, the most recent being their cohabitation of a studio in Chelsea where Ida Baker was often hidden behind a set of curtains when visitors came to call. Murry lived elsewhere. Mansfield was more sophisticated in the ways of the world, particularly the sexual ways of the world, than Woolf was. She had directly considered the question of her own sexuality, but was obviously unsettled about it, had no answers but would have been more able than Woolf to name her feelings on this score. She and Middleton Murry had spent several years in varying degrees of intimacy with D. H. Lawrence and Frieda Lawrence. They had recently, in fact, lived near the couple in Cornwall while Lawrence wrote *Women In Love,* in which Mansfield and Middleton Murry form the basis of the characterizations of Gudrun and Gerald.

There had, by the time of the dinner party, been several important women in Virginia Woolf's life: her mother, stepsister Stella Duckworth and sister Vanessa Bell, her Greek tutor Janet Case and her friend Violet Dickinson. In these relationships, Virginia had been the child, the daughter, and her uncertain sense of self had grown, slowly, in relation to the women. Mansfield was not a likely candidate for mother-lover in Woolf's life. Neither would show the other the way, neither would be caretaker to the other.

But attraction was clearly possible between them. The question was, would it be recognized?

A dinner party is created. No one wrote down how it came about, but convention would dictate that Virginia's interest in Mansfield caught up with her and that she, befitting her role as the elder, the pursued (Strachey said Mansfield was an admirer and wanted to meet her) and the hostess, invited Mansfield to dinner and, with equal submission to convention, invited Mansfield's man, John Middleton Murry. Sidney Waterlow, a diplomat whom the Woolfs had known for some time, came along. Five people at dinner, three men and two women. Leonard Woolf is the most "established," rooted, solid. Virginia is beginning to rebuild, has a social life controlled by Leonard, is protected by him and seen in need of protection. Mansfield is well known and notorious, as is Middleton Murry. There is nothing about Mansfield in 1917 of the ravaging illness that would buffet her in the next five years; Middleton Murry is not her caretaker, never would be, by temperament, has no need to be in 1917. Three men, two women. Where did the weight fall? Along what lines did the conversation run? How eager was Katherine, how reticent Virginia? Did the men dominate? What kind of tentative reaching, what forms of exploration took place between the women writers?

There is no record of the first impression.

And so we also meet, to return to the geography of our relationships at dinner parties. Often, we are surrounded by men. Often, a woman has created the dinner party, attends to the food and the service as the conversation gallops gaily on. Sometimes the woman has a housekeeper, another woman to do these tasks, freeing her to partake in conversation as well as the meal. How rare, at a dinner party, for the women to latch on to one another, to become rapt in conversation, to exchange or debate this or that, to go on and on as the plates are mysteriously cleared, the coffee brought. Women attend to these things, whether we do them ourselves or not. Assume that Mansfield and Woolf looked each other over, were tentative for personal and cultural reasons. After the dinner party, decisions would be made: Who would offer to extend the relationship? Would it be a relation between couples—the Woolfs and the Mansfield-Murrys—or between the women alone?

The couples or the women? This has continually to be

negotiated. Is it "I" or "we"? Do I or we want to see you singular or you plural? This goes on in my own life, this shifting, this deciding, and it always has to be articulated. We women living near the end of the twentieth century have learned to be careful and precise on such subjects, for we have known the chagrin of telling a woman friend we want to see her, arriving, finding her man involved as though it went without saying when it did not. It needs saying among women as it does not among men, who, married, attached or not, behave as though they are single.

Virginia Woolf was married; Mansfield had been living with Middleton Murry off and on for as many years as Virginia had been married to Leonard and would marry him the following year, when a former marriage was finally, officially ended. But Mansfield, married or not, operated as "I" more than Virginia Woolf did at this point in her life. It was from Mansfield that the first energy about making a relationship had come and it is Mansfield's enthusiasm that is documented. She describes herself as "ardent" for friendship, haunted by Virginia and she names quite accurately the reticence on the other side:

> My God, I love to think of you, Virginia, as my friend. Don't cry me an ardent creature or say, with your head a little on one side, smiling as though you knew some enchanting secret: "Well, Katherine, we shall see"...But pray consider how rare it is to find someone with the same passion for writing that you have.

The passion for writing was out in the open. It was clearly what they had in common, what they visibly had in common. There were other things between them, but neither noticed. One such thing was the marriage relation. Virginia Woolf had, in the work already published and in *Night and Day,* which she was soon to begin writing, been meditating on what it meant for a woman to be married—what it gave, what it took, what it was for her. Mansfield was turning over the same questions, turning and acting, living with Middleton Murry and leaving him, living with a woman, coming back to the man. Woolf and Mansfield were women without children—today we would say "child-free," but "childless" is more appropriate to the ways in which both of them saw this issue. It is unclear to what extent childlessness was chosen by Woolf, for she envied her sister, Vanessa, that mother's life and Leonard, it seems, had decreed that Virginia should not have children. Mansfield had chosen one abortion, perhaps more, but was not resolved, for several years later she was to hallucinate a child and write painful letters to Murry about that child and write in her journal about being "child denied." And then there was illness. Woolf struggled perpetually with illness and what it meant, being deprived of her powers; Mansfield was to spend the remaining five years of her life in the same struggle. Yet they hardly spoke of it. They spoke of the "passion for writing."

They shared, too, an awareness of gender, particularly of gender differences in intellectual matters and in literature, but they hardly spoke of that either. Mansfield's stories are full of the bitter ironies of "marginal" women struggling for economic survival, intent on autonomy and often, at the last moment, buckling, as Miss Ada Moss does in a story called "Pictures," desperate to "go," as they would have said then, with the man who had the price of a good meal. Mansfield wrote brilliantly about male pomposity, masculine rigidity. The man in "The Man Without a Temperament" has a wife who is ill, frail, whom he cannot nurture, whom he must hold himself away from, keep from. The story was written during one of Mansfield's most agonized bouts of illness, three years after she met Woolf, three years before she died. It is aimed at, is about, and exposes much of what she must have felt then about Middleton Murry, who alternately came and went. Murry had chosen, when he chose Katherine Mansfield, a woman who, for all her "Bohemian" ways and her affinity for George Sand, took care of him. He could not adjust to a change of roles. Mansfield became like Chopin, suffering, in need of a mother-lover, but Murry could not play Sand to her Chopin.

This constellation of female illness, masculine nurture, and the price of being taken care of, the abandonment of not being taken care of, is an uncanny mirror in the lives of Mansfield and Woolf. Neither chose to look in that particular mirror, not squarely in 1917, not in relation to each other. Woolf, of course, came more and more to look, but 1917 is some distance away from the deepening consciousness of the later books, of *Mrs. Dalloway, To the Lighthouse, A Room of One's Own,* and *Three Guineas.*

"Eliot—Virginia?" Mansfield writes. It must be two years later, upon publication by the Hogarth Press of T. S. Eliot's poems:

> The poems *look* delightful but I confess I think them unspeakably dreary. How one could write so absolutely without emotion—perhaps that's an achievement. The potamus really makes me *groan.* I don't think he is a poet—Prufrock is after all a short story. I don't know—These dark young men—so proud of their plumes and their black and silver cloaks and ever so expensive pompes funèbres—I've no patience.

It was not the first time Mansfield thought or wrote or said something about masculine arrogance and what she called the "Male Mind." One aspect of the tension in her highly complicated relationship with D. H. Lawrence was about that. She and Murry had lived with the Lawrences while Lawrence was at work on *Women in Love* and it had been a tortured time, with Lawrence urging on Murry his idea of "blood-brother-hood" and Murry resisting, Mansfield trying to find her footing in that menage, unable to write, struggling to name that thing in Lawrence that she called the "Male Mind."

Close to the time of Mansfield's letter about Eliot and "these dark young men," Woolf recorded in her diary a similar impatience with Middleton Murry, and his "orthodox masculine ways":

> I think what an abrupt precipice cleaves asunder the male intelligence, & how they pride themselves upon a point of view which much resembles stupidity.

But here, as elsewhere, Woolf is ambivalent on the subject, desirous of approval from the "Male Mind":

> I find it much easier to talk to Katherine; she gives & resists as I expect her to; we cover more ground in much less time; but I respect Murry. I wish for his good opinion.

At the dinner party of 1917, Mansfield and Woolf had, as an additional affinity, attempted to think through something about the "Male Mind" and their relation to that. If they ever spoke about the subject directly, the record is lost. All their affinities, in the few years of their relationship, would be lightly touched on, withdrawn from and returned to.

Theirs, as it turned out, was a summer friendship. The following summer, both Mansfield and Woolf report many meetings. Virginia asks Katherine for a story for the newly set up Hogarth Press. "Prelude" is delivered. They walk, they look at sunsets, they talk about writing and Mansfield writes to Woolf—"we have the same job, Virginia." Virginia is in and out of this relation—the wariness and reticence Mansfield has named. The person she most often shares her thoughts on Mansfield with is Vanessa, not surprisingly, for Mansfield must have evoked something of Vanessa to her. What draws Woolf is a woman who takes writing seriously; this is more important to each of them than whether the writing is exactly what one would like it to be. And this, along with a tension possibly sexual between them, is what is frightening.

A woman artist of any kind is a bobbin on the sea, in danger of drowning. She feels herself in danger. She has behind her centuries of civilization in which the known and celebrated artists were male, in which the idea of a female artist was sneered at as often as the idea of female as an authentic whole person was sneered at. Misogyny takes its toll. She is in danger of feeling that men are the real artists, that the male mind exists and is good and right and that it is not hers. She bobs in the sea. She holds fast to scraps of evidence of other women who have crossed such seas—the painter Gentileschi in the seventeenth century, the Brontë sisters—whatever evidence happens along, saving notes in the bottle, bouncing by. She is made to worry and often to choose which kind of femaleness she will live out, what she will do about marriage and motherhood, how she will do it or not do it and become, remain, survive as an artist. The waves rise. She nearly drowns. She strikes out again, swimming. Can a woman be an artist? Her swimming may take the form of writing a book like *A Room of One's Own* or another kind of book, looking backward, looking around, looking for a likeness, a friend, other women, for embodiment of the Great Permission, the idea that it is all right, for strength for courage. She writes a book that surveys all women poets from Mary Sidney to the present day or considers the grandmother who was a painter who stopped painting and went mad or a biography of Joan of Arc, Edna St. Vincent Millay, Mary Astell, Virginia Woolf,

Charlotte Brontë, always looking for something about her own life, her own swim.

"You write a book," says Gertrude Stein, and while you write it

> you are ashamed for everyone must think you are a silly or a crazy one and yet you write it and you are ashamed, you know you will be laughed at or pitied by every one and you have a queer feeling and you are not very certain and you go on writing. Then someone says yes to it, to something you are liking, or doing or making and then never again can you have completely such a feeling of being afraid and ashamed that you had then when you were writing or liking the thing and not any one had said yes about the thing.

Who will say yes?

Thomas Wentworth Higginson claims to have said yes to Emily Dickinson, but he also said she was half-cracked. Robert Browning said yes to Elizabeth Barrett, many kinds of yes. The Male Mentor puffs himself up with his own yes, too often acquiring in the unlikely figure of the struggling woman artist yet another female dependent. But women are not passive in this matter, many of us assign to men the role of mentor, major yes-sayer. Dickinson, after all, sent her work to Higginson. We send, show, display our work to men, many of us especially in the first stages of our artistic lives. Men are in positions to help us, they edit the magazines and sit in the editorial chairs of publishing houses. There was no woman who could bring the poems of the Brontë sisters from manuscript to print, after all. So often in history we have been forced by circumstance to seek this yes from men, to receive it wholeheartedly or ambivalently, for the yes carries conditions. This seeking gets written up in history, but similar seeking and offering from woman to woman does not.

Will you say yes to me?

This was in the air between Mansfield and Woolf. If one sees the other as the only serious woman artist she has encountered, one is asking for a yes. The possibility is raised. If a woman is neither wife nor mother but artist, she is "wrong" in society's terms, "unnatural," but if she knows another woman, has read about her, seen her, written letters, looked at a manuscript, she is less alone, less subject to the accusation from without or the self-doubt from within.

"We have the same job, Virginia," Mansfield wrote to Woolf in the summer of 1917. Woolf said yes and no. Her first remark on the subject of Mansfield was that the other had "dogged her steps" for three years. The specter of jealousy—another writer, a younger woman. And the specter of class, the snob in Virginia withheld itself—Mansfield smelled like a civet cat. Most of what was important in Mansfield's life at the time was not seen by Virginia. The woman called L.M., Mansfield's "companion," is barely mentioned by Woolf and then only derisively—"that Rhodesian woman." Woolf saw Mansfield as the steady dogger of her own steps, while Mansfield's frailty and vulnerability escaped her.

A scandal arose in the fall of 1917. It had something to do with Ottoline Morrell, Middleton Murry and sex. Clive Bell appears to have been the agent who brought the gossip to Virginia Woolf. (He did like to divide women, that man.) It roused something in Virginia about Mansfield the civet cat. The relationship froze. By the winter, Mansfield had become so physically ill that she had to leave London for the South of France, where she had the first hemorrhage of the tuberculosis that would kill her. She wrote desperate, raving letters to

Middleton Murry, imagining a son who was living with her, waiting for his father to visit. And she wished she had a press of her own, one of the few indications of her envy of Woolf. Some of Mansfield's letters to Murry, written in the spring, caught in the Big Bertha bombardment of Paris as she tried to make her way back to London, were considered "too painful" to print, by Murry.

Woolf knew none of this. She was irritated, hearing Mansfield was back in London, that they did not meet until, at last, they did, in the spring. "I have been kept in since I saw you," Mansfield wrote, "and cannot fly, cannot fly, cannot fly." Virginia told her diary that Mansfield looked "ghastly ill" and that they "came to a complete understanding." Mansfield went to the country—she felt banished by Murry—and the warmth of their friendship flooded back. Her letters urged Woolf to visit:

> If you do come down here and I do meet you at the station I think the Heavens will open. . . . You'll see, we'll go for picnics. Yesterday, I saw you, suddenly, lying on the grass and basking. And then I saw us sitting together on the rocks here with our feet in a pool—or perhaps two pools.

Woolf sent strong Belgian cigarettes, another thing they had in common. Two scribbling women, two hard-smoking scribbling women.

It froze again. Mansfield, back in London, moving into a house that she called "The Elephant," where she would live with both L.M. and Middleton Murry, wrote to Woolf of her mother's death and Woolf did not reply. Knowing the intensity of Woolf's feeling about the death of her own mother, knowing its remnant in her mind and how she tried to work it out in her writing, we understand why Woolf did not reply, but Mansfield did not. She was grateful to her women friends for their support, but Woolf was not among them. The freeze was on in August, when Woolf complained that "the Murrys have put us off" and read Mansfield's story "Bliss" in the *English Review,* flung it down and said, "she's done for."

What hurts us?

Neglect hurts us. Abandonment hurts us. Fear of abandonment haunts us, is denied, burrows in, pulls us back into long, unbreakable silences. Woolf is silent then hurtful when she feels hurt by Mansfield. It is not only the sense of being on a life raft together—and that is a powerful sense—but something to do with expectations. Everyone in this culture comes to women for nourishment, for varieties of mothering, for understanding and comfort, for selflessness. Women come to women for these things as much as men do, as much in the shadow of the ways in which we would like to have been, to be mothered as men are, perhaps more in the shadows. Woolf and Mansfield transact exchanges of caring and then silences set in. Mansfield's removal leaves Woolf abandoned in ways she does not know and the sense of what there is in common, the shared job, if nothing else, submerges only to surface, as it always does in tragedy, with death.

Woolf was in London. Mansfield journeyed, desperate for relief, into profound places in her own psyche and into various forms of medical and spiritual practice that she believed would help her. Middleton Murry was increasingly put off by Mansfield's directions, abhorred mysticism and spirituality. Ida Baker remained constant and Mansfield involved herself with various Russian healers, eventually, in 1922, putting herself in the care of Gurdjieff at the Institute for the Harmonious Development of Man near Fontainbleau. Ida Baker lived nearby.

Between Woolf and Mansfield there was no communication left
on record, the last exchange that can be documented having been
in 1920, when Woolf went to say good-bye to Mansfield and
wrote in her diary that she had to pinch herself "as if to make
sure of feeling" and Mansfield promised to send Woolf her diary.

At the beginning of 1923, Woolf read of Mansfield's death
in the newspaper. She picked up her own journal and began a
long, painful, complex meditation, describing shock, confusion,
then "blankness & disappointment; then a depression which I
could not rouse myself from all that day. When I began to write,
it seemed to me there was no point in writing. Katherine won't
read it."

Gorky said about Tolstoy: As long as he is alive, I am not
alone.

Woolf resurrected Mansfield as she wrote, imagined her,
saw her move about the room among medicine bottles and
books. "Sometimes we looked very steadfastly at each other, as
though we had reached some durable relationship, independent
of the changes of the body, through the eyes." Her mind moved
between the idea of durability—what now is left—and the old
contempt, the vulgarity, as Woolf called it, she could never quite
make peace with, the old jealousy and rivalry—and then, "Did
she care for me?" Woolf blamed herself for not making the
move, not going to Paris when she knew Mansfield was there,
and from guilt—"I could not take the step"—she moved to
regret:

> The surroundings—Murry & so on—& the small lies &
> treacheries, the perpetual playing & teasing, or
> whatever it was, cut away much of the substance of
> friendship. One was too uncertain. And so one let it all
> go.

Woolf faced her jealousy squarely—"the only writing I have ever been jealous of"—and began to see for the first time what she had overlooked—"I think I never gave her credit for all her physical suffering & the effect it must have had in embittering her."

Mansfield would not be exorcised. Woolf seemed to know that something was being learned. She kept Mansfield alive, kept working out what was important for her to work out, by writing to Ottoline Morrell and to Mansfield's friend Dorothy Brett, turning it over and over, checking her perceptions against theirs, apologizing, saying that she had found it too difficult, looking at her own fault in the matter, seeing herself as easily swayed by gossip and other people's opinions and her own insecurity. "I felt that I no longer knew where we stood together," she wrote to Dorothy Brett, and "she gave me something no one else can."

Woolf kept Mansfield with her in the years that followed. She began to translate Russian literature with Koteliansky, as though she had lifted the torch that Mansfield dropped. She read Mansfield's journal, when it was published, with "sentiment and horror," understanding more deeply than before how little she had seen of her friend's actual pain, how blinding the jealousy had been. Publication of Mansfield's letters "desolated" Woolf. The pain was unbearable. And yet there was no redemption. What Woolf learned she took with her into other relationships with other women. Mansfield prepared her for Vita Sackville-West, to whom Woolf wrote: "What odd friends I've had, you and she."

Stress marks on a friendship—a ripe theme rarely plucked in a literature that sees friendship as masculine and turns aside from female friendships because of their ostensibly miasmic nature, what men see as overwhelming sentimentality, obscure emotionalism and unspeakably trivial content. Women have not got the wholeness and definition, except in relation to men, that Emerson searched for in a friend. Women have no enterprise, in masculine literature, except men, and so that part of our heritage is short on substantial, developed female exchange that does not involve romance.

Mansfield and Woolf offer an alternative, an example to be absorbed, an interaction that shows in actual life a subject skirted in literature. The obstacles to friendship between them are in part personal and in part transpersonal, roadblocks set up in patriarchal culture. The failure of the friendship tells what the obstacles were as well as what each woman ran into in the privacy of her own heart and mind. Elsewhere, in both life and literature, there are examples of obstacles overcome, for the obstacles never disappear. Although Susan B. Anthony said that failure was impossible, the failure of female friendship is easily possible, for it lives in a minefield.

Propaganda claims friendship to be a relation among equals, but facts show otherwise. The ancient Greek model, for example, portrays the friendship and love of a younger man for an older one, a disciple relation, a power differential. We know how to maintain good feelings as the dominant ones in relations—teacher to pupil, mother to child—or as submissive ones—supplicants, disciples. But to be lateral is difficult. Mansfield and Woolf could be neither child nor mentor to one another. They had no experience in the lateral.

If only Susan B. Anthony had been a novelist. If only Elizabeth Cady Stanton or Lucy Stone or Antoinette Brown had turned their hands to drama or short story, had made into literature what they so vividly lived. If only the letters and diaries of any of those women, their historical analyzing and reporting, had not been so dismally ignored by modern readers. If only, in short, their friendships had made a greater impact on the cultural record as we now look at it, things would be seen differently. To rummage around in the history of the women's movement in nineteenth-century America is to come across a dazzling indication of the possibilities of female friendship and the success of it in the face of culture.

Stanton reminds Anthony to "dress loosely" so that she can retain her health and mobility. To Lucy Stone, she writes, "All you need is to cultivate your power of expression. Subjects are so clear to you that you can soon make them clear to others." To Antoinette Brown: "Don't hesitate, but in the name of everything go forward." On her way to Oberlin College, a man warns Antoinette Brown that she ought to stay away from a woman named Lucy Stone, so Stone is the first person Brown seeks out, and although one likes stark Quaker clothing and the other dresses up in fanciful dresses and hats with artificial flowers, they become good friends. Stone becomes a public lecturer for temperance, abolition and women's rights; Brown is the first female divinity student in America. "Don't be afraid of anybody," Brown writes, "but speak as though you had a right to." And:

> My heart has just been called back to the time when we used to sit with our arms around each other at the sunset hour & talk & talk of our friends & our homes & of ten thousand subjects of mutual interest until both our hearts felt warmer & lighter for the pure communion of spirit.

Thirty years after that, each having married a man of the Blackwell family and had several children, Brown is writing, this time about her oldest daughter:

> If Florence were either settled that she was not to marry, or if she were happily married, she would begin to unfold naturally in new directions. She has mother-wit enough; but it is as you suggest her mind is elsewhere.

The conventional geography of female friendships takes a new turn. Women encounter each other at colleges, at meetings and congresses, on the backroads of Kansas, knocking on doors, carrying petitions, agitating for passage of the Fourteenth Amendment. They have an enterprise and a common cause that points to the need to acknowledge and focus on what they have in common as women rather than to ignore it. The business to be done requires cooperation *and* autonomy, purposefulness, the use of the whole self, both intellect and passion. It also requires courage and strength of all possible kinds—the physical stamina of traveling, speaking, riding in a rainstorm in an open cart to a lecture hall where one will be ridiculed and perhaps attacked, the strength to ride in a cart and overcome opposition, not to be docile, passive, servant to husband and children, separate, private and silent.

Women must belong to themselves before they can be friends to one another; culture conspires against it. Female friendships that work are relationships in which women help each other belong to themselves. Elizabeth Cady Stanton, who insisted on birthing and raising her children according to her own instincts and in defiance of the misogynist masculine theories and practices of the day remarked on "how much bondage and suffering a woman escapes when she takes the liberty of being her own physician of both body and soul." Lucy Stone insisted on belonging to herself in the face of the conventions of marriage, which robbed a woman of her self, removing her name, property and the right to her own body. Lucy Stone retained her name. In a culture that defined a good woman as a prone woman—prone in the marriage bed and the child-bed, prone on the invalid's couch—Stone insisted, "I am determined to maintain the perpendicular position."

A friend needs to be perpendicular.

Women friends help each other to remain perpendicular in the face of cultures that attempt to knock them over with the hurricane forces of ideology about what a woman should be or pull the ground out from under them by denying the validity of their experience, denigrating their frame of reference, reinforcing female masochism, self-doubt, passivity and suicide. In friendship, women do for each other what culture expects them to do for men and in that way, female friendships are subversive. What passes for trivia and gossip in the masculine eye—a self-denigration in which we often participate much as the black race kept up the "ole time shuffle" for white audiences—is, in fact, profoundly philosophical. These are exchanges among us about ways of being, about ethics, about existential authenticity, modes of perception, ways of knowing.

To remain perpendicular. To act. To be. These are the subjects of conversation among the women who worked first for abolition of slavery, then for female suffrage, the female "comrades" of nineteenth-century America. These are the ways in which their friendships are a paradigm of what is possible, what, in fact, has often *been,* but remains unnoticed. The conventional division of wife/mother against "independent" woman has so often set us against one another. We eye each other over such barricades and are wary, dubious about what we might have in common, we different "kinds" of women. I am this; you are that. Elizabeth Cady Stanton and Susan B. Anthony showed, in their living, that this/that can be a complementary division, not a description of impossible alienation. Stanton said with gratitude that her friend Anthony prevented her from "becoming wholly absorbed in a narrow family selfishness," that her friend and the purpose they both saw would "turn any woman's thoughts from stockings and puddings."

The capacity of a married woman with children to be a friend to another woman depends on decisions she has made about how much she will belong to herself. Practical arrangements have made such friendships difficult. The stress of marriage on female friendships resembles the breaking points in relations between sisters. One resents the withdrawal of the other's attention. Over and over, women worry about whether or not their friend will be accessible, about how much, in the changing ground of their new relation, a satisfying and familiar intensity will survive.

Some mock, as the twentieth-century British novelist Stevie Smith did:

> I have had trouble with married women friends and with those who are living free-like and unmarried with their darling chosen-one. I have had trouble for two reasons, because sometimes I like the chosen-one too much, but mostly and the most trouble, because I do not like him enough, and because I think it is so wonderful of the women to be so unselfish and so kind. But I can see that they have to do it, if they are going to have a darling husband and darling children, they have to do it, there is no other way, and if you do not then you will live lonely and grow up to old solitude. Amen.

Troublesome ghosts intrude on this sober discussion. Among Anthony, Stanton, Lucy Stone, Elizabeth Blackwell, the Grimké sisters, one can see the assertion of the importance of women friends alongside or in spite of commitment to husbands and children. There is an ancient anger and a more ancient hurt in the pit of my stomach as I write this. There is jealousy. The abandonment that comes with the turning away of a friend's attention, and the rueful question, what's he got that I haven't got? It rings heartily of adolescence, seems regressive, childish as it floods back. Freud says what he's got is a penis. There is more to it. What he's got is power. He offers to buy her dinner, build a chateau for her in the countryside, make her an editor of his magazine, introduce her to someone...

An echo of the loss of mother, to be sure. She turns to him, away from me, and what's he got.... On this score, Freud described something I recognize. We carry it with us, all of us, this early loss, and it makes us more vulnerable than I think anyone knows to what happens between us and our women friends in the way the world is structured as we grow up. It is "immature" to retain this jealousy, this hurt, this fury. Women rarely mention it, resign themselves to losing other women to men, say it is the way of the world, part of growing up.

The ghost of the childhood friend is the ghost of a passionate love. Simone de Beauvoir wrote about hers in *Memoirs of a Dutiful Daughter:*

> I was dazzled by her originality.

> I loved Zaza so much that she seemed to be more real than myself.

> Zaza did not suspect how much I idolized her...my affection for her was fanatical.

In *Sula,* Toni Morrison describes the complex agony of a friendship between Nel and Sula, who "met in dreams" because

> each had discovered years before that they were neither white nor male, and that all freedom and triumph was forbidden to them, they had set about creating something else to be. Their meeting was fortunate, for it let them use each other to grow on.

Their girlhood friendship develops into the most profound bond, intimacy, validation and identification:

> They never quarreled, those two, the way some girlfriends did over boys, or competed against each

other for them. In those days a compliment to one was a compliment to the other, and cruelty to one was a challenge to the other.

In Morrison's novel, Sula leaves town. Nel marries. Sula returns and Nel thinks of that return as being "like getting the use of an eye back, having a cataract removed." The cataract is her married life. With Sula, she laughs and of that laughter Morrison says:

> It has been the longest time since she had had a rib-scraping laugh. She had forgotten how deep and down it could be. So different from the miscellaneous giggles and smiles she had learned to be content with these past few years.

To the rib-scraping laughter and the fanatical affection of these adolescent friendships, add the shared life of the mind. "Bookish" girls record the friend with whom they first read this or that novel, discovered certain writers, began to be aware of themselves thinking. De Beauvoir says this about Zaza and Lillian Hellman tells, in the story called "Julia," about the New Year's Eve she spent with her friend when she was twelve years old, how they lay in twin beds while Julia recited Dante in Italian, Heine in German, Donne's poem "Julia" and, in response to Lillian's plea for more, Ovid and Catullus.

A bulwark against foot-binding and paternalism—in a world that discourages female growth or extracts (encourages) female dependency as the price for being shown the wonders of the city—it is no wonder that attachments between girls grow so fierce and that they survive though driven underground by everything that goes by the name of maturation.

1957: I go to Nora for what I then called "culture" much as de Beauvoir did to Zaza and Hellman to Julia. Her house is full of "art books" and "classical music." Our friendship is four years old. We share clothes and get our hair cut together and we talk about boys. Our aspirations are similar, from the trivia of high school life, like sororities, to the confused stretching of our minds at work, to the determination to "make something of our lives," be something in the world, be, and be *something*, which means not JUST wives and mothers. We have arranged to go to the movies together on Friday night. On Tuesday, Marty calls, asking will I go out with him on Friday night. It is "only" Nora. It is "only" a girl friend. By breaking my date with her, dismissing it, choosing him, I fulfill his expectations, my own and hers.

We are not, beyond adolescence, expected to like one another. We are not meant to respect one another, to stand on solid footing facing one another with public issues in the air between us. So privatized are our relations that Lillian Hellman's "Julia" comes as a larger surprise than it ought to be. In that story, grown women struggle with moral and political issues, not with whether a man will call or whether the kitchen floors will shine. It is a picture of one of the few adult relationships between women that has the complexity and integrity Woolf so rightly missed in literature. "Julia" is full of conventional kinds of tension: Hellman faces danger as she carries a large sum of money into Germany so that her friend Julia can use it to ransom Hitler's prisoners. The intrigue between the women, though, is deeper than the "foreign intrigue" trappings of their external adventure. Childhood friends have grown apart but remained connected in feeling. One has become a revolutionary, the other is on the road to artistic success in conventional ways. Their differences are political. What Hellman is asked to do tests her loyalty and her courage, her ability to act in spite of difference.

Can she be counted on? How strong is the bond across divided and distinguished worlds? How strong is her love?

When it became a film, "Julia" underwent a small but significant change. Dashiell Hammett appeared on the screen in larger proportion than he occupied in Hellman's story. He became a participant in the action, subtly diluting, by his presence, the intensity of the female friendship that was, in fact, the plot. Two women are alone in an adventure. Is a man necessary to make it significant?

1638. Boston. Anne Hutchinson leads a rebellion within the church, demanding that women be allowed to preach. She holds meetings of women in her home and because she is a midwife, is accused, obliquely, of witchcraft. She is put on trial; the sentence is banishment. Mary Dyer, a generation younger, wife of a milliner, stands at the moment of banishment and follows Hutchinson—before the eyes of the congregation, in tense silence—out of the church. In 1660, Mary Dyer is hanged in Boston.

1937. Berlin. Julia asks Lillian Hellman to risk her life.

The sixties. New York. Working my way through college. The work is "women's work"—in a department store, in the typing pool. I am surrounded by women, but full of a sense of my "separateness," my "difference," a fraudulent and defensive class contempt. I make no connections with women at work. At college, my writing class is taught by a man; there are several well-known male writers around; they play volleyball in our gymnasium and the girls with literary aspirations act as unofficial cheerleaders. After graduation, we go in different directions, many of us with men, some on our own. Linda, my roommate, who came from the same place I did, married Steve. I went to graduate school in Berkeley and drove there with Joan, whom my friends warned me was a lesbian.

1850. Charlotte Brontë describes her friend, Ellen Nussey:

We were contrasts—still we suited—affection was first a germ, then a sapling, then a strong tree.

At the same time, in America, Lucy Stone and Antoinette Brown write letters to each other. They swear never to marry; they see marriage as interference, deflection from the path, quitting, and severance of their bond with each other. In fact, each marries, but they marry brothers and their friendship and correspondence survive fifty years.

Myself again. The late sixties. An Ivy League graduate school, studying literature, which is male, taught, still, by professors who are male, with several exceptions. One is a famous woman scholar, formidable and seen by me through male eyes as "unattractive." I cannot imagine that this woman has to have a body. Her undergarments must have been as antitactile as my grandmother's. There is no sense of pleasure or amusement about her, no spaces, everything dense and intellectual. She wears sensible shoes and genderless, bland clothing. I respect her enormously, but it is hard to learn from her anything about being a woman of intellect, retaining both woman and intellect. This terrible lesson is true, too, in popular films, where career women are ugly bitches. It is clear that women must choose in a way that men need not. There are girl friends for "girl" things and intellectual women for intellectual things.

"Girl" things are driven underground, become as secret as compulsive eating binges. Charlotte Brontë had two friends.

With Ellen Nussey, she shared family life—thought of her as a fourth sister—daily domestic detail, relational subtleties, asking for nurturance, for cradling. With Mary Taylor, a feminist who eventually left England because it was too oppressive to women and struck out boldly for New Zealand, she shared a great deal more about books and politics. Taylor criticized *Jane Eyre* for not being political enough.

The underground aspect of female life is all too often mythologized, romanticized when it is not being ignored. In those experiences that isolate us from men, we want the companionship of other women. There are and have been societies where this wanting is institutionalized—in the menstrual hut, in those places where childbirth is a female affair. Whether men are banished from these sacred female places or whether they avoid such encounters depends on which end of the telescope is held up. It depends on who wrote the record of those ostensible "facts," whose values and point of view were recorded. In modern, industrial societies, we struggle for ways to retain the camaraderie of those sacred places, to experience them as metaphors, not to be bound, as men have bound us, to our bodies, not to have bodily connection and empathy as our only common ground. In *The Golden Notebook,* the writer Anna Wulf has parallel experiences with a man and a woman who represent the world of television and are attempting to buy Wulf's novel for adaptation to that medium. Wulf is battered by the wrench in values expressed by each of those television people—they both want to tone the work down, to de-politicize it. Neither speaks her language, yet she experiences the woman with a double sensibility: "I liked her as a woman," she says. Wulf is attuned to a small sexual drama being played out during her interview in a hotel dining room, a flirtation on the woman's part with a man at another table. She senses that there is an arrangement between them, the television woman waiting for her "work" to be done, anxious whether the man will remain waiting for her.

"I liked her as a woman." Although in other ways, she is

"the enemy" and not to be liked, not to be seen as human, I could think of her as a woman—apart from everything else. Whether her husband beats her or not. How she feels with a child at her breast. The tension before her menstrual period. The moment when the rice is burning on the stove, a child demands her attention, the telephone rings. Waiting for a man to call. Her jealousy of other women, wanting a mink coat or wanting to write something brilliant.

Myself in graduate school in the company of many other women like myself and not knowing them. We stayed away from each other. We tried, in the privacy of our student apartments, to be smarter on the subject of John Donne or The Victorian Novel, than anyone else, but especially smarter than other women—because there was room for only some of us, because the jobs that might be waiting were limited and only a few women would get them, because the struggle to be taken seriously by our male professors was relentless. Because our culture had taught us to deny what we had in common, to put out the fire of our identification and empathy with each other, to pretend not to know each other's vulnerability and the cosmic implications of the political arrangements against which every one of us was struggling to survive and grow.

A decade later, the world is beginning to be different. My world is different, but the rest of the world is, too. We have made it different. Simone de Beauvoir helps organize a delegation of women from all over the world to go to Iran, where they protest the massacre and repression of women in that country. Intimacy is no longer underground nor solitary. Our connection is not only bodily—although we often remark on the mystery of women who spend time together having their menstrual periods at the same time. We nurture each other as we have through all history. On a particularly depressed evening, I take myself to my friend's house, where she cooks a beautiful dinner for me and shows me her theatre piece in progress. She is for me mother/sister/lover/friend, but the categories do not apply, are hollow. I spend the afternoon with Priscilla and only at the end, only in a cursory way, do we mention the man she lives with, the children who absorb a fair share of her attention.

A summer's night on an avenue crowded with restaurants. The man walking beside me observes the great numbers of women out for the evening together. I have ceased to think of this as remarkable. I have come to think of this as a period in history, like one or two others, in which women find each other the most interesting people around, in which women find new thinking, new ways of looking at the world, in other women far more than they do in men. I have come to feel my own life as one in which women are an enormous delight, at least most of the women I know, and that to cancel an appointment with a woman because a man had called would now not only violate my own expectations and hers, but is unthinkable and would diminish my life. The man beside me is envious. He does well, I think, to be so.

5

Lovers

PARIS IN THE TWENTIES

Some say alright all but one way of loving, another says alright all but another way of loving ... I like loving. I like mostly all the ways any one can have of having loving feeling in them. Slowly it has come to be in me that any way of being a loving one is interesting and not unpleasant to me.

Gertrude Stein, *The Making of Americans*

Now what would happen if I let myself go over? Answer me that. Over what? you'll say. A precipice marked V.

Virginia Woolf to Vita Sackville-West

You will then tighten your arms about me and if the cradling of your arms is not enough to soothe me, your kiss will become more clinging, your hands more amorous, and you will accord me the sensual satisfaction that is the surcease of love, like a sovereign exorcism that will drive out of me the demons of fever, anger, restlessness.

Colette

Sensuality, wanting a religion, invented Love.

Natalie Clifford Barney

The window opens wider and the breeze blows. We have come to love. One woman sits on the bed in her college dormitory and tells her roommate that none of the men she is dating have her roommate's sensitivity, humor, whatever qualities she likes so much, and the roommate echoes the thought and then it occurs to both simultaneously that they have been in love with each other all this time. A spring breeze fills the room with relief, a summer breeze brings passion. Women kiss in a restaurant and walk through the snow with their arms around one another. Strangers lock eyes in a room and it begins. But the air grows dank. Just when the window ought to open wider, the air become fresher, it closes. Love between women is not permissible. Men grow resentful of exclusion, women become frightened. Love comes to mean exile. A clamp shuts the window.

She loved her.

A hundred things happen when I write that sentence, when you read it. It depends on who I am, who you are, where you read it.

I loved her.

My feelings for other women are a turbulence, like clothes tumbling in the wash, a spot of hatred flopping over love bunched up, some care, some respect, some passion. To divide "friendship" from "love" is arbitrary, yet here it stands. I see skeins, cordiality beside affection beside deep connection, and somewhere along the line I ask myself to mark where one feeling ends and another begins, but I cannot. The line between friendship and love melts.

She loved her.

The culture makes it hard for women to love each other, just as it makes it hard for us to like and respect one another. Harder. The territory is mined with danger. The tribunal comes with its punishing hand, the Inquisition comes, the lawyer for the estate of the father. Women spend their lives with other women and call them "companion" or "friend." Historians say "benefactor" or "roommate." Evasion has been necessary for survival. In spite of the childhood chant: sticks and stones can break my bones but names will never harm me—they can and do and we know it. Fear of harm makes for distorting, not knowing and lying.

Well, I didn't exactly love her.

Sometimes, she loved her the way he loved her in the movies. The way he came clattering up on his horse, dust flying, grabbed her and headed west. She loved her is different from he loved her. Or from she loved him. Another kind of weight falls on the sentence. Which kind of weight and where it falls relates to history, to how many other books I have written or you have read in which she loves her, how easily the words trip off the tongue or the pen.

The varieties of female love lie hidden by fear.

I never told Mavis I loved her, but I certainly did, in a time when I was frightened and frenzied, came home to her solidity, counted on her. There was much of the motherless child in my loving her, gratitude for her steady nurturance. I occasionally adore Nancy the way I would a movie star, more often love her in real ways, feel familiar and intimate, accepted, accepting. I have watched women I love in rooms full of people, feeling myself beside them and alone with them.

They say that love is eternal, but looking over the record, it does not first appear to be so. Oddly enough, love between women seems confined to certain moments in time, certain periods in history. Whether or not she might love her, might let herself love her, might have understood her love, has to do with history. What expression her love might have has to do with what is permissible in her culture, as do the varieties of meaning she might give to her love, the impact it will have in her life or the life of the woman she loves. At some points in history, the social conditions are such that love can thrive, that the window can be thrown wide open.

Elizabeth Stanton wrote to Susan Anthony: "No power in heaven, hell or earth can separate us, for our hearts are eternally wedded together." A year later, having heard one of the many rumors of division in their friendship from those who wished it divided, she wrote: "Have you been getting a divorce out in Chicago without me?" Charlotte Brontë sent Ellen Nussey locks of her hair. Antoinette Brown called Lucy Stone "my dearest little cowboy" and Susan Anthony addressed Anna Dickinson as "Dear Chick-a-dee."

This is said to be a matter of "style," a phenomenon of the nineteenth century, an intensely romantic expression of friendship condoned by the culture, necessary, in fact, to the smooth functioning of the culture. The reverberations of a single self and its personal feeling into the external world has something to do with acceptable "style." The language of love and marriage used by women in relation to one another has been, at various times, tolerated, understood or punished, recognized or repressed. Personal sensation takes root and grows or is crushed under a brutal heel, depending on what need there is to nurture or crush it. At the intersection of the personal with the social, the inner response and public custom, we come up against the idea of history.

The story of women in love requires not only geography— the intersections of various lives, the bends in the road, the detours—but temporality. At what point in time did she love her? Was it a time when women gathered in bars and danced the night away? Was it a time when women were not able to own property, thereby increasing the risk and the punishment if one woman fled the house of father or husband for another woman? Was it a time when the literature at the local bookstand showed women embracing or marrying one another, where a female stroller might find a reflecting image of the way her own heart beat? Was it a time when the female body was acknowledged to have its own course of passion and need, when it was understood that women desire, whatever their object? Or was the body corseted in the cultural mind?

In *Orlando,* Virginia Woolf called "society" "one of those brews such as skilled housekeepers serve hot about Christmas time, whose flavour depends upon the proper mixing and stirring of a dozen different ingredients." *Orlando* is, itself, the product of a delicate mixing, a certain society that belongs to a moment in history. Woolf's novel is a love letter to Vita Sackville-West, doused in wit, a rollicking consideration of profound questions about gender and love. It was published in 1928, several days after Radclyffe Hall's *The Well of Loneliness,* which depicts what its author called "inversion" and its audience called "Sapphic love." In the same year, Djuna Barnes published *Ladies Almanack,* as rollicking a piece of writing as Woolf's, peopled by the well-known and recognizable lesbians of her day.

To say that something was in the air in 1928 is to put things mildly. A phenomenon of history was in the air, had been for some time, lingered in the air all through the decade and partly into the next. The phenomenon mixed attitude with event and affected·both literature and women's lives in ways that were to go underground for half a century. Women have fallen in love with each other in all periods of history, in all countries, in various ways. Women have loved each other passionately whether or not the culture would allow it. Often, in defying the culture, they have hidden themselves away. What happened at the beginning of this century is an extraordinary emergence into public life of such loving and the equally extraordinary literature that came of it.

In both Paris and London, in life and in literature in the 1920s, the love of women for other women seems, from the perspective of our own time, to have thrived, to have established a context, to root itself in history, to spin out a literature in all modes, all shades of attitude, all genres, to have had both participant and audience on a substantial scale.

This part of the story is missing from conventional accounts of the literature of the first part of our century. Paris and, somewhat less, London, we have been told, were aglitter in the twenties with a group of writers now called "The Lost Generation." Hemingway, Fitzgerald, Joyce and Pound dominate the history of the time, with Eliot still in the bank and Miss Stein, when she appears, being quite large, incomprehensible or silly. Anyway, she was Miss Stein and she had an Alice, but that was not very much part of the picture, except when it came to food, which, along with liquor, seemed as important to the period as the writing of books and the founding of small magazines.

A group of Americans were "searching for identities" in Europe, principally Paris, after the First World War. I always understood this search as a detective novel, picking up a clue on the platform of the metro, receiving bizarre messages on tablecloths at various cafes on the Left Bank, deciphering hieroglyphs on the endpages of books sold in stalls along the Seine. The protagonist in this sort of story in my mind resembles Inspector Maigret. At least, he is always male.

Now some peculiar patterns emerge as I reshuffle the deck and look at writing and writers from the point of view of women. Women's lives and literature undergo a radical transformation in the period under imagination here. Gertrude Stein, the poet Hilda Doolittle, who always signed her work "H.D.," Virginia Woolf, Colette, Kay Boyle, Edith Sitwell, the great classical scholar Jane Harrison, the women who became publishers, like Harriet Monroe at *Poetry* and Margaret Anderson at *The Little Review* and Sylvia Beach, who is responsible for the existence of *Ulysses* as a printed work—this is their time (this is the time of their time) and they are but a few. Looking at all the arts, widening the lens, there is Isadora Duncan, Sarah Bernhardt, Eleonora Duse on stage, Berenice Abbot making photographs, and Janet Flanner writing her "Letter from Paris" in *The New Yorker,* signing it "Genêt." This is the period between two world wars. In America, it is the time of the Provincetown Playhouse and Edna St. Vincent Millay and of the Harlem Renaissance. But I am looking at the women and wondering, as the details emerge, at the hand touching the hand, the actual connections among these women, their literary and personal relations and how much of this emergence has to do with both love and power.

Begin with the idea of an American in Paris. Although the image of Gene Kelly clackety-clacking along the cobblestones intrudes, it is clear that a great many Americans, especially women, went to Paris in the early part of the twentieth century, either permanently or on long visits. There was a magnet in the cultural climate; Paris was the intellectual center of the world, hospitable to artists. There was a community there, and it was not America, which each of these travelers saw as Puritanical, repressive, materialistic and bourgeois. Both Gertrude Stein and Alice Toklas came, separately, from California. Hilda Doolittle came from Pennsylvania. Sylvia Beach grew up in a clerical family in New Jersey and Natalie Barney, who affected the course of literary life in Paris for half a century, was a midwesterner.

It begins to sound like a Henry James novel. It is not. There is no Daisy Miller in this group, no Lambert Strether, no American "innocence" up against the Old Order. There is, in fact, exile, but it seems to work in reverse. In Paris—or London—many women managed to create a literary culture in which they were full citizens. They left behind them an American culture in which they would have been exiles.

At about the same time that James' Daisy Miller scuttled off to Europe, three fictional women made a similar voyage with very different consequences. Gertrude Stein wrote, in *Q.E.D.,* a novel of extraordinary numb anguish—about Mabel, Helen and Adele, three high-spirited American girls. Aboard a ship, these college friends debate various Jamesian themes, including the morality of the bourgeoisie, the ability or inability to feel, questions of how feeling is experienced and how it is acted upon. The feeling at stake is subtle at first, then less so. On a cold and beautiful night, Adele "suddenly felt herself intensely kissed on the eyes and on the lips." The relationship continues, triangular, Mabel often remote but apparently "in control" of Adele.

1903. The writing was done in Paris; the events behind the novel had occurred some years earlier. It was not published until later, partly because Alice Toklas jealously resented the book and would not allow its publication, but also because, before Gertrude knew Alice, she knew that no one would have published it. Stein's novel is a prologue to the decade and so, too, is Colette.

1907. Colette in a pantomime with the Marquise de Belboeuf, whom she calls "Missy," who is her lover. The women kiss; the police arrive and shut the show down. Colette and Missy live together for five years.

> In our house there is only one bed, too big for you, a little narrow for us both. It is chaste, white, completely exposed; no drapery veils its honest candor in the light of day. People who come to see us survey it calmly and do not tactfully look aside, for it is marked, in the middle, with one soft valley, like the bed of a young girl who sleeps alone.

Among the people who come to see them is Renée Vivien and a host (hostess? the language conspires against accuracy) of women in trousers, all of whom Colette caught on the page. Renée Vivien died in 1909. It took Colette twenty years to be able to write about her.

Alice Toklas moved in with Gertrude Stein the following year and Leo Stein, who had led the way, who had set up brother and sister in Paris among painters, referred to her as "the typist." Three years later, Leo left. Gertrude wrote about the dissolution of her relationship with her brother—"It was not a community in that belief"—and of her relationship with Alice Toklas—"some one who was loving her." Colette left Missy for Henri de Jouvenel, whom she married and with whom she had her only child.

It is often said that the First World War resulted in a new freedom for women and that the woman-loving culture in Paris, with connections to literary lives in London, was an offshoot of the war and the new freedom. Obviously, women were living together in love before the war and, especially in Paris, living within a culture they had made. The war did its part in eroding a great deal of Victorian paternalism. "New" ideas about women, from less restricted clothing to openness about sexuality, were in the air more after the war than before, but the war did not simply pry open Pandora's box and release something that had been bottled up for decades. In fact, most of the "new" ideas had been around a long time. Greater freedom for women had been a collective effort as far back as the American suffrage movement and as recently as the passionate recurrence of that movement in England. George Sand wore trousers, but not many other women did. Women are freer to waltz in each other's arms or set up housekeeping together in some historical times and not in others, but women always do it. In the twenties, it became a major cultural style.

1917. A woman called Winifred Ellerman, daughter of one of the richest men in Europe, reads a book of poems called *Sea Garden* by the American Hilda Doolittle, and eventually finds its author: "H.D. was the most beautiful figure that I have ever seen in my life, with a face that came directly from a Greek statue and, almost to the end, the body of an athlete." They became—I hesitate, the history of the world is full of such hesitation—they became friends. Two years later, H.D. is pregnant and has pneumonia. Winifred Ellerman, who has taken the name "Bryher" to dissociate herself from her family, saves H.D.'s life:

> I found H.D. in bed and looking feverish, even to my inexperienced eyes....I was so alarmed by her appearance....I have just found you, suppose I lose you, was the thought running through my head...."If I could walk to Delphi," H.D. whispered with an intensity that I knew I was seeing for the first time, "I should be healed."

1917. Gertrude Stein has written a piece called "Ladies Voices" in which she says: "Genevieve does not know that it is only in this country that she could speak as she does." Gertrude is in that country. She speaks as she does. She writes a long poem called "Lifting Belly," a delectable, erotic poem, one of many that captures the love-play and domestic banter of herself and Alice: "Kiss my lips, she said. I did. Over and over and over I did." Sylvia Beach arrives in Paris and opens her bookstore with the help and advice of Adrienne Monnier, a Frenchwoman who also runs a bookstore. Colette is going to Proust's dinner parties at the Ritz and Proust is interested in "Sapphism," eventually goes to ask American expatriate Natalie Barney, known throughout Paris as "L'Amazone," about the subject. Barney publishes her book, *Pensées d'une Amazone,* in 1920.

Call it a decade, spilling over a bit on either end. In the decade or more after the First World War, two structures of literary life dominate Paris—Gertrude Stein's entertainments and Natalie Barney's Fridays. Both women are lesbians, but that is the end of their similarity. The structure of the Stein/Toklas household is thoroughly domestic. Husbands bring their wives— Hemingway, Fitzgerald. Stein is very interested in the men, in taking her place in literature alongside the men. Natalie Barney describes her "still envying her knights errant: Thornton Wilder, Scott Fitzgerald, Hemingway, Carl van Vechten, Bernard Fay, Max White, for being initiated and able to spin, undazed, around her circles." She helps them and she requests their help. Barney gives the best description of what Stein did for people:

> How many spilt lives came to Gertrude with their misfortunes, due to some inextricable situation or sentimental rut? She, instead of offering helpless sympathy, often helped them out, by changing an idée fixe or obsession into a fresh start in a new direction.

which describes, among other things, the difference between friendly behavior and mothering behavior. It is unfortunate that so few records remain or were ever made that would tell us how women saw Stein. Mostly, we have what it was that frightened Hemingway and the stolid monument that Picasso painted. For the tenderness and vulnerability, her fragile doggedness in pursuit of her own road—"Let me listen to me and not to them"—in spite of a chorus urging otherwise, a pursuit entirely encouraged by Alice Toklas, we need to read Stein herself.

Still, the Stein household was in many ways conventional and heterosexual married couples were the norm, although Picasso brought each of his mistresses to have them looked over by Stein. Natalie Barney was engaged in an entirely different enterprise. Although men did come to the Barney salon, the focus of her Fridays was events for women and did not emphasize couples any more than they emphasized masculine culture. Mata Hari danced there for women only. The atmosphere of Barney's salon seems, from the impressions of those who recorded them, to have been full of *esprit,* waltzing, music, decorativeness, certain kinds of grand extravagant gestures—these dictated by Barney, who once had herself sent to Renée Vivien dressed in a nightgown in a box of white lilies. She once stuck a long-stemmed red flower in the spokes of Gertrude Stein's motorcar. Theatrical. Defiant, too, as though Barney flung herself in the face of a tradition of silent suffering, martyrdom, and morosity in lesbian culture, against the cloud that shaded many lives and much writing—a cloud shaped by the homophobia of the surrounding culture. This spunk is one strain of life and letters in the period.

Vita Sackville-West comes into it now and after her, Virginia Woolf. In 1919, Sackville-West was in Paris with Violet Trefusis. They were passionately in love and Sackville-West dressed in trousers, called herself "Julian," and had a wonderful time. The story of Violet and Vita, their mad escape and desire to elope together, the pursuit by unnerved husbands and the eventual end of the affair is told in *Portrait of a Marriage.* The opposition and triumphant destruction of women's love for each other by husbands and fathers is not unusual. Both literature and life are replete with it. A year after Vita and Violet returned to their husbands, Freud published his essay on "The Psychogenesis of a Case of Homosexuality in a Woman" and the first aspect to engage his attention in the "case" was the attitude of the subject's father, whom Freud describes as conventionally remote and stern:

When he first came to know of his daughter's homosexual tendencies, he flared up in rage and tried to suppress them by threatening her.... There was something about his daughter's homosexuality that aroused the deepest bitterness in him, and he was determined to combat it with all the means in his power; the low estimation in which psycho-analysis is so generally held in Vienna did not prevent him from turning to it for help. If this way failed he still had in reserve his strongest counter-measure; a speedy marriage was to awaken the natural instincts of the girl and stifle her unnatural tendencies.

Although Freud was later to analyze Hilda Doolittle, he was not yet acquainted with her in 1920. Still, his description of the father is close to what Bryher, who had begun to live with H.D., said about her own father. In 1921, those women traveled to America and at the end of that trip Bryher ended up proposing marriage to Robert MacAlmon, for reasons that she flatly explains in her autobiography:

I had happened to meet a young American writer, Robert MacAlmon, who was full of enthusiasm for modern writing. He wanted to go to Paris to meet Joyce but lacked the passage money. I put my problem before him and suggested that if we married, my family would leave me alone. I would give him part of my allowance, he would join me for occasional visits to my parents, but otherwise we would lead strictly separate lives.

The ensemble returned to London. Bryher had accomplished the kind of protection she sought, although there was to be trouble and pain among everyone involved for quite some time.

1922. The protection of father or husband is still required of women, although the requirement has somewhat lessened. Women are making their own connections and this web of connection spreads to London. Aldington, married to H.D., is to begin a campaign to free T.S. Eliot of his job at the bank, and one whom he will most seek to enlist is Virginia Woolf. Katherine Mansfield has disappeared, as far as Woolf knows, and will soon die at Fontainebleau. Bryher knows the Sitwells. Both know Gertrude Stein. Radclyffe Hall has been living with an elegant lady in London; the lady has died while Hall was running off with the wife of an admiral. In Paris, Natalie Barney's salon is in full swing. Hemingway goes to visit Gertrude Stein for the first time. And Clive Bell tells Virginia Woolf that a Mrs. Nicholson thinks her the best writer.

Context returns as something to be considered along with personal timing in terms of what course a relationship might take, what the options are. Clive Bell introduced Vita Sackville-West to Virginia Woolf, but what happened afterward did not follow the course of his other introductions. Mrs. Nicholson refused to be called Mrs. Nicholson, partly because she lived in a world where women claimed their own names, their own lives, quite naturally and most likely with one another as example. Both Woolf and Sackville-West, at this point in their lives and at this point in history, knew women who loved each other. They read books by these women, spent time with them. It was possible.

Woolf is taken aback. Sackville-West is "an apparition" who begins sending a book every other day. The women meet in the company of their husbands. Most letters from this period are about herself and Leonard wanting to see Vita. Arrangements are made to suit him—for example: "Could you come on Saturday 13th not Sunday 14th, as Leonard has to disappear Monday at dawn, and therefore wouldn't see you at all." Woolf is impressed with her friend's legs, as many have quoted, but impressed, among other things, because she sees Vita as "stag like or race horse like." She responds to strength, motion, and class. Unlike Mansfield, who belonged, in Woolf's eyes, to "the underworld" —partly through her connection to Middleton Murry—Sackville-West is an aristocrat—partly through her connection to her family: "All these ancestors & centuries & silver & gold have bred a perfect body." Woolf is a ragamuffin, a virgin, shy and schoolgirlish.

Time, as Woolf wrote, passes. The descriptions of Sackville-West in diary and letters come more and more to resemble the knight in shining armor: the trunk of Vita's body is "that of a breastless cuirassier," which, the dictionary says, is a cavalryman wearing a breastplate, close-fitting armor originally made of leather. Her aesthetic and erotic admiration is apparent from the first descriptions and so, too, is the direction of her imagination, which couches Vita's beauty in metaphors of masculinity—she is "grenadier; hard; handsome; manly." This is the beginning. This is Virginia admiring.

From the earliest days of life with Vanessa at Gordon Square, Virginia Woolf lived in a culture where male homosexuality was out in the open, where sexuality was one of the more popular topics of discussion and aspects of life's action. Some of her best friends, as they say. Although she had been sardonic on the subject of "buggery" from time to time, Woolf was not homophobic and her context, on this score, was one in which many of the shapers of culture were male homosexuals. Virginia was more acerbic about the male-dominated aspect of that culture than she was about what those men did in bed with one another. She had entertained the idea of marrying Lytton Strachey, who was homosexual.

Female homosexuality was then, as it had always been and still is, far less visible, partly because women were less visible. Early in 1925, she had this to say in a letter to a friend:

Have you any views on loving one's own sex? All the young men are so inclined, and I can't help finding it mildly foolish; though I have no particular reason. For one thing, all the young men tend to the pretty and ladylike.... Then the ladies, either in self-protection, or imitation or genuinely, are given to their sex too. My aristocrat...is violently Sapphic.

Her aristocrat is Vita Sackville-West. The friendship and then love coincides, for Woolf, with intense thinking about relationships with women:

Much preferring my own sex, as I do, or at any rate, finding the monotony of young men's conversation considerable, and resenting the eternal pressure which they put, if you're a woman, on one string, find the disproportion excessive, and intend to cultivate women's society entirely in the future. Men are all in the light always: with women you swim at once into the silent dusk.

Woolf is hardly encyclopedic on the subject of loving women. She never writes directly, for example, about physical passion, although she does, in diaries and letters, express a tenderness and erotic playfulness that belie the "frigidity" of which she is so often accused. She also does not write about guilt or self-hate, one of the most insistent themes in the literature of women's love, and she does not write about it because she seems not to have known it. What Woolf does portray, brilliantly, over and over again, is the sensation of being attracted to a woman and the politics of it. This is what begins to grow in her writing. The politics of it comes to the forefront. Her relationship with Vita begins at the same time and contributes to a deeper and deeper consciousness of the range of human feeling and the politics of women's lives.

Her aristocrat was violently Sapphic at the beginning of

1925. In the spring, Woolf published *Mrs. Dalloway,* in which Clarissa Dalloway, withdrawing for a moment from the business of life as wife of a man of the world, withdrawing to an attic room, a narrow bed, thinking of herself as a nun or a child—in other words, thinking of life removed from the need to be with men in adult, female ways—remembers her friend Sally Seton and remembers her love for women:

> Yet she could not resist sometimes yielding to the charm of a woman, not a girl, of a woman confessing, as to her they often did, some scrape, some folly. And whether it was pity, or their beauty, or that she was older, or some accident—like a faint scent, or a violin next door (so strange is the power of sounds at certain moments), she did undoubtedly then feel what men felt.

Woolf describes what Mrs. Dalloway imagines men felt; she describes male orgasm:

> It was a sudden revelation, a tinge like a blush which one tried to check and then, as it spread, one yielded to its expansion, and rushed to the farthest verge and there quivered and felt the world come closer, swollen with some astonishing significance, some pressure of rupture, which split its thin skin and gushed and poured with an extraordinary alleviation over the cracks and sores!...But the close withdrew; the hard softened. It was over—the moment.

Then she remembers Sally Seton and a specific time when Clarissa was trying to decide whether or not to marry a man she did not marry, a charged time. She remembers her excitement about Sally—"She is beneath this roof!...She is beneath this roof!"—Sally's dark beauty, her way with flowers, Sally's abandon and energy, "the most exquisite moment of her whole life" when Sally kissed her, and "she felt that she had been given a present, wrapped up, and told just to keep, not to look at it." Then Clarissa Dalloway's reverie is broken just as the event she is remembering was broken—by the intrusion of a man, the man she does not marry, Peter, and she begins to think about him. But she has named the feeling:

> The strange thing, on looking back, was the purity, the integrity, of her feeling for Sally. It was not like one's feeling for a man. It was completely disinterested, and besides, it had a quality which could only exist between women just grown up.

Woolf's description of Clarissa's feeling for women as "disinterested" is materialistic. The economic dependence of women upon men leaves women "interested"—for survival—in male approval and Woolf sees relations between women as free of that. Money buys freedom, to some extent, as everyone knows, to some extent, especially those without money. The freedom Woolf admires in Vita Sackville-West is related to money. Have five hundred pounds a year and live by your wits, Woolf will recommend in a *A Room of One's Own*. Woolf does not understand very clearly—although she can portray it in fiction—how little "disinterested," psychologically, feelings among women are, especially in her own life. Clarissa and Sally are "in league together" as Virginia and Vanessa, according to Virginia, were. She brings her sister—a person of most intense "interest"—to this description, as she will bring her mother in relations among women in her next novel, *To the Lighthouse*.

Between 1925 and 1928, Virginia Woolf fell in love with Vita Sackville-West and the love was reciprocated, if the letters

between them and the observations of onlookers are any
indication. It is said that they first went to bed together in
December 1925—this comes primarily from Vita's letters to her
husband. Between 1925 and 1928, changes came over Virginia,
best reflected in her letters. The masculine descriptions disappear. Vita becomes "honey" more often than breastless Amazon.
She becomes comforter: "Why do I think of you so incessantly,
see you so clearly the moment I'm in the least discomfort? . . .
Like a child, I think if you were here, I should be happy." She
becomes the object of delight and the delighted, playful tone
sparkles:

> I'd like 3 days doing nothing but eat and sleep at Long
> Barn more than anything. An occasional kiss on
> waking and between meals.
>
> I like your energy. I love your legs. I long to see
> you.
>
> If I saw you would you kiss me? If I were in bed
> would you—
>
> I feel like a moth, with heavy scarlet eyes and a
> soft cape of down—a moth about to settle into a sweet
> bush—Would it were—ah but that's improper.

By the fall of 1928, Vita and Virginia are about to go to
France together. Virginia writes:

> What clothes do you expect me to take? None, I hope.

During the time they are away, Virginia sends her husband
letters full of descriptions of delicious meals the two have shared,
descriptions full of appetite and delight—this from a woman
who has been called anorexic, whose distress on her honeymoon
most certainly took the form of refusal or inability to eat, whose

"cures" for madness at that time, prescribed by her doctors, included force feeding, which she never forgot, which she mentioned when she sent *Mrs. Dalloway* (into which she had put much of that early madness in the character of Septimus Smith) to Vita and remarked how hard it had been to face the material, that part of her life, especially "being forced."

But the letters are not linear. Like life, they do not proceed in a straight line from attraction to loving to continuation, but have a countercurrent, a pulling away, drawing back, and this is most usually in sexual terms. They are not always Virginia's own terms, for Vita Sackville-West wrote that she was afraid of arousing physical passion in Virginia and obviously both Leonard Woolf and Harold Nicholson were looking on with concern. Virginia calls herself a "eunuch" who does not know "what's the right side of the skirt" (this, she says, makes it easier for women to confide in her) and she advises Lytton Strachey to stop short in a love affair that intoxicates him:

Stop, stop! I cried, thinking instantly of you. Now what would happen if I let myself go over? Answer me that. Over what? you'll say. A precipice marked V.

Virginia will not go over, or everyone around her thinks Virginia should not go over and she inherits that worry. Although the precipice is clearly erotic abandon—she says always that she is more interested in intimacy than she is in sex, with everyone—there is also the aspect of the precipice that Vita went over once: running off with a woman, leaving the man. "Throw over your man," she writes, playfully, as she once said to a friend that she would like to elope with her Sapphist. The boundaries are quite set between them—they are married women who will not throw over their men—and these boundaries contribute to the sense of safety that is in the record of the relationship. In other quarters—when women are poorer,

have no husbands, have not established literary reputations—
there is great danger in women loving women, but Woolf did
not live it and never risked it.

1925–1928. Woolf was extremely productive in her writing.
She felt that she had found an audience in Vita; she was feeling a
more secure sense of audience altogether. She did some of her
best work in these years. *Mrs. Dalloway* was published in 1925; *To
the Lighthouse* in 1927; *Orlando,* which Nigel Nicholson calls "the
greatest love letter in history," to Vita, about Vita, in 1928. In
her stories and essays, she worked on the ideas that culminated in
lectures on women and fiction at Cambridge and then in *A Room
of One's Own,* which was published in 1927.

1929. The culmination of a certain kind of common life for
women—for some women. A ground swell has been churning
for over a decade—for some women. Woolf is, in some ways,
that creature whose birth she prays for in *A Room of One's Own,*
Shakespeare's sister. And the paver of the way for more sisters.
In 1929, there is a female culture, exactly the kind she speaks of
in that book. There is a common life with shared friends, a
loving life, sometimes erotic, always loving. Books pass from
hand to hand, have an audience, an understanding of language
and the ways in which it is being used. Stein's more "obscure"
erotic writing would not have been obscure to the women of this
culture. The lives of these women are both separate and joined.
They have made, to some degree, the habit of freedom their
own. They have cut their hair and put on trousers as a mark of
that habit. They have gone alone to Paris, to London, to the
countryside, to opium dens, to theatrical shows on tour in the
provinces, printer's shops and bookstores, across the Channel and

to America. they have made a "we" out of separate lives, to greater or lesser extents. It is a fragile "we" and it will disintegrate before another decade has passed, but it did exist. It was made up of women who had five hundred a year (at least) and rooms of their own, inherited. Without the legacies of their fathers, they would not have been free to make what they made, but without the ideas and examples of each other, they might have spent their lives under lap rugs on steamers.

Out of this culture came *Orlando, The Well of Loneliness,* and *Ladies Almanack,* all in 1928. *Orlando* appeared six days after the London court decision to suppress *The Well of Loneliness* for its "immorality" and Woolf was involved in opposing the suppression. She did not instigate the opposition, but joined it. This was the "liberal" thing to do, although some of Woolf's companions in this protest had their own more personal reasons. E. M. Forster had written and self-suppressed a novel about homosexuals, *Maurice,* which had not only his own homosexuality to move him to action, but the example of his sister, Dorothy Bussy, who would later write *Olivia,* a novel about lesbianism in a girls school, set in the very school attended by Natalie Barney. Woolf signed a letter and offered to testify in court, but no literary testimony was taken, since the court considered the issue moral and not literary. Privately, Woolf thought *The Well of Loneliness* a "meritorious dull book." She wrote to her nephew that

> At this moment our thoughts centre upon Sapphism—
> we have to uphold the morality of that Well of all
> that's stagnant and lukewarm and neither one or the
> other; the well of loneliness.

and to Ottoline Morrell:

I have already wasted hours reading it and talking about it. . . . The dullness of the book is such that any indecency may lurk there—one simply can't keep one's eyes on the page.

But when she wrote to Vita Sackville-West, "about your friend Radclyffe Hall," she concentrated on the things she liked.

Leonard Woolf said that the furor over *The Well of Loneliness* was the turning point in Virginia's career as a novelist—that it awakened interest in the subject and prepared the way for the huge popular success of *Orlando*.

The difference between the two novels reflects not only the extreme difference between their authors but something more cultural, more archetypal. They stand as entry points for looking at the experience of one woman loving another, the fate of that experience in the world, the efforts to translate that experience into literature. The novels raise or embody most of the interesting questions, shed light on the female imagination and how it shapes things, are magnets around which theme and language can cluster.

The Well of Loneliness is about exile. Its mood is apologetic; it is meant as a plea for tolerance (of "inversion") and it is dense with self-hate. "Stephen Gordon"—the name given the girl at birth—wants to be a boy. She feels like her father's son, goes fox hunting, lives on a large estate, and eventually falls in love with a married woman nearby, who teases her, rejects her, calls in the irate husband, exposes Stephen, who is banished by her mother, becomes a writer, and then the First World War descends. The war frees Stephen in that it allows her to *be,* to use her strength. She becomes an ambulance driver, much as Gertrude Stein and Alice Toklas did. In this milieu, she meets and falls in love with a young girl, but hesitates, because of the exile that her love implies. Mary Llewellyn persists and the two women set up a life together in Paris. Their house is, in fact, the house that Natalie

Barney lived in. Stephen is "husband"; Mary is "wife." Stephen is content with her work and her "wife"; Mary's life shrivels. Prescriptively, Stephen "brings" Mary into the Barney circle, wanting her to have friends, but the prescription fails and Stephen, at the end, for love, gives Mary up to a man.

Orlando is about triumph. It is a romp, in which the character of Orlando, aristocrat, heir to the family estates, begins life in the court of Elizabeth Tudor, where he is favored by the Queen, loves and loses a Russian princess (the details of which are based on Vita Sackville-West's affair with Violet Trefusis), falls into a Sleeping Beauty-like trance, awakens in the late seventeenth century to a life of solitude, reading, and writing, falls in love with a Romanian archduchess, panics, has himself sent to Constantinople as an ambassador. In Constantinople, he lives like a typical colonial, receives a dukedom, and falls into his second deep slumber, from which he awakens as a woman, returns to England as a Lady in the reign of Queen Anne, is deprived of her hereditary lands (Vita Sackville-West could not inherit her family lands because she was female), tries to write, and faces the absolute social necessity of marrying. She attends the salons of the "wits," which is boring, and becomes part of a "female society," which is better. In the nineteenth century, she suffers in her crinolines, breaks her ankle, sighs and marries. She struggles with being both a woman and a writer and has a son. Then it is 1928—just like that—and Orlando smokes cigarettes, drives a motorcar and publishes what she has been writing for three centuries.

Shadow and sunlight, clouded and free, victimized and defiant—these are the terms that come to mind as *The Well of Loneliness* is placed beside *Orlando* and both placed in historical context. Shadow, clouds, victimization, emanating from self-hate, which itself emanates from the contagion of homophobia in the surrounding culture. This characterizes not only Radclyffe Hall's novel, but the diary that Vita Sackville-West kept about her affair with Violet Trefusis. This is "monster" literature—the lesbian as deviant, deformed, sick—in which ethics require her defeat. Most masculine literature about love is in this vein. The woman must be vanquished; the man in the story triumphs.

The context is homophobia. Opposition comes from all quarters. Definitions are made—heterosexuality is the norm in language and culture—applied and, often, internalized. Whatever the core of the love experience, its encounter with the world ends in devastation. Shakespeare showed this in *Romeo and Juliet,* and those lovers remain in readers' minds with benign grace and the youthful aura of tragedy. Not so lesbian lovers, who, like Radclyffe Hall's protagonist, must parade their pain, express anger at heterosexual tyranny by passivity: look what you have done to me.

Opposition comes from all quarters, even in the period under consideration, the only time in history, except, perhaps, for Sappho's, when a culture to support the literature thrived. E. M. Forster, for example, indignant as he became at the suppression of *The Well of Loneliness,* told Virginia Woolf that he did not, in fact, approve of lesbians because he "disliked the idea of women being independent of men." William Carlos Williams, in his *Autobiography,* recounts his visit to Barney, barely able to contain his own unconscious anger:

> Out of the corner of my eye I saw a small clique of them [the women] sneaking off together into a side room while casting surreptitious glances about them, hoping their exit has not been unnoticed.

It is certainly in the eye of the beholder. Williams' next sentence is a gem, a howler if you don't mind the perversity of it:

> I went out and stood up to take a good piss.

Ah. Then he cannot help but tell his readers a story about a member of the Chamber of Deputies, and using the member as a screen, he tells us:

> To his annoyance, as he stood lonely in the center of the dance floor, he saw women about him, dancing gaily together on all sides. Thereupon, he undid his pants buttons, took out his tool and shaking it right and left, yelled out in rage, "Have you never seen one of these?"

Phallic-centeredness takes on actual meaning. This is the root of male anger against lesbians and it appears in all times, all cultures dominated by that particular tool. D. H. Lawrence is the god of this ideology, and although no one has yet assembled the evidence, we can probably think of masculinity in this period as divided into two camps—the homosexual men who might have objection to women leaving the room together but generally kept quiet about it and the heterosexual men, like Hemingway, Williams, Fitzgerald, Pound, Lawrence, who insist on going out and taking a good piss. Much of their literature devolves around the theme: "Have you never seen one of these?"

Opposition comes also, and perhaps more painfully, from women. In *The Well of Loneliness,* it is Stephen's mother who reviles her and sends her into exile. In their confrontation, the mother begins with her own physical revulsion—"a desire not to touch or be touched by you—a terrible thing for a mother to feel"—and moves, as tyrants always do, from the personal to the universal with no thought or feeling in between. The mother, enforcer, in this novel of patriarchal values, says easily that Stephen is "unnatural" a "sin against creation," but especially "a sin against the father who bred you." Stephen defends herself against her mother and against the world by accepting their terms and trying to put herself into the existing scheme of things. "As a man loves a woman," she says, "that was how I loved."

And it is women who range themselves against Karen and Martha in Lillian Hellman's play *The Children's Hour,* from the confused little girl who first makes up the story that there is something "wrong" between the two women friends to the rich grandmother who becomes the agent of their destruction. She proceeds differently from Stephen's mother, but her tactics are equally conventional. The sin against the fathers is dealt with by annihilation. It was not to be discussed. It will not be named. Everyone will take a step backward from the two women as though they were carriers of typhoid. Nothing will be said, named, or looked at. The love whose name dare not be spoken. Extermination by silence.

She loved her. She looked around and the world said it doesn't fit the scheme of things. Those who love women marry them, protect them. It doesn't fit the scheme of things. So she denied that she loved her, so she pretended she was a man to fit into the scheme of things, so she killed herself one way or another. This is one course of love in the world.

Another is to sin against the fathers and be free of the whole mess, which is what Virginia Woolf struggles for in her own writing, approaches, retreats from, observes. In 1920, Vita Sackville-West had written the diary eventually published by her son in *Portrait of a Marriage.* In it, she describes herself as a Jekyll and Hyde, a person torn by a dual nature, which she names "masculine" and "feminine." Her diary is full of agony and self-hate. The only time she is at peace is when she marries Harold Nicholson, has a child, is the dutiful wife of a prominent man. This fits the world. But the "dual nature" acts up and the battle begins. If Virginia had not read the diary, she did know Vita, she

did know these things. *Orlando* is addressed to it, appears to have
been written to show Vita that the author of *Orlando* understood.
There was a dual motive behind this, or two aspects of the same
thing, for the book was begun while Virginia worried about
Vita's new love affair with Mary Campbell (which, in fact,
ended when Roy Campbell threatened to kill his wife) and it is
meant to win Vita. The book is also addressed to Vita's pain; it is
meant to assuage the self-hate. Two aspects of the same thing.
The loving motive, the way of winning a lover, here, on the part
of a woman, is not to conquer but to understand. Virginia offers
the book as understanding. She takes up what Vita had said in her
diary:

> I hold the conviction that as centuries go on, and the
> sexes become more nearly merged on account of their
> increasing resemblances, I hold the conviction that
> such connections will to a very large extent cease to be
> regarded as merely unnatural and will be understood
> far better, at least in their intellectual if not their
> physical aspect. I advance, therefore, the perfectly
> accepted theory that cases of dual personality do exist,
> in which the feminine and the masculine elements
> alternately preponderate.

Orlando makes this true. And rather than apologize or plead
for understanding, *Orlando* sets Vita free, makes her amalgam of
masculine and feminine a cause for celebration. The book is an
escape from oppression. Gertrude Stein's poetry often has this
quality—free at last, outside the gender system, away from the
world of the fathers and the brothers. Natalie Barney had it. In
our own time, Rita Mae Brown has it. One of the things that
makes *Rubyfruit Jungle* so appealing is its freedom, which takes the
form of refusing self-hate, moving outside and laughing.

The laughter of the Medusa. Humor is one way out of the

cul-de-sac. Cosmic laughter, not the kind of joke that turns tyranny inward. *Orlando* is the light strain.

She loved her and they laughed.

A woman looking at another woman sees differently from a man. Sometimes. Often, we wear their lenses, so it is hard to see. On the whole, we do not see mythologically. We do not see Eve, the mother of evil and seduction. We see less Sacred and Profane Love, Madonna and Whore, Good Girl and Bad. Fewer red red roses. Less "loveliness." We see beauty and strength and we struggle to name these qualities in our own ways, but, lacking a language, our words are often read as "feminine" and "masculine." Often, beauty resides in strength and this we love in women the way conventional masculine lovers in literature (and, one would assume, in life) do not. So our literature is full of Amazonian imagery, by which we mean strength and often, particularly, courage. Female strength, which patriarchal culture often tells us must come breastless. So Woolf first sees Sackville-West as a cavalier with a breastplate. Joan of Arc insisted on male clothing. The masculine body—and the masculine name—become the only way of surviving. Masculinity becomes, in the eyes of many women, not an inner experience, but a mediating one, a strategy for relating to the world.

When Vita Sackville-West put on male clothing and called herself "Julian," she felt freer than she ever had. Gertrude Stein refers to herself as "husband." A woman looks at another woman and sees strength, sees it admiringly. She speaks of Amazons, racehorses, stags. Romaine Brooks painted Natalie Barney with a small figure of a horse in the foreground.

She also sees feeling far more than men do. Mythological figures, archetypal "feminines," have no feeling, do not change. When Colette describes a female body, which she does often and in great detail, she sees the scars and she sees attitudes instead of universals:

> But I can see her reflection in the slanting mirror, her reflection with which she has just exchanged an anxious look, an irritable movement of her eyebrows. ... She threw off her dress and her little knickers, her Valenciennes lace brassiere, scratched her bare arms, stroked her rumpled chemise with the flat of her hand, with the shocking immodesty of one woman undressing in front of another.

"Sometimes," Virginia Woolf wrote in her diary, remembering Katherine Mansfield, "we looked very steadfastly at each other, as though we had reached some durable relationship, independent of the changes of the body, through the eyes." A woman of my acquaintance described the difference between making love with a woman and making love with a man as the difference between keeping her eyes opened or closing them. Romanticism tells us to keep our eyes closed; tells us that love is transport, which, for women, is a swoon, eyes closed, falling backward, passing out.

The literature of passion between women does not resemble the literature of heterosexual passion, except when the authors of that literature adopt a disguise—for their own or cultural reasons—and pretend that it is the same.

Female love exists in a phallus-free world. Even women who have dressed like men and used men's names do not—this simple fact does bear saying—have phalluses. A woman is a woman, however she cuts her hair and whatever she does in bed. The language of love between women is, on the whole, not the language of—I took her, the earth shook (only once!). Women use little of the imagery that purports to express eroticism but in fact expresses domination and conquest.

H.D. describes, in *Tribute to Freud,* how she began to have a vision, to see handwriting on the wall and was afraid, wanted to pull back, resist the powers, but Bryher, who was with her, helped, urged her on, gave her the strength not to resist. In *Briefing for a Descent into Hell,* one woman helps another go mad and come out the other side. Because of Alice Toklas, Gertrude Stein had the courage to refuse to be "normal," as defined. These are gestures of women in love. It is conceivable that men in love might do these things, although they don't seem to in the literature available to us, being too busy sweeping women off their feet. This leaves women with no leg to stand on, much less push beyond the "normal."

Love literature about women's mutual eroticism often revolves around the kiss and the caress. This may be attributable to reticence, to knowing how much one might express on the page. Vita Sackville-West describes her thralldom beginning when Violet Trefusis kissed her. Clarissa Dalloway remembers Sally Seton's kiss. What Woolf called her "Sapphic story"— "Slater's Pins Have No Points"—ends after several pages of brilliant description of erotic tension between a music teacher and her student, accompanied by the student's meditations on what happens to women who choose not to marry, this way:

> Julia blazed. Julia kindled. Out of the night she burnt like a dead white star. Julia opened her arms. Julia kissed her on the lips. Julia possessed it.

A kiss changes the action in Gertrude Stein's novel, *Q.E.D.,* forcing one woman to confront how she feels about another, making manifest what has been latent and vague between the two.

She loved her. She loved her and she kissed her. She kissed her and caressed her and then...

The image of the mother appears. The mother and child.

Tenderness between women calls up ancient association of this kind, best expressed by Colette:

> For I know quite well, that you will then tighten your arms about me and that, if the cradling of your arms is not enough to soothe me, your kiss will become more clinging, your hands more amorous, and that you will accord me the sensual satisfaction that is the surcease of love, like a sovereign exorcism that will drive out of me the demands of fever, anger, restlessness. . . . You will accord me sensual pleasure, bending over me voluptuously, maternally, you who seek in your impassioned loved one the child you never had.

She loved her and when she wanted to write about the ways in which she loved her, she read other women writing and she saw that they were sometimes in pain and sometimes delighted; she saw that they wrote multiorgasmically about sex and not the way men did. She saw the mother and the child, the kiss and the caress. She saw sex and food on the page, friends and enemies. When she wanted to write about the ways in which she loved her, she read the novels and essays of Virginia Woolf and Colette, the thoughts of Natalie Barney and Radclyffe Hall, the poems of H.D. and the work of Djuna Barnes. She saw that Una Trowbridge, who lived with Radclyffe Hall, was the first to translate Colette into English, and that Sylvia Beach was a friend of Bryher's, who lived with H.D., and in Beach's bookshop not only was Joyce published, but Edith Sitwell came to speak about Stein.

She thought there would be a way to express what she felt and what she had in mind. For a little more than twenty years, she thought that.

H.D. wrote a poem about the Second World War called "The Walls Do Not Fall," but in fact the walls did fall. They fell the way walls do, a chip here and there, the tumble of a loosened brick and then the inevitable wholly destructive thud. The rise of fascism was the fall of European culture and especially the ruin of the culture the women in this chapter had created and kept alive. It was over when the war was over and it never took root again. The further we get from the Colette-Barney-Stein-Sitwell-Beach-Woolf connection, the more extraordinary it appears and the more final its death is in the desert that came afterward.

Women saw the rise of fascism and the war differently from the way men did. Stein, who is always said to have lacked a mind for politics, who is said to have objected to the war because she did not want to be disturbed, was, in fact, the person who first named this female vision of the war:

> There is too much fathering going on just now and there is no doubt about it fathers are depressing. Everybody now-a-days is a father, there is father Mussolini and father Hitler and father Roosevelt and father Stalin and father Trotzky [*sic!*] and father Blum and father Franco is just commencing now and there are ever so many more ready to be one. Fathers are depressing. England is the only country now that has not got one and so they are more cheerful there than anywhere. It is a long time now that they have not had any fathering and so their cheerfulness is increasing.

This is *Everybody's Autobiography,* 1936, which ends: "The periods of the world's history that have always been such dismal ones are the ones where fathers were looming and filling up everything." In a sense, the women artists of the early part of the century had banished the fathers and were therefore free to build their own culture, to some extent, to live as they pleased and to love one another in various ways as they pleased. Now the fathers came back to haunt them, to put their feet down, to express their displeasure at the heretical banishment by the daughters. The ideology of fascism is, among other things, reprisal against women. Woolf, like Stein, saw fascism and the coming war as too much fathering and she wrote *Three Guineas* in 1938 to say so.

> The creature Dictator as we call him when he is Italian or German . . . believes that he has the right, whether given by God, Nature, sex or race is immaterial, to dictate to other human beings how they shall live; what they shall do. Let us quote again: "Homes are the real places of the women who are now compelling men to be idle. It is time the Government insisted upon employers giving work to more men, thus enabling them to marry the women they cannot now approach." Place beside it another quotation: "There are two worlds in the life of the nation, the world of men and the world of women. Nature has done well to entrust the man with the care of his family and the nation. The woman's world is her family, her husband, her children, and her home." One is written in English, the other in German. But where is the difference? Are they not both saying the same thing?

Imagine the effect of an ideology that insisted that a woman's world was husband and children on women who had rejected both. It is not an ideology that arose in the 1930s—since it describes most of world history—but it did, then, thunder as it had not for some twenty years. It did cut off the routes of escape from that ideology that women had relied on those twenty or more years. It weakened the walls around a women's community within which women might be heretics against this particular ancient religion. Woolf says that the fight against this aspect of the Dictator must wear down a woman's strength and exhaust her spirit.

That is what happened.

The impact of the war, its coming and its inescapable presence, was personal to everyone. Woolf's nephew, Julian Bell, was killed in Spain. Ottoline Morrell died in the year *Three Guineas* was published, which must have sealed the passing of an old order for Woolf. The following year, her London house was scheduled for demolition, the area around it slated for redevelopment. With the declaration of war and the coming of the bombs, the Woolfs stayed permanently in the country. Virginia talked to Vita on the telephone and heard the destruction in the background. She, like Colette, had particular demons because she was married to a Jew, and one of the things the Woolfs did in the country, with the specter of concentration camps in their minds, as it was in Colette's mind and Gertrude Stein's, was to stockpile morphine and plan to use that along with the fumes of their car to commit suicide together. Vanessa's studio was demolished. *Three Guineas* had expressed Woolf's vision of war as the stress disease of patriarchy—an analysis made even more explicit in H.D.'s long poem "The Walls Do Not Fall" and in some of Edith Sitwell's writing. More passionately, *Three Guineas* embodies the indignation women feel at destruction not of their own making. To be barred from deciding the course of action of the State and then to sit in one's house while the bombs fall—this Woolf delineates with knife-sharp wit and this, with all the frustration and impotence implied, is what Woolf lived through, what everyone attempted to live through, as too much fathering obliterated everything.

Stein lost the lease on her flat at 27 rue de Fleurus in 1938. Although everyone urged her to escape to America, she went with Alice Toklas to the South of France, lived quietly in a village and sold her Cézannes, threatened always by the camps and protected, it appears, by the mayor of the village, who had her name on no list of residents. Natalie Barney left her house behind and fled to Florence with Romaine Brooks to lead a life similar to Stein's, equally cut off but slightly less threatened, although the house was poked around in by the occupying Germans and the housekeeper left behind was interrogated. Radclyffe Hall planned to sell her property and, with Una Trowbridge, join Barney and Brooks in Florence, but escape was cut off by the war and they remained in England. H.D., like Stein, refused to return to America. Colette, saying, "I'm used to spending my wars in Paris," stayed put, quite isolated, for her friends were either dying or hiding out.

There was no culture in exile. Everyone retreated to her private life, cut off from common life. Houses were invaded and occupied, as were the cities in which the common life had taken root. The fathers not only dictated, but bombed and invaded. A woman would feel this as rape. As Woolf said, it wears down a woman's strength and exhausts her spirit.

Virginia Woolf walked into the river with her pockets loaded with stones in 1941. Radclyffe Hall died slowly and was dead in 1943. Gertrude Stein returned to Paris in 1944 and was dead two years later. Colette survived, confined by arthritis to her couch. Bryher wrote that although H.D. had physically survived the war, it killed her spiritually. Natalie Barney survived like an Amazon, returning to Paris in 1946 and starting it up again, establishing her salon to which many of the next generation came because Natalie Barney was a legend, not because Mata Hari danced or Stein read her poems or Colette performed in a play. It was over.

And not replaced. In addition to historical and economic consideration, in addition to the fact that Europe was altogether devastated by that war, that most aspects of the culture were wiped out, there is one important and concrete phenomenon in the obliteration of women's culture in the twentieth century that calls for attention. These were not women who married or had children—with the exception of Woolf and Colette. Natalie Barney spent fifty years with Romaine Brooks; Gertrude Stein spent forty with Alice Toklas; H.D. the same with Bryher. I am asking now about influence, which is what Woolf asked about in *Three Guineas*—how do women influence history and culture? In that book, Woolf pointed to the minimal influence of the class to which she belonged—the daughters of educated men—and the ironically greater influence of the courtesan or the uneducated Great Lady.

Women, for the most of history, influence culture through men, as women have acted through men. Autonomy in the past bred exile from the future or at least this is the painful lesson of history, although our own period brings hope that this is not a description of Eternal Fate. Without husbands, without children, what are the roads of connection to culture? To posterity? They are, to learn something from what happened in the twenties, collective roads built by women who refuse to disperse. Had the miraculous happened, had Woolf, Stein, Colette, H.D., Bryher, Hall, Barney and scores of others managed to endure the state of seige together, perhaps, impossibly, in the same place, the wrecker's hand might have been weakened.

But it was over. The love of women for women, which formed the bedrock of a culture that nourished art, that encouraged women to create it and saw that it had a hearing in its own time, was obliterated. It does not appear in our history books, is not pointed to as the great moment in the history of culture that it was, no longer leaps to mind as example or inspiration. Modernism was not a male enterprise. We need the women, but not each in isolation. We need them in their connection, which were many forms of love.

6

Conflict

OFF WITH HER HEAD

At the ancient feast of the Nonae Capratinae, "the women are feasted in the fields in booths made of fig-tree branches and the servant-maids run about and play; afterwards they come to blows and throw stones at one another."

Plutarch, *Lives of the Romans*

An envious thing for sure is the female mind
And always hateful to its rival for men's love

Euripides, *Andromache*

Deep into Madame's secrets I had entered—I know not how: by an intuition or an inspiration which came to me—I know not whence. In the course of living with her, too, I had slowly learned that, unless with an inferior, she must ever be a rival. She was my rival, heart and soul, though secretly, under the smoothest bearing, and utterly unknown to all save her and myself.

Charlotte Brontë, *Villette*

I am walking down a street where a women wearing a mink coat waits for someone, leaning against a building. She is not looking in my direction but opposite, where another woman comes toward us. The other woman is wearing a more expensive, more glamorous sable coat. The waiting woman winces. A look of pain crosses her face and she turns away, now seeing me in my mere sheepskin coat. She is relieved.

This is the world we have been raised to participate in. These are the moves on the chessboard.

We are caught in a crossfire on the subject. Literature is a moving picture show of women in constant conflict. So, too, is folklore. *Ad nauseam* we see and hear how women do not like each other, cannot get along, how women snipe and begrudge and look at one another with envy, jealousy, and resentment gleaming in their eyes. It gives comedians a lot of material to work with. That is half the crossfire. The other half is another stereotype. This one says that little girls are sugar and spice, that "femininity" means being nice, avoiding conflict. How is it possible to be creatures of such clawing and such gentility?

Myself against her.

Tradition tells me that we compete for men, that our conflict takes the form of envy, jealousy and pettiness. We are brought up to think of other women as enemies, to be in a state of conflict with them, but not to express it directly. We hardly stand toe to toe and do battle with one another. Most intellectual conflicts in history and in public life are between men. From the presidential debates to the street-corner fistfight, we can imagine varieties of masculine conflict, their terms and their resolution. When it comes to women, there is less information, fewer images of anything aside from what comes up in "Cinderella," more choking on the subject.

Helen. She stumbled from one hotel to another at the beach resort in Spain, carrying a coffeepot with her from room to room. (Generally isolated, caffeine-high, and appealing. I liked her; I pitied her; I saw much of myself in her.) We were lying beside a swimming pool and I, moved to dive in, invited her. She demurred, worried about her wig. Blind fury on my part. The blackout. I was running toward the beach, her wig in my hand, and flinging it into the ocean, gleeful as it was swept away. We did not speak for many years. I don't blame her. What arrogance on my part, what self-righteousness. I look under the layers—why is that woman running toward the sea with her friend's wig in her hand?

Marlene would not swim. She tells me she had been an enthusiastic swimmer at seventeen, then stopped. "When you started worrying about makeup and hair?" I asked. "Yes." I wanted to smash her in the face. The perpetual ideologue. A new version of Mrs. Grundy, in different terms, and something of a Stalinist. What churns up is my hatred of that woman in myself. Every acquiescence, every artifice of my own comes back to me.

Anger is easier to talk about than pain. Because we are seen by each other as well as by men as nurturers, we ask much of one another. Conflict between myself and another woman often reduces to mother-conflict, to issues of engulfment and abandonment. She asked too much of me. I asked too much of her. One of us was a mother, drained by other people's demands, unable to respond to the ordinary needs of friendship. A woman expresses need to another woman with a culturally sanctioned feeling of entitlement that she does not have in relation to a man. Conflict comes from unconscious playing out of mother and daughter, too close, too far away, too desirous of the other's approval, too tied, too suffocated.

Many of us spent our childhood and youth imagining that there were no other women like us. Our mothers were mothers, most of them without avenues of expression outside the home. Many of us were surrounded by what Kate Chopin calls, in *The Awakening,* "mother-women," whether they were actual mothers or not. We dreamed different dreams. This dreaming left us lonely and precarious, out on a limb, with no reflections, no support. We coped with those feelings by becoming "special" in our own eyes—heroines. The imagined fact that there were no other women like us became a special attachment to our own "difference," which existed alongside its loneliness. Then we met one another and were overjoyed and validated, but, I suspect, a bit irrationally and neurotically disappointed. There *were* other women like us. What a relief. But still...But still...I know, because of what I know about her life and what she has written in her books, that George Eliot felt this way. And it goes a long way toward understanding why Simone de Beauvoir, when she met Simone Weil at the Sorbonne, kept her distance.

Two Queens on a chessboard and something of their reflection in actual life, this time in the life of the sixteenth century, other times elsewhere, often in dream life. The metaphor of the chess game overflows. The Queen is the most powerful figure on the board. She can go in all directions, hither and yon, excessively mobile. Control the center of the board and look to the Queen. Yet her power is in the service of greater aim, of what it means to win, namely to capture the King, who is, in the end, the object, the most valued. An immobilized king is the end of the game. This, after all, is transposed war.

The Queen of England and the Queen of Scotland move differently, although they stand on the same chessboard. Elizabeth Tudor will pass into history as the Virgin Queen and it will be reported that she said, emphatically, that she refused to bleed and then proceeded to live accordingly. She meant not the blood of battle, but the blood of woman. Elizabeth refused to marry, refused to bear children, refused to live what is thought of, within the narrow limits that such things have been thought of, as a woman's life. Mary Stuart did otherwise, marrying the French Dauphin at twelve, then the Englishman Lord Darnley, then the infamous Scot James Bothwell, the accused murderer of Lord Darnley—which turned her into Clytemnestra in the public eye. She bore a son who became King James and, later, a child conceived in what appears to be rape by Bothwell, lost in miscarriage. From a distance, the Queens appear to embody the

War of the Roses all over again. Elizabeth is the white rose, Mary most red. One is chaste and virginal, one passionate, bodily. From a distance.

Closer, the fact that they stand on the same chessboard becomes more apparent. This is the King's war still. This is a masculine game. Many people do not like the idea of a woman ruler. Although women have ruled, some well, some badly, it is still up for question, open for discussion in some quarters, still open to criticism and attack. This applies equally to the Red Queen and the White Queen. Elizabeth makes a most conventional solution. She will rule and not be a woman. This is difficult for a female to do, but Elizabeth's strategy, echoed before and after her in history, literature and life, is to adopt the masculine. She calls herself "Prince." She will not bleed. Mary does not make the same refusal. Questions of marriage and birth are not personal questions but ones of power in the State and succession. A woman's body is not her own. This is doubled for the woman ruler. Will she be educated? What will she know of the world? How much will her decisions be her own, how much of her power is authentic and how much only apparent and controlled behind the scenes by ministers or benefactors or kings of other countries? These issues surround Elizabeth Tudor and Mary Stuart.

Elizabeth's mother, Anne Boleyn, went to the scaffold so that her daughter might rule. King Henry, desiring a son, wishing to supplant the daughter, ordered Anne executed for refusing to relinquish Elizabeth's claim to the throne. This left Elizabeth motherless, with martyrdom in her heritage and a particular urgency about redeeming the idea of a female ruler. Mary Stuart is said to have been close to her mother, although the child grew up in France while her mother, Mary of Guise, remained in Scotland. She had "a virtual nervous breakdown" upon her mother's death. These are different paths, different kinds of evolution in the lives of Elizabeth and Mary long before their lives so concretely crossed. How these differences were manifested in their interaction remains conjecture. No one considered matrilineage. This is not the stuff of history. No one asked; no one answered; no one wrote it down.

Four hundred years have passed. There are records, but still it is hard to locate the personal in one of the most famous conflicts between women in history. Other forces are at work in the story. Immense political questions are at stake and are not to be discounted. There are interests having nothing to do with either Mary or Elizabeth, but with conquest and alliance, with Catholic and Protestant struggle, with political and economic power. The Queen moves. But does the Queen move under her own power?

What happened?

In May 1568 Mary Stuart arrived in England with a small group of followers, fleeing Scotland and asking for refuge. There had been a rebellion against her in Scotland. Entwined with the struggle for control of Scotland was the accusation that Mary had been an accomplice to the murder of her husband, Henry Darnley. Bothwell was the supposed architect of this murder. Mary had married him, been forced to sign papers of abdication, and had been imprisoned for a year. She asked Elizabeth's protection. Elizabeth refused to receive Mary unless she was purged of the stain of her husband's murder. Mary refused to submit to the inquiry that Elizabeth—or her advisers—ordered, but it was held anyway, with neither Queen present, inconclusively. For nearly sixteen years afterward, Mary Stuart remained in England, Elizabeth's prisoner. In 1586, she was tried for treason, accused of plotting Elizabeth's murder, found guilty and, early the following winter, executed.

What happened?

The severed head is held aloft while the body lies warm and bleeding still on the block. This is ceremonial. There is triumph in the raising of the head, gloating. The spectators cannot make out every nuance of facial feature, yet the hair holds their attention, the long auburn hair of Mary Stuart, the tresses by which she could be recognized, the mere follicle and coloration that came to mean "Mary Stuart." Long auburn hair and a beautiful woman. Passion, they thought. Many kinds of recklessness. On a winter morning in 1587, the tresses hold the eye but briefly, then they fall to the ground, loosen from the scalp, it appears. Decomposition before the very eyes of the assembled executioners? The truth is less supernatural: Mary Stuart wore a wig to her death. Underneath, the natural hair is short and gray.

What happened?

When Mary arrived in England, she was twenty-six years old. Elizabeth was thirty-five and had been on the throne since she was exactly Mary's age. Mary was extremely tall, athletic, famous for her dancing and trained in feminine obedience. She had been known for years for her beauty, particularly her complexion and the red-gold hair. Elizabeth was more hidden, and although she had set aside what she considered debilitating aspects of "femininity," she was obviously ambivalent about that and known in court for her vanity—her insistence on flattery and flirtation. Elizabeth eventually had the mirrors around her covered so that she could not see her aged face, which she, along with everyone else, thought ugly. And there was the truth or myth of Mary's beauty; the *femme fatale* interpretations of Mary's life and conduct, coexisting with later ideas of Mary as Catholic martyr. The sensuous hair coexisted with the severe nunlike headdress Mary adopted during her captivity.

Elizabeth was caught in the world's bind about femininity. Mary elicited the ambivalence. This much it is possible to conjecture. Upon the birth of Mary's son, two years before her flight to England, Elizabeth is reported to have said: "Alack, The Queen of Scots is lighter of a bonny son, and I am but of barren stock."

The Queens are at opposite ends of the chessboard.

Their past relations have been mixed, the question of succession to the English throne being part of the mixture. When very young, Mary Stuart was in France and subject, she would say later, to the political aspirations of the men in her family. A claim to the English throne was made on Mary's behalf. She later disowned the claim, but it would never leave the mind of the Queen of England. Yet there was friendship or amiability between them—how much was protocol and courtesy and decorum is difficult to take into account. Consider the friendship in part, at least, genuine. They were close in age. They, ironically enough, resembled one another in the complexion and coloring so praised as it appeared in Mary. They were cousins. And Queens. Tokens of friendship and letters of affection had passed between them. And yet there had been skirmishes. While Mary was still in France, the poet Ronsard published a book of poems two thirds of which were dedicated to Elizabeth, one third to Mary. One poem suggested that Elizabeth rivaled Mary in beauty. Ronsard, a good friend of Mary Stuart's, received, after publication, a glittering diamond from the Queen of England.

The beehive, they say, can contain only one Queen.

Is Mary Elizabeth's enemy?

Opposite ends of the chessboard?

OFF WITH HER HEAD!

Mary Stuart fled to England because she believed Elizabeth would protect her. It would have been wiser for her to have gone to France. Her choice has been called "romantic." Upon arrival, she wrote to Elizabeth that she had come to England

being assured that, hearing the cruelty of my enemies, and how they have treated me, you will, comfortably to your kind disposition and the confidence I have in you, not only receive for the safety of my life, but also aid and assist me in my just quarrel. . . . I entreat you to send to fetch me as soon as you possibly can, for I am in a pitiable condition, not only for a queen, but for a gentlewoman.

For years and years and even more painful years, Mary holds to these feelings. Elizabeth had a kind disposition. Mary had confidence in her. They must meet, come together, see one another. A personal encounter will solve everything. Mary knows that the communication between them passes through many hands—the coldest of Elizabeth's few letters to Mary are actually written by Lord Cecil—and she wishes to remove the hands, establish an actual connection. She is fighting for her life, but she is also thinking and acting in conventionally feminine ways.

A woman who loved her mother so deeply and whose love was reciprocated is often "romantic" about other women. Mary holds to the idea of female "succor," asking it over and over of Elizabeth, seeing what is happening in terms of female family:

For I honour you as my elder sister, and, notwithstanding all the grievances above mentioned, I shall be ever ready to solicit, as of my elder sister, your friendship before that of any other.

Her letters are signed: "Your very affectionate good sister and cousin."

"Madame—" Elizabeth writes, the abruptness of the dash very much the style of her letters. She describes what is happening between them as "one Prince and near cousin regarding another." "Prince" is the way she always described herself and there is not in her language any break in this most public, formal and masculine discourse.

Mary writes a poem about what is going on, describing herself as a ship attempting to enter a port, beaten back by strong winds, kept from safe harbor. Later, Elizabeth, too, writes a poem about it, calling Mary "the daughter of debate that discord aye doth sow," and resolved, firm, like a prince, turning to her own power, her sword:

> *My rusty sword through rest shall first his edge employ*
> *To poll their tops that seek such change or gape for*
> *future joy.*

Mary remains the supplicant, increasingly powerless and increasingly rebuffed. She clings to the idea of a meeting. Not only was the Queen of Scotland reputed to have enormous personal charm—and all the hint of magic that the word implies—but this is very much the conventional female way, this reliance on the personal, the relational. Not only would interfering hands and tongues be swept aside, but, Mary seems to believe, that if Elizabeth were to see her, to encounter her, to demystify her, their common blood and bond would be undeniable.

Elizabeth refuses. From time to time in the course of this very long ordeal, Elizabeth shows mercy. She prevents Mary's execution at an earlier date. But she refuses to see her. She also continues to exert her power by humiliation, sending tattered rags when asked by Mary, who came to England without a wardrobe, for aid. The part that sees Mary as enemy in personal terms, the irrational part that sees the other woman's beauty as threatening to herself (her position aside, her politics aside, as they must at times have been)—this part of Elizabeth in conflict with that part of Mary withholds beautiful clothes.

The Queen can move in any direction on the chessboard, but she must remain on the chessboard. This is what we are given; these are the possibilities laid before us. Female power—

this is the way the squares are laid out—is the kind of power that Cinderella has when she walks into the ballroom gorgeously garbed. Everyone must go to charm school. Female power and value depend on pleasing men—who hardly seem to imagine beauty for whatever its own sake may be, but admire beauty to possess it, turn it into decoration, show it off, showing themselves off in the capacity of owner and conqueror.

Mirror, mirror on the wall. Who is the fairest of them all?

Beauty knows no pain

Here she is, Miss America.

The chessboard of female competition allows us to move only in the direction of who is more beautiful. Her breasts are bigger. Oh dear. Her breasts are smaller. Oh dear. If I could only be as thin as she is. Oh dear. As tall. As long-legged. As clear-skinned. As blonde. As raven-haired. As slim-hipped. Oh dear, dear, dear and damn damn damn—what? Damn IT? That is too vague. Damn HIM? Damn him for choosing Miss America, for being the one to say who is more valued, for devaluing me? That is too frightening? Well, then, damn who? DAMN HER.

If Mary Stuart's beautiful hair fell from her severed head and, revealing the actual short gray hair underneath, shocked the crowd, that is understandable. In death she was, in this way, demystified and revealed as an aging, mortal woman. It must have caused someone's heart to shrink. Elizabeth Tudor, they say, on hearing of Mary's execution, wept, had her secretary jailed for daring to use the death warrant that she had signed, protested that she hadn't meant it to be used, and was stopped in all this by Lord Cecil, who reminded her of the State, the chessboard.

In Greek mythology, the goddess Eris—which means "Strife"—tossed an apple marked "for the fairest" among Hera, Aphrodite and Athena. They argued and turned the decision over to Paris, who was the most handsome mortal. Each goddess tried to bribe Paris, offering her own particular gifts: Hera offered divine power; Athena offered wisdom; Aphrodite offered the most beautiful mortal for his bride. Paris chose Aphrodite and her gift, winning Helen for his wife. Aphrodite helped Paris to kidnap his prize and this was the cause of the Trojan war.

This is the original beauty contest, debased in modern life so that wisdom and power cannot compete with beauty. The contestants now need not offer anything beyond what they look like to be called "the fairest." Athena's wisdom and intelligence do not lead a man to choose her. Hera's power wins her nothing in masculine eyes. All that matters is being beautiful; there is no other "virtue" comparable to it. No woman, in this vision of the world, is both beautiful *and* powerful or beautiful *and* intelligent. Beauty stands alone. Mirror. Mirror.

Male painters love the theme. You can hardly walk through a museum without feasting on some version of the Judgment of Paris, entirely physicalized, embodying female competition for male approval. This arrangement glorifies the man who will choose, makes him the center of the painting and the action, sets all power in his hands.

In her book about the backgrounds of Greek religion, Jane Harrison, relying mostly on evidence from the visual arts, traced the evolution of the "three goddess" theme. Originally, a single female deity was worshiped, the familiar Great Mother. Then the goddess was divided and two female deities appeared. The two were called "Maiden" and "Mother" and show up most vividly in the story of Demeter and Persephone. Then the two became three. Harrison associates this division into three with a decline in female power, shows how the evolution of patriarchal conditions transformed cultural artifacts of women from those of glory to those of shame, from inspirers to temptresses. She says that female goddesses became "sequestered to a servile domesticity, became abject and amorous." The three amorous goddesses, then, represent a real diminution of the image of female power. Not only does one become three, but the three are in conflict, and trivial conflict at that. They argue about who gets the man's attention—rather than who rules the world. The single masculine godhead, not incidentally, *increased* in power when it became threefold—in the Christian trinity, as Father, Son and Holy Ghost.

In addition to the ancient beauty contest, classical Greek literature, from which later storytellers of all kinds have taken their themes, is a crazy quilt of female conflict. It is also a relentless catalogue of rape and the two facts are connected. If this is a literature made as conditions were changing from matriarchal to patriarchal, as female power was being suppressed—the argument of many anthropologists and classical scholars—the two go hand in hand and serve the same end. Female strife is one way of diminishing female power. Rape is another, the instrument, as Susan Brownmiller showed in *Against Our Will,* of masculine domination.

The Trojan war is depicted, not as the activity of men bent on conquest, but as a struggle between Athena and Aphrodite. In the *Iliad,* the goddesses engage in the kind of "catfight" that seems to thrill audiences so much:

> *Athena caught up with her and drove a blow at her*
> *breasts with her ponderous*
> *hand, so that her knees went slack and the heart*
> *inside her.*
> *These two both lay sprawled on the generous earth.*

In Ovid, Athena and Arachne, who is mortal, have a contest to see who is the best weaver and Athena loses her temper, slashes Arachne with her shuttle. Arachne would rather hang than bow her head and hangs herself. Abashed, Athena turns the girl into a spider so that she may live.

Aphrodite is angry at Circe. Athena turns Medusa's hair into snakes and helps Perseus kill her. Circe turns Scylla into the monster who haunts the *Odyssey*. Aphrodite torments Psyche. Hera, Zeus' wife, is the embodiment of sexual jealousy, wreaking vengeance on the females who sleep with Zeus, who are numerous. Vengeance is delivered whether the women are willing in their sexual encounters with Hera's husband or not. Callisto is turned into a bear. Io becomes a heifer. Echo has her speech taken away from her by Hera and can only repeat the last words she heard.

Conflict between women, the kinds just described, becomes a carnival. Masculine writers love to describe these scenes and, interestingly, set them in stories where women are passive in relation to men, hostile to each other. Female conflict, seen in this kind of structure, works conveniently—it takes note of aggression in women and sets it against other women. Men are spared. The audience applauds. Everyone loves a catfight. This cattiness, they say, is typically feminine. No one speaks of the deprivation out of which those kinds of conflict are made; no one notices the narrowing of the female sphere so that all that is left to a woman are her clothes, her looks, her husband. No one sees that energy misdirected misfires in the direction of the nearest victim, another woman.

Charlotte Brontë stood in all the crossfires.

Villette was her last novel. In it, Brontë reworked the material that she had been trying to articulate since her first book, *The Professor*. The "events" behind *Villette* and *The Professor* are the two years Brontë spent teaching in a Belgian pension where she developed—I hesitate about what to call it—a passion, I am sure, but one whose sexual nature Brontë was oblivious to. She developed a deep feeling of connection to M. Heger, husband of the woman who owned the pension. That the connection was mostly on Charlotte's part seems established, although it is said that M. Heger was capable of flirting with the young women around him and might have encouraged her. At any rate, it meant something to Brontë that it did not mean to him. She carried this connection home with her to Yorkshire as need. She wrote. He replied coldly. She controlled herself, restrained, pained, waited months to write again. These letters are among the most unbearable to read because they are a starving soul's pleading for crumbs. She asks for some small recognition. She has invested M. Heger with the power to help her, to keep her alive. He is silent. Hers are not the letters of a woman in love, but of a woman drowning in solitude and isolation:

> If my master withdraws his friendship from me entirely I shall be altogether without hope; if he gives me a little—just a little—I shall be satisfied—nay, I shall have reason for living on, for working.
>
> It is humiliating—to be unable to control one's own thoughts, to be the slave of a regret, of a memory, the slave of a fixed and dominant idea which lords it over the mind. Why cannot I have just as much friendship for you as you for me—neither more nor less? Then should I be so tranquil, so free.

He denies, never writes. And of course there is a woman in the story, the Wife. Charlotte wrote to her friend Ellen about Madame Heger's "coldness" to her. Madame—from the accounts that can be pieced together—did interfere while Brontë was in Brussels, did sense trouble in the house, and did put an end to it, going so far as to escort Charlotte Brontë to the train herself. As readers, we owe Madame a debt, for it was she who lifted the torn letters of Charlotte Brontë from her husband's wastebasket, where he had tossed them, and hid them away so that later, they might be known and this part of Brontë's life, whose full effect she kept to herself, might be revealed.

Villette is a reworking of what happened. Like *Jane Eyre,* it is the story of the growth of a young girl, a journey and a sentimental education. Lucy Snowe, who narrates her own story, sees her life as a sea journey in which she is both the passenger and the ship itself. At the start, she asks the reader to imagine her as "a bark slumbering through halcyon weather ... buried, if you will, in a long prayer. A great many women and girls are supposed to pass their lives something in that fashion; why not I with the rest?" She answers her own question—why not? "Circumstances," she says, "create storms on this calm sea" and "there remained no possibility of dependence on others; to myself alone could I look." One aspect of the narrative is the tension between stasis and activity, the desire to lie on the deck and the desire to steer the ship. Things external to herself force growth, stimulate action. Her own mind is "homeless, anchorless, unsupported."

Lucy Snowe finds a kind of home, a temporary anchor and a complicated kind of support at the pension in Villette and in the person of Madame Beck, its proprietress. This is the original Madame Heger in a different aspect. Although Brontë draws on many actual details, she has changed Madame's status, for Madame is not married and the man in question—called, in the novel, M. Paul Emmanuel—is her cousin, not her husband.

Quite a difference. By removing Madame from her actual position as wife, Brontë, in her imagination, has changed the terms of the conflict and turned them to her own advantage.

Years of brooding suffering resulted in this extremely intricate way of providing herself with a gratification that life did not bring. Because Madame Beck is not a wife, her "interference," as Brontë portrays it, loses some of its legitimacy. It also allows Brontë to let Lucy Snowe "win"—becoming the architect of a reparation through the imagination that was denied in actuality. Madame tries to crush the growing amity between Lucy Snowe and M. Paul, but she fails. Lucy defies her. M. Paul slaps her in the face. What pleasure Brontë must have had creating a scene in which not only is the "obstacle" toppled, but the man in question made to show his alliance with the young woman, to stand against Madame, to choose Lucy. But it is not actually romance that Lucy Snowe wins. She does not marry M. Paul. This is not *Jane Eyre*. Lucy wins what Charlotte Brontë yearned after in her relations with M. Heger—the "master" recognizes her value, procures for her a small house in which she can have a school of her own, sets her on the road to autonomy and fulfillment, frees her from servitude and submission, puts her on the path. He becomes the Enabler. The interference of the other woman in this process is vanquished.

These are Lucy Snowe's lines in the only scene of open confrontation between the two women:

> "Neither you nor another shall persuade or lead me."

> "If you have any sorrow or disappointment—and, perhaps, you have—nay, I know you have—seek your own palliatives in your own chosen resources. Leave me, however."

> "Let me alone. Keep your hand off me, and my life, and my troubles."...

> Two minutes I stood over Madame, feeling that the whole woman was in my power.

It is interesting that she does not mention the man. The focus of her defiance—which is part of her growth, an indication of her conviction that she has a road of her own—is that she will not be controlled or stifled. The man disappears, in a sense, revealing another reading of the conflict, exposing other layers.

Let's go back to the beginning of the story. Madame Beck is not perceived by Lucy as a rival until the single confrontation scene. She is, first, a mother. Lucy arrives, close to desolate, in a strange city, is led by a man to the pension. She speaks no French; Madame no English. Nevertheless, Madame gives her a job and shelter. (M. Paul is called in for his opinion, suggests taking a chance.) Lucy admires her, ambivalently:

> Madame was a very great and a very capable woman. That school offered her for her powers too limited a sphere; she ought to have swayed a nation; she should have been the leader of a turbulent legislative assembly....
>
> Had I been a gentleman I believe Madame would have found favour in my eyes.

Madame becomes the focus of Lucy's own conflict—the desire to lie on the deck or steer the ship, to be passive or active, to go, as she says, "backward or forward." She stands, in one scene, on the threshold of an opportunity that she feels insecure about meeting—a chance to teach a difficult class, a risk that will bring advancement or humiliation. Madame challenges her, nearly taunts her, pushes her forward. Lucy meets the challenge. What she wins at the end of the novel—a school of her own—is exactly what Madame has.

As long as she plays "by the rules," Lucy keeps Madame as mother. But the desire to go forward causes her to break the rules—literally, by staying up all night, pacing back and forth in a classroom, waiting for M. Paul to come to her. At this moment Madame interferes, tries to send her to sleep, and Lucy grows defiant, breaks the rules, refuses the mother.

Leave me.

Let me alone. Keep your hand off me, and my life, and my troubles.

OFF WITH HER HEAD.

"She eclipsed me," Lucy says. Madame is large; Lucy has felt like a child beside her, obliterated by her shadow. And this is no longer tolerable. Self-assertion in the face of another woman's eclipsing presence—this is a more accurate description of the conflict in *Villette*. It resembles life with mother more than it does the Gothic romance.

The Eternal Triangle, they say, nodding their heads sagely, presuming to acknowledge something about human nature. The Eternal Triangle usually has a woman at each side, a man in the middle. It is the Wife/Mistress theme, the "Other Woman" idea. From time to time we do get stories, sometimes great, tragic stories about a woman in the middle, but something very different happens. Madame Bovary, like Anna Karenina, is a wife who "takes" a lover, puts herself at the apex of the Eternal Triangle. But how different is the fate of the woman in the middle from that of the male hero shuttling between wife and mistress. The conflict—this man or that man—is usually a representation of the woman's conflict about marriage itself. The wife in the middle stands between husband and lover. Her "problem" has less to do with the qualities of either man, more to do with what it means to be "wife." Husbands hardly seem so divided about the duties of husbandry, but, then, "husband" hardly carries with it the same sense of restriction that "wife" does. The wife in the middle always suffers and usually dies. Anna Karenina is finished off at the railroad tracks and Madame Bovary's death scene is one of the most exquisite in the novel.

By removing Madame Heger in her imagination from the role of "wife," Charlotte Brontë changed the terms of the conflict or invented a different lens through which to see it. Without one of the women bearing the wife-title, the idea of position, which is so important to the triangle theme, is diminished. Position is what most of these struggles turn out to be about:

> But since my master has wed the Spartan Hermione,
> Abandoning my bed (I'm nothing but a slave),
> She drives me cruelly, treats me worse than any slave.
> She says I've made her childless with my secret drugs
> And hateful to her husband; that I wish to take
> Her place and live here, casting out her marriage right
> By force. I never wished that from the very first.

Andromache is speaking, in Euripides' play. There are many others in Greek drama, but Andromache is the clearest on the subject of what the conflict between wife and mistress is about. Hermione fears being supplanted. Hermione's "right" is in question: she is afraid Andromache will take her place. That place is defined by men—husband and father. Her role as wife—defined by her husband, recognized by the State—is, Hermione thinks, in danger. The power she threatens to bring against Andromache, usurper, is the power derived from Menelaus, her father. Andromache is vulnerable because she lacks male protection. Her father is, in the words of a servant, "too old to help you even if he came," and her vulnerability, according to the servant, is final: "But now you haven't any friends at all."

Although Queens may not do what they like on the chessboard, their position is always relative to the King's.

Hermione is determined to hold her position and to drive Andromache back. This she attempts to do by humiliation, then by force: "You must drop those haughty thoughts you had before and crouch submissively,/ Fall down here at my knees,/ And sweep this house of mine." To best another woman, you get her to sweep your floors. In other words, you make it clear what the hierarchy is, who stands where. We most often see this happen between wife and husband, but Hermione, here, is acting in the best interests of her husband's world and so her method is derived from his. You best another woman by robbing her of her self-respect.

The chorus blames all this trouble on a mysterious "they":

> They have hemmed you and Hermione in with hate
> And strife.

and Hermione blames other women:

> The visits of evil women it was that ruined me.
> They puffed me up with vanity; they said these words:
> "Will you endure to have that rotten slave girl here
> To share your husband's bed, with you right in the house?
> By Hera queen, she wouldn't look upon daylight
> One moment in my home or wallow in my bed!"

Andromache is the only one who can see that the rightful object of blame is the man:

> I've gone to bed by force
> With masters; then you slaughter me, you don't kill him,
> The cause of all these things?

No one shares this point of view. The invocation of Hera by the malicious women—"by Hera queen"—reminds everyone of Zeus' jealous wife, who so tortured the victims of her husband's raping. But anger, in these plays, turns against women and not against men. These are plays of the patriarchy and they take place in a world in which women have lost their own power. Now it is derived from husband, father or son; previously it belonged to oneself. The anger of women is indeed about position—women are angry at the loss of their own power—but now the anger is trivialized and set in domestic jealousy, now the anger is turned upon one another, now it is the wife-position worth protecting at all costs.

In *La Seconde (The Other One)*, Colette calls this "the remains of a pure religion."

Fanny sees her husband, Farou, kissing Jane, his secretary, her tentative friend. It is a scene out of melodrama—the door is ajar; they do not see her. Fanny broods. She is a "tolerant" wife, married to a bombast of a man—Colette's own former husband M. Willy, to be sure—who has had many mistresses. Fanny turns the event and its meaning over and over in her mind, pushes down the jealousy and anger. Together, Fanny and Jane, who have spent most of the novel together off in the country waiting for Farou, watch a rehearsal of his latest play—*No Woman About the House*. Onstage, two women are fighting over a man:

> All the virgin strength, all the untapped innocence I bear within me, the heinous sin I could commit, the finest deed I could perform—I hurl them all against you, I cast them into the battle for him.

Yes, the onstage bombast is meant. Fanny has often said that her husband's lines for women reflect a man's thinking. As she watches, Jane, beside her, slips an arm in her arm. No one is better than Colette at this kind of irony.

What churns in Fanny, however, churns again. She thinks of asking a woman friend for advice, but rejects it:

> This old Clara would give me advice in accordance with tradition, her tradition, in a manner it makes me sick to think of.

We know what traditional advice would be. OFF WITH HER HEAD.

Fanny and Jane are alone in a room:

You see, Jane...I've found out that you...that Farou...

The wife is very dark; the mistress is very ash-blonde. Light to dark and dark to light the conversation goes, back and forth between them. But tradition does not hold. The blonde mistress cares more about the wife than about the man.:

It's unbelievable that anyone should make such a fuss about love! A man isn't so important; he isn't eternal! A man is...a man is only a man!...A man is never alone, Fanny—and indeed it's rather horrible that he should always have a woman, another mistress, a mother, a maid, a secretary, a relation, a female of some sort.

This has its effect. Fanny is agitated and Farou comes in, sealing it by "acting like a man"—"Fanny sought for a manly decision, a trace of the emotion which Jane's words had roused within herself." He remains calm and rational, firm in the mode that analysts would call Logos as opposed to Eros, supercilious, patronizing, speaking of ideas, exhibiting no feeling for the kind of feeling relationship she has with Jane: "She would willingly have dug a knife into Farou so as to see something spontaneous, irrepressible, gush out of him—blood, curses, suffering."
Her mind turns, after Farou leaves, to his emotional cowardice, to her actual loneliness with him, and to her sense of connection to Jane. The traditional solution disintegrates. The wife-position is not worth holding on to, nor destroying another woman over. The female conflict is seen in a different light:

She turned again to the help which could spring only from an alliance, even if it were uncertain and slightly disloyal, from a feminine alliance, constantly broken by the man and constantly re-established at the man's expense.... Where is Jane?

In Gertrude Stein's novel *Q.E.D.*, the Eternal Triangle is composed of women—Helen, Adele and Mabel. They are three American women traveling abroad. There is an attempt to anchor what happens in such settings as aboard ship, in Morocco, in New York, but the effect is bleary. The action does not occur in places, but in feelings. Stein cannot bring it out in the open. The novel is dense with pain. Aboard ship, at the beginning, Adele's pain emerges first: "Nestled close to the bare boards as if accustomed to make the hard earth soft by loving it." No one in the novel can soften anything by loving it. Helen kisses Adele. Helen embraces Adele. Adele learns there is something between Mabel and Helen: "I had no idea of your pain."

Stein captures a pain so severe that the one who is suffering can hardly make sense of what has happened to her and still try to think or talk or, as Stein did, try to write it down. It is hard for someone else to follow, but not hard to feel. What exactly happened here? The novel provides impressions: "I felt"; "she felt"; "I thought"; "there was a third"; "she said"; "she did"; "she gave the other one a present"; "I thought it was prostitution"; "I could not provide bread and butter." What recurs are the feelings: "I had no idea of your pain"; "I do not know what I mean to you"; "I am afraid of being abandoned."

The women discuss morality, what is "right," but ideas fall away—this is one of the things Stein wants to show—when a person is "deeply stirred." They are deeply stirred, all three. In Adele's eyes, Mabel has the power men usually have; Adele watches Mabel give Helen a present and laments her own inability to provide Helen with "bread and butter." It is not narrative, but a dirge. Stein put the book away. Adele says: "I have neither the inclination nor the power to take Mabel's place." Adele cannot make the hard earth soft by loving it.

This pain, this rejection, the sharp nail and the silent cringe—all this is corralled and a fence called "lesbian" built around it. Our feeling for each other, our tenderness, need to be loved by each other, cared for, the shrinking from neglect, the inability to say "You hurt me" falls dangerously if at all from a woman's lips in relation to another woman. In a lesbian novel, it is part of the landscape. Outside the corral, articulation falters, inhibited, fearful.

I tell a woman I do not know very well that I am writing about relations among women. She tells me about a woman teacher, a long time ago, and as she goes on with the telling, she touches the pain. The teacher did not care for her enough. She never told the teacher how much she cared. And she cared, she cared. "I've never told this to anyone," she says. She thinks the power of the feeling makes her a lesbian. She chokes on it. She pushes it away and goes about her business.

Pain between women that comes from caring is an aspect of conflict consigned to cobwebs, except in overtly lesbian literature. It is the antithesis of the popular catfight and its mirror, perhaps its actual and hidden truth.

Djuna Barnes' novel *Nightwood* takes up the abandonment of one woman by another, the jealousy and the devastation. Nora is explaining the intensity of the pain, how it differs, for her, from what happens between a woman and a man:

A man is another person—a woman is yourself, caught as you turn in panic; on her mouth you kiss your own. If she is taken you cry that you have been robbed of yourself.

A man is another person. Colette was on this road when she wrote of Fanny's loneliness with Farou, her alliance with Jane. We arrive at the double standard, the evolution of different sets of ethics, often different languages, gestures and expectations, on the part of women toward other women and toward men. We arrive deeper, at different undercurrents of conflict. The ghostly mother reappears and plays her part. Many women say that their conflict with other women is more devastating than their conflict with men. This is not actual mother, but mother-as-construct, the expectation of constant mother-love, the experience of absolute dependence on a female, the uneradicable memory of it. This is about the sense of men as "Other"—the experience of great distance which affords, paradoxically, great protection. A woman in a soap opera who fights with her husband threatens to go home to mother. In fantasy, the feminine alliance is permanent and given. What shatters fantasy creates conflict.

1978. The world of different expectations. The highway heading west from Florida, Cynthia behind the wheel, myself beside her, the start of a junket long planned, an alliance on the road with a CB radio crackling. This is not ancient history. This is the present good old summertime and she drops a bomb. Unknown to me and without my consent, Cynthia has packed into the Jeep a quantity of drugs that could land us in jail for a very long time if we were caught. She is playing with my life. She tells me this when we are well under way, when it is difficult to open the door and walk out. And why? Cynthia is bringing these drugs to her boyfriend, who will sell them. "The feminine alliance constantly broken by a man." I am enraged. She gambles with my life. It is true that hell hath no fury like a woman scorned. In this case, I am scorned by Cynthia, my life scorned, my right to make my own decisions about the course of this life absolutely scorned. I know that under exactly these conditions, when such scorn for my self-determination appears on a man's lips, in his eyes, or in his actions, I walk away. I am exceedingly vigilant on this score. I am prepared, watchful, alert to such dynamics of domination and usurpation of power. And—naïve— I have not absorbed the idea that such conflict is possible with women. I am particularly trapped in my understanding of why she has done this, for Cynthia is not evil and the demands of her relationship with her lover have led her to it. I never lose that understanding, but it cannot lead to forgiveness. The conflict, the rift, the betrayal are unresolvable. We are at the end of the road before the trip is a day old.

In Jane Austen's last novel, *Persuasion,* we are on the side of Anne Elliott, facing, with her, a conflict with another woman, Lady Russell. We face, in fact, several kinds of conflict— abrasion between herself and her sisters, for one—but the central dissension is what makes the novel proceed, her relationship to Lady Russell. We are in Austen territory, the English country-side, the gentry, the world of manners and social standing and concern about money. We are in a world where marriage is a woman's whole life, where whom she marries is cause for general concern, for the choice affects family and fortune. And we come up against the spirit of independence of Austen's heroines—Anne Elliott thinks for herself, sees the sham that is the world of manners. Set this heroine against a woman with whom there is a deep sympathetic bond—"*almost* a mother's love, and mother's rights." Lady Russell was the friend of Anne's dead mother. Were she Anne's mother, the conflict between them would have evolved differently—the "almost" makes a large difference. Were she Anne's mother, Anne might defy or comply more completely. As it is, she is left, Austen is left on her behalf, to work the conflict out by other means.

It is about marriage. It is about a man. There is a difference of opinion between the older woman and the younger on the subject of captain Frederick Wentworth, a sea captain, whom Anne fell in love with, who loved her, whose proposal was refused by Anne's father and opposed by Lady Russell. Father and friend objected on similar grounds with slightly different nuance: "He thought it a very degrading alliance; and Lady Russell, though with more tempered and pardonable pride, received it as a most unfortunate one."

Anne could take on her father's power more readily than Lady Russell's. She is an Austen outsider—the female who does not fit because of her *vision,* because "appearance" is not the beginning and end of the story for her. Anne is quite alienated from her father—he does not see her value. As exile, the strength to defy the world of the father is just about given. But the woman—and a woman who loves her, at that—there it is harder:

> It might yet have been possible to withstand her father's ill will, though unsoftened by one kind word or look on the part of her sister—but Lady Russell, whom she had always loved and relied on, could not, with such steadiness of opinion, and such tenderness of manner, be continually advising her in vain. She was persuaded to believe the engagement a wrong thing.

She was persuaded. By making it her title, Austen points her readers to the idea of persuasion—the force that can move a person—to the idea of influence. Someone in the novel says Lady Russell is "a woman of the greatest influence with everybody . . . able to persuade a person to anything." Female influence, so lightly ignored or disparaged, is the subject of this novel. The conflict between Anne and Lady Russell does not revolve around the man one might marry—that is only the excuse—but about, in fact, the theme of separation, the development of one's own influence over oneself, the ability to differ from and stand one's ground against the persuasion of another woman. We have many such stories on this theme between women and men. What is different here—because it is Jane Austen and because there is always this dimension to the conflict when it occurs between women—is the lovingness that coexists with the conflict. "It might yet have been possible to withstand her father's ill will." Yes. The dissonance is there between daughter and father to begin with. "But Lady Russell, whom she had always loved and relied on..."

Anne is given a second chance. The captain returns, seven years later. The drama is replayed and has a different outcome. A rival comes into the picture, much suited to Lady Russell's way of thinking. He is Walter Elliott, a cousin, a man who brings with him all the prospects of the world which could repair the family's disrupted fortunes and Lady Russell sets herself on the side of this reparation. Here she attempts to persuade Anne, who has already said that she and Mr. Elliott "should not suit." Lady Russell sets before her the prospect of regaining the family home and something deeper, more bound to appeal:

> "I own that to be able to regard you as the future mistress of Kellynch, the future Lady Elliott—to look forward to see you occupying your dear mother's place, succeeding to all her rights, and all her popularity, as well as to all her virtues, would be the highest possible gratification to me....My dearest Anne, it would give me more delight than is often felt at my time of life!"

This is nearly irresistible. Lady Russell offers the ties that bind, the things that stand women side by side, that prevent dissent. You will take your mother's place. You would please me. You would have approval of the entire female line, the female community.

Anne is "bewitched" by this talk, but comes to her senses, rises from the irrational appeal of it to the rational. She sees that Lady Russell believes what Anne does not. Her "feelings" and her "judgment" stand against the idea of Mr. Elliott and against Lady Russell's persuasion. She has come to know her own mind—an integration of "feeling" and "judgment"—and, more importantly, to risk the loss of Lady Russell's approval. The sea captain, having been accepted by her, is worried about Anne's friend:

> "The knowledge of her influence, the indelible, immovable impression of what persuasion had once done—was it not all against me?"

Anne has understood differently:

> "If I was wrong in yielding to persuasion once, remember that it was to persuasion exerted on the side of safety, not risk. When I yielded, I thought it was to duty; but no duty could be called in aid here."

It is not the marriage that ends the novel, for it is not the marriage that is at stake. It is the resolution of female conflict, which is lovingly accomplished. Anne faces the anxiety implied in Lady Russell's "opposition of feeling," resolute, and, "There was nothing less for Lady Russell to do than to admit that she had been pretty completely wrong, and to take up a new set of opinions and of hopes."

Two Queens on a chessboard. Mary Stuart and Elizabeth Tudor face-to-face, the imagination making possible what history denied. Mary Wollstonecraft goes to speak with the wife of the man she is in love with, imagining that they can take things up between themselves, hoping for the kind of conversation that occurs in Colette's novel, where the women attempt to deal with their conflict. Wollstonecraft is rebuffed. There are a limited number of moves available. Myself against her. The legacy of jealousy, envy and hate in a very specific context—female passivity that gives over the power of judgment to a male arbiter, says that Paris will decide the matter. But the issue spins and comes out differently on the other side.

I say this conflict is hard for me. You say it is hard for you. I say there is respect between us, you say so too, that we stand here on our own two feet, alone in a room together, and that only then can we begin to name the tempest, the dissent, only then are we prepared to risk mother's love, to coexist without a cord to bind us, to risk the persuasion of safety and take our chances. I say you hurt me. You say I scorned you. We say we care. It begins. The conversation begins.

7

The Light and the Dark

WHITE WOMEN
ARE NEVER LONELY
BLACK WOMEN
ALWAYS SMILE

"Look, Madam, at the baby's arms. We shall want a sunshade certain."

"Oh Nanny, do let her tan! I love these beautiful brown people. They seem so free of secrets."

Zelda Fitzgerald, *Save Me the Waltz*

The curve of the soul of the Jewish women was still unbroken. Female, fertile, yolky, fruitful as the earth, and ready for the plow, they offered to the famished wanderer, the alien, the exile, the baffled and infuriated man, escape and surcease of the handsome barren women, the hard varnished sawdust dolls, the arrogant and sterile women, false in look and promise as a hot-house peach, who walked the streets and had no curves or fruitfulness in them.

Thomas Wolfe, *The Web and the Rock*

For she realized what she had been taught was that nobody wanted white girls except their empty-headed, effeminate counterparts—white boys—whom her mother assured her smelled (in the mouth) of boiled corn and (in the body) of thirty-nine cent glue. As far back as she could remember it seemed something understood: that while white men would climb on black women old enough to be their mothers—"for the experience"—white women were considered sexless, contempt-ible and ridiculous by all. They did not even smell like glue or boiled corn; they smelled of nothing since they did not sweat. They were clear, dead water.

Alice Walker, *Meridian*

A dark woman looks at a light woman. A light woman looks at a dark woman. Each of them has an idea. They have each read books, been to the movies, sat before a television screen. They have been to school at the kitchen tables of their own homes and in the streets where they live. The men of their families have gone off to war, to bars, to schools and to foreign countries, returning with stories about how it is out there, what other women are like. The women are looking at each other with stories in their ears. The Jewish woman has an idea about the Christian woman; the Puerto Rican woman about the black woman; the blonde about the brunette.

The storytellers are chanting in the background. They tell about the beginning of the world.

"In the beginning God created the heavens and the earth."

Now we know. Now it begins. Versions of the story in which the force called God is a woman, dark or light, disappear, as do stories in which God is dark. Voices saying such things drift on the wind. We are left with the white man God, maker of things.

"The earth was without form and void. And darkness was upon the face of the deep."

Everything is empty and dead. There is foreboding in the nothingness, the nightmare aspect of sleep.

"And the spirit of God was moving over the face of the waters."

Ah astir, awake, form, shape and, possibly, meaning.

"And God said, 'Let there be light,' and there was light."

Authority.

"And God saw that the light was good."

A sense of value. Gone the darkness and nothingness and newly arrived this illumination, pushing away the terror, the deep, the dark.

"And God separated the light from the darkness."

The issues between us change shape.

A dark woman looks at a light woman. Their mouths twitch, but they have only the language of Genesis with which to speak. Therefore, they are silent. Around them, the storytellers, loving contrast, tell about the light and the dark. The light and dark women of literature and popular culture are paired, almost always in opposition. Theirs is not an active opposition, though, not an engagement, but an invention, set down in opposite corners of the cosmos, described as the dark lady on the one hand, the light on the other. It happens a lot in cowboy movies. As stereotypes, dark/light female characters represent attitudes: the dark is bad, the light is good; the dark is wanton, the light obedient; the dark woman is all body, the light woman mind or spirit—and so on through the country of polarity.

In Hebraic legend, the first woman created as companion for the first man was made from the earth, which means she was dark, refused to subordinate herself to the man, Adam, and was banished. Her name was Lilith and she is one of the most resilient of the dark lady archetypes. Lilith's story was replaced by one more suited to patriarchal thinking: Eve emerging from Adam's rib, thriving until she encounters the serpent who seduces her into seducing Adam. Eve, a fair maiden in her later depictions, had no rebellious instinct of her own, but was urged on by another force—phallicism embodied—into disobedience. Eve leaves the garden hand in hand with Adam; Lilith is banished from God's universe into solitary and restless nonexistence.

Medea, like Lilith, is a dark lady outlaw, known in Greek legend as a barbarian and a sorceress. Dark is uncivilized, disrespectful of the laws and manners of the light civilization. Medea, transplanted from her own culture to Corinth with Jason, is the essence of the dark lady outsider. Her association with sorcery is another convention—the lady of dark powers. Medea is "clever" and "cunning." The "cleverness" of the dark characters means, to the white mind, duplicity; white is suspicious of dark cunning. Medea's form of discourse—her very language is called "loose speaking"—is not the language of the culture in which she finds herself trying to survive. In Euripides' play, Medea, exile, outsider, stranger, is asked to accept her husband's "taking" of another woman, a virgin bride, daughter of the King, a fair woman. Obviously, she must be fair, because she is daughter to the King, a woman who *belongs*. Jason, like most men in the middle between dark and light women, wants to have both Medea's darkness and his new wife's lightness, his past and his future, his own darkness and his own light.

Medea is a dark woman dwelling in her darkness, refusing to accept the white terms, refusing to repress the dark and refusing to respect the light. "Let the whole house crash," she says, and so it does. The order of the house, the ordinary ties of civilized life, are destroyed by Medea's "barbarism" and "sorcery," by her refusal to knuckle.

A similar theme in a different literature is embodied by Tituba in Arthur Miller's play *The Crucible*. The power of Tituba's "darkness" infects the white girls. The combination of Tituba, sorceress, woman from Barbados, and Abigail, white girl, member of the community made outsider by her sexuality, can bring the house down. Because of darkness, Salem tumbles. Frenzied purifiers want to make the world white again.

Cleopatra, too, is history's dark dark lady, representing in literature and legend the river Nile itself, fecund, sensual, Egypt as seen through Western male eyes. She is a gypsy, lustful and passionate, always cunning. The opposition, in Shakespeare's *Antony and Cleopatra*, that works on the hero and determines the structure of the play and the meaning of events, is between light and dark, Rome and Egypt; the life of duty and order, the life of pleasure and abandon are represented by two women, the Roman wife, Fulvia, and the nonwife, Cleopatra. Fulvia embodies "civilization," Cleopatra barbarity. The wife-mistress theme here, as elsewhere, aligns itself with the light and the dark.

Since light and dark are always compared by men, the comparison turns sexual. The idea of sexual competition between dark and light women appears, takes root, never departs. It makes its way into the visions of light/dark expressed by black men as well as white men and remains in the language used by women when women, both light and dark, take up the task of telling this story themselves.

> Under a compelling occasion let women die. It were pity to cast them away for nothing, though between them and a great cause they should be esteemed nothing. Cleopatra, catching but the least noise of this, dies instantly; I have seen her die twenty times upon far poorer moment. I do think there is mettle in death, which commits some loving act upon her, she hath such a celerity in dying.

Antony's servant, Enobarbus, is speaking. An Elizabethan would readily recognize the pun on the word "die," which meant to have orgasms. ("Experience orgasm," say the footnotes in the passive voice.) Cleopatra can die twenty times. Fulvia, on the other hand, is mocked by the men when her actual death is reported—jostling each other in the ribs, asking can Fulvia *die?* This orgasmic capacity of Cleopatra's is also the power and the terror for men of the dark lady. The frigid wife and the sexy mistress. The asexual light and the extreme sexuality of the dark. The white white wife, mocked, also, in these terms, by Cleopatra, and the eroticism of the "exotic" woman. These terms do not disappear. They antedate Shakespeare's play and they live well beyond it into our own literature and popular mythology.

Light and dark personify halves of a whole experience and consciousness, split by their creators to externalize an inner conflict. This is white man's culture. This is the design of the white male Christian, imagining, in the loneliness of his study or the solitude of his drawing board, objectifications of his discontent or, perhaps, his pleasure. Knowing the doubleness of his own instincts and attempting to convey, in syllable or brush stroke, his vision of how things are, he comes up doubled. His story or his picture sets the light and the dark at opposite corners of the room. He stands planted in the center, leaning first this way, then that way, toward life or death, toward good or evil, the mind or the body, consciousness or unconsciousness.

The light and the dark are at opposite corners of the room masquerading as women, but they are not women, they are options, directions, potentialities for the man in the middle. They are Satan as John Milton experienced him and Eve, the fair English girl who gets the hero—Adam, the first man, the race of white men—to disobey, to question and to fall. Stories of light and dark women are stories of a struggle for the soul of the hero. Even when these stories appear to be about romance, they are closer to theology, to a man's version of his own salvation or damnation. There are no women in the room. They only appear to be women.

The man in the middle of the room is not only worried about the state of his immortal soul, but is swelled, too, with arrogance about his ability to colonize either of these forces, to choose one over the other and make it his own. His agony comes in deciding which way to turn. He is concerned about his seed, which comes to represent his soul, whether the seed be planted in light soil or dark. That is his problem, and his resolution of the problem determines the future of the race.

God separated the light from the darkness.

The white man's literature separated the light woman from the dark woman. He said, this is opposition, corners of the cosmos, women with nothing in common, no connection, no communication, no bridge. Likewise, the white man's religion, his governments and the actual life he lived. There is no bridge between light and dark women except himself. Opposite ends of the cosmos, he said, because I know. I have been there. I have traveled. I can say there is the woman of my own race and the women of other races, that they stand apart, their *essences* stand apart, because it is I who have seen and I know women.

A woman is alone in her room. She tries to imagine another woman alone in another room in some other place. Say that this takes place before our time. The woman has very little experience of the world. She cannot travel because her father or husband won't allow it. Travel is dangerous for women. She stays at home. As Gwendolyn Harleth says in George Eliot's novel, *Daniel Deronda:*

> We women can't go in search of adventures—to find out the North-West passage or the source of the Nile, or to hunt tigers in the East. We must stay where we grow, or where the gardeners like to transplant us.

But she can read. So she holds in her lap a book by an explorer, a journeyer, someone who has seen the world, been to another country, observed other women. He finds other women and other places "exotic," which, she knows, means "outside." Outside what, she asks? Where is the inside?

The traveler is the insider, carrying his insides with him as he journeys to foreign lands, foreign to his culture and his mind. For centuries, the literature of travel, as well as the literature of invention, was written by white men, men who left their native lands in the interests of commerce and conquest. In the Middle Ages, the motives for masculine moving from one place to another were essentially or ostensibly religious—the pilgrimage and the Holy War. By the sixteenth and seventeenth centuries,

Protestant Englishmen bent on business of nefarious kinds roamed the world and recorded what they found.

Often, they found what they had brought with them. Repressed white men found sensuality and vice in the often bare-breasted women of foreign countries, especially eastern countries—which is the direction in which Jason traveled in search of the Golden Fleece and the direction in which he went to find Medea. Call it glamorous or romantic, it was the women who embodied exotica for the traveler. Most particularly in the Renaissance, the "great age of exploration," the literature in which the traveler reports what he has seen is imperialist, and especially sexually imperialist. In the hands of the white Christian Englishman, inside/outside is also good/bad, clean/dirty, rational/sensual, civilized/savage, godly/pagan. This applies when any white man looks at a less white, non-Christian woman—from the Spanish conquistadors in Mexico to the marauders who "tamed" the American Indian to the Yankee soldier in Vietnam.

Inside looks at outside as a "thing"—other, remote, distanced, tantalizing and terrifying. Inside cannot enter easily into outside to discover what it is like, how it feels, what it thinks. We know Pocahontas as John Smith saw her; Tituba as Arthur Miller created her; Justine as Lawrence Durrell saw her; the women of Tahiti through Gauguin's eyes.

Historically, men move and women stay put. This is our heritage and shapes what we, until quite recently in human history, have known of other lands and the women of other lands. Our awareness of what is "out there" comes from the perception of Odysseus and not Penelope. My most vivid understanding of how much women have stayed put is an architectural detail, drawn from the period in English history when men were out conquering unknown continents and dark peoples.

There is a Jacobean estate in the English countryside still standing and typical of the building of its time. On the top floor of the mansion is a large, empty room, windowed. Here the ladies of the mansion walked, enclosed, taking their exercise on the several hobbyhorses scattered about. You need only to walk about that room yourself to understand the historical enclosure of women and to feel the straining against it.

Closer to home, Nantucket Island stands as a monument to grounded female culture, with its houses looking to the sea and the widow's walks upon which women waited. It is a small leap to thinking, too, of the architecture of female clothing, the sixteen-inch waists, the hoops, heels, and corsets that represent female enclosure and grounding.

Restriction and the pressing against it is the recurrent and insistent theme of most female literature. "Let me out to the night," wrote the English poet Anna Wickham, "let me go, let me go." Women do not want to be houses.

Shakespeare's sister, whom Virginia Woolf invents in *A Room of One's Own,* has a taste for the theatre, much like her brother's. She wants access to that same theatre, access to the world of experience. But says Woolf:

> She could get no training in her craft. Could she even seek her dinner in a tavern or roam the streets at midnight?

Isabelle Eberhardt might be this aspect of Shakespeare's sister come to life, a woman who found a way to satisfy her "lust to feed abundantly upon the lives of men and women and the study of their ways." Eberhardt, of Swiss birth, spent most of her life in Algeria among Arabs. She managed to do this, at the beginning of the twentieth century, by dressing in men's clothing, much as other women managed to do things by adopting male pseudonyms. The female disguised as a male in order to move in the world appears in literature and life. The illusion of masculinity is a certain kind of passport. Isabelle

Eberhardt wrote, in *The Oblivion Seekers,* of the barriers that keep women from knowing the world:

> A subject to which few intellectuals ever give a thought is the right to be a vagrant, the freedom to wander. Yet vagrancy is deliverance, and life on the open road is the essence of freedom. To have the courage to smash the chains with which modern life has weighted us (under the pretext that it was offering us more liberty), then to take up the symbolic stick and bundle and *get out!*

She agonized over what it felt like to

> feel the torturing need to know more and see for oneself what is there, beyond the mysterious wall of the horizon.

Although Eberhardt went beyond the blue wall of the horizon, the lives that she actually got to know in Algeria, or the lives that she chose to write about, were men's lives. The foreign woman remained foreign.

Other women, from time to time, have gone to see for themselves what is there. The very act of going represented rebellion against social conditions. It is no accident that the literature of the open road, from the troubadours to Kerouac, is a masculine literature. When women left the Jacobean walking room of the house, they filed strange reports about what they saw. Since they did not travel in the interests of any kind of colonization they did not see the women of foreign countries as potential erotic slaves. As "outsiders"—I am speaking of the women on their own, with minds of their own, who left records in their own voices, not the legions of wives who accompanied imperialist men and whose visions we simply do not know—they saw differently.

Most travel literature by women has a surprising dose of social consciousness and most women writing in this vein have paid particular attention to "other" women. As a graduate student, Margaret Mead overrode the objections of Franz Boas, her mentor, to travel to Polynesia and study adolescent girls. Fanny Kemble, an Englishwoman who wrote a diary of life on an American plantation in the nineteenth century, was horrified by the institution of slavery and her husband's participation in it. Harriet Martineau went from England to America to observe the condition of women. Dorothy Wordsworth recorded a tour of the Continent in 1820. The first thing to catch her eye in Calais was this scene:

> A line of women and girls, seated beside dirty fish-baskets under the old gateway and ramparts—their white nightcaps, brown and puckered faces, bright eyes, etc. very striking... even in the countenances of these fish-women, the very lowest of the people, there is something of liveliness, of mental activity, interesting to me.

Margaret Fuller wrote, in 1847, about the value of travel for Americans:

> There is a gradual clearing up on many points, and many baseless notions and crude fancies are dropped. Even the post-haste passage of the business American through the great cities, escorted by cheating couriers and ignorant *valets de place,* unable to hold intercourse with the natives of the country, and passing all his leisure hours with his countrymen, who know no more than himself, clears his mind of some mistakes—lifts some mists from his horizon.

Crude fancies and mists on the horizons stand between the actual light woman and the actual dark woman. The shuttling man in the middle stands between us. We are interpreted to each other by men. We read about each other in the books of men, look at one another through masculine eyes. And we have taken it in, thinking of ourselves and each other in the language of this white masculine tradition.

I walk around in the world wearing my own skin and carrying my own mind, looking with my dark eyes. In the literature of the white male Christian, I am exotic, which has a certain kind of power and a certain kind of price. In any case, I carry all this with me as I walk and I encounter many women. Some look like me and emerged from similar situations. Some look like Nancy, with long blonde hair and blue eyes, or like Honor, with fair skin and brown hair. June, Wendy, Inez, Harriet. The Irish bank clerk. The supermarket cashiers. To a black woman, my idea of myself as "dark" is laughable. A jumble of ethnicity appears when I look at this aspect of things: the female self and the female "other." Whether self and others are perceived ethnically, racially or in terms of class difference, the white man's descriptions offer me no mirror for understanding the ways in which "otherness" manifests itself, what tensions it creates, what perceptions it encourages, what it lends to our fantasies and fears about one another.

"Is he Jewish?"

They ask me this over and over as I am growing up, about each boy who telephones or drives up in his father's car. Is he Jewish? Disapprobation rests on layers of fear. This is still an immigrant family, mine, uprooted, ashamed of roots. The question comes from worry about the world, comes more, as I understand it, from concern for my happiness than for the perpetuation of the race, which is its most conventional motivation. We are in a hostile world. We must hold together.

"We" is both family and tribe. The hostile world can, at any moment, send soldiers into an implacable life, test the ingenuity of the grandmother who fed seven on a single potato and remnant soup. Non-Jews are "They," not to be trusted. Because it is a middle-class ghetto by now, the family surrounds itself with other Jews and has no need to teach the children that we must get along with "Them" to make do in the world, but does teach that intimacy is dangerous. In earlier times, those were severe lessons, now omitted, except, of course, to ask if he is Jewish.

When I think of "Them" I see a man. I see a Nazi guard with a flat sadistic face and large feet cased in storm boots holding a rifle at his side. In this fear, I am small, thin, with large dark eyes, very much like Anne Frank, the only image of a Jewish female person that I had in my imagination for most of my life. Jewish girls get locked in attics. Nazis are just outside the door.

I am a dark woman alone in the corner of the room, aware of my darkness and what it means in the culture I have inherited, in the books I read and the films I see. I say the word "Jewess" out loud and it reverberates around the room, accumulating overtones of disdain until it returns to my own ears wrapped in mockery and contempt. I hear the sound of the white male voice.

Now we face the silence. Take away the white man and you remove the pressing masculine need to invent Dark Ladies and Fair Maidens, you remove the motivation and thus the stereotype, but you are left with an eerie silence. Now women have begun to be the recorders. Now there are more women. Now there are stories about mothers and sisters and friends and lovers. Now Mrs. Dalloway thinks excitedly about Sally Seton; the spiritual daughters of Jane Eyre find various women along their solitary, growing travels, women to point the way; the girls in the girls' school have their map-makers and diarists; the community of women sits down at the campsite to tell stories of things that have been and are to come. It is not too simple anymore.

The complexity shows. The direction of attention has been described for those who will attend: I think sometimes . . . often . . . of her. She has this effect on me or that. I love her. I hate her. I learn from her. I avoid her. She and I, the many she's, the many I's, are characters in our stories. Yet there is an arena of experience we have not named or have mentioned in passing and shrunk from.

Let's not talk about it.

Let's not have Ellen say that she knew no Jews in her midwestern town until she came to college and then, there, the boys teased her that she was not as aggressive as the Jewish girls at school and she shrank from it. Let Nancy not say there were no Jews in Fairfield; there was only one black woman at college. Let Honor not tell about being beaten up by a black girl in Jersey City. Let June be silent on the subject and black writers confine themselves to black people and the black community. Let everyone speak of racism but never tell what they have known as a dark woman and a light woman, black and Caucasian, Jew and Christian, eye each other, in a book or an office building, perhaps meet at some crossroads, speak, feel, exist together.

Let me avoid the issue. Let me not say that the school district in which I grew up was changed from year to year so that there were no black hands clutching pens at the desks next to mine. (And the things that were said in my household—shall I write a new saga in which those malicious comments are exorcised?) And life in the university, the first step out of the Jewish ghetto, the rows of white faces, the several black male students, the occasional female, and my own absorption with Jewish-Christian tensions, issues, implications. There were, with the exception of Kafka, no Jews in the curriculum, no women.

Busily, I studied, many of us studied, and never asked about the chasm.

Take away the white man and you are faced with a story that has little precedent, no convention to guide you, an absence so complete you might wish to deny that there is a story there at all. The experts speak of race and class. From much of what they say, from the ways in which consciousness is stirred, some part of the shape of literary things reaches my mind. Sartre speaks of anti-Semite and Jew. Fanon speaks of race. They do not speak of myself and Honor or Nancy, myself and June or Barbara. They speak of male interaction, male ideas, masculine institutions.

Our heritage is a tradition in which light and dark women are at opposite ends of the cosmos. Do we feel ourselves so separate from one another? Our heritage says that the dark woman is sexual, the light woman not. Do we believe this? Our heritage reduces character to physiology. Do we? Our heritage says that our difference is chemical, has to do with essences, is created so by the white man, God, and is forever so. Is this our experience? Is this what we imagine? Our heritage prevents us from imagining, indicating that men will tell us what we need to know of other women. Do we then cease to know or to imagine? Do we leave each other out of our literature? Our heritage insists on the paradigm of domination, that dark must be controlled by light. Do we take this on, turn it upside down and emerge with other forms of domination, urge that light be controlled by dark?

What can women do with the Book of Genesis?

A dark woman and a light woman are alone in a room. Will one send the other for tea? Will one make the other afraid? Will there be an accusation; who will make it? Will they touch or have a meal? Anne Frank meets Nancy Drew. Will they speak of suffering or drive off in a roadster? Aunt Jemima, Mrs. Portnoy, Faulkner's Dilsey and my Yiddishe mama sit on overstuffed chairs, discussing the care and feeding of the young, the number of times to stir the batter, the hot flashes of menopause.

Virginia Woolf wrote so movingly about the electricity between women, the spark of identification, recognition and love that touches one hand, then another, and Colette is stirring when she writes about, when she shows us the process of alliance between women, the bonding, the overcoming of obstacles which is the overcoming of culture. We can live with these visions. The rest is unspeakable. The anger. The betrayal. The obliteration. Things run smoothly if we close our eyes. Pretend that between the black woman who works in the white woman's home and the white woman herself there is harmony. Pretend that the smile on the black woman's face—as white people have always created smiling blacks and smiling women—is genuine.

Let's not talk about it.
Let's pretend it doesn't exist.
There is nothing here to talk about.

Two women are not alone in the room in which they find themselves alone. There are ghosts. There are murmuring voices. The white woman looks at the black woman. Have the voices affected what she sees? Will she tell us if they have? The white woman, for whom the black woman, true to convention, works as the domestic, orders books she does not read, magazines she never opens, clothes she rarely wears and constantly replaces. The black woman looks at the white woman and sees waste, a profligacy bordering on the spiritual. Will she speak? Will she say what she sees? Will either woman address what is between them?

Both the actuality and the mythology of relations between races appear in the literature of the American South, and interestingly enough, the interaction of black and white women is the heart of the story in two of our earliest novels about slavery. *Gone With the Wind* and *Uncle Tom's Cabin* were both written by white women and they set, as they must, black and white women in the fixed relation of slave and mistress. Although Margaret Mitchell's novel perpetuates mythologies of all kinds and Harriet Beecher Stowe's is progressive, both embody the white woman's point of view, show the light looking at the dark.

Women are at home together again, and again the man is far away. Father may run his world benevolently, as Mister O'Hara does in *Gone With the Wind*, or viciously, as Simon Legree does, but run them he does. He buys and sells horses and slaves. He might be mean or he might be desperate. *Uncle Tom's Cabin* begins with Mr. Shelby fallen into debt, forced to sell the slave Eliza's child, which precipitates the action of the novel. The women have different ways of manipulating the man in charge—Scarlett wraps him around her little finger in conventional feminine ways, Mrs. Shelby tries to influence him with decency and purity—but the authority remains his. The arrangements of the larger world, from the torching of Atlanta to the raising of a whip on a naked back to signing the Emancipation Proclamation or fixing the price of cotton, are in his hands.

The house is the woman's domain. Within the house, a familiar enterprise is under way. In *Gone With the Wind*, the daughter of the house is being educated in the ways of femininity and the black women have a large role to play. The relation of dark and light women at home is extremely intimate. Scarlett's mammy fed the white girl from her breast, bathed her, knows her body, dresses her, pulls the laces tight until Scarlett's waist measures no more than seventeen inches, brushes her hair, observes her freckles. In the bodily intimacy of women at home, there is always a black female present in a white woman's life, from Mammy's lacings and dressings to young black Dilcie nursing Melanie's baby. It is commonplace and crucial to arrangements between the races. Ironically, it supports a culture of extreme female "delicacy" about bodily things, a corseted code of behavior based on reticence about the actual female body. Even Scarlett, who begins to free herself from this code, hides under shawls and coverings when she is pregnant. The intimate connection to black women allows delicacy, in relation to all men and to other white women, to bloom into the flower of southern womanhood.

The white girl's coming-of-age novel has as its dramatic focus her acceptance of, accommodation to, or aquiescense in the code of femininity. What does it mean to become a woman? How can a girl make her way in the world of adult life? What is the direction of her freedom and what price is she called on to pay? Will love mean marriage, will marriage mean submission, is loneliness the price of autonomy? What worlds can she conquer; what preparation is needed; what opposition stands against it? These are the issues in the education of a young white girl. These are the turning points in the literature that traces her passage from girlhood to womanhood, that determine whether hers is the story of growth or despair, suicide and suffocation.

The issues in Scarlett O'Hara's life are the same issues in Carson McCullers' *The Member of the Wedding* and *The Heart Is a Lonely Hunter*, in Harper Lee's *To Kill a Mockingbird*. Novels of adolescent white girls set in the South incorporate the figure of a black woman as crucial to the white girl's growth. The black woman is not there because the author is drawn to depicting black life, but because she serves a purpose in the life of the white character.

Black Mammy and White Mother are allied in the task of socializing the young white girl. Mrs. O'Hara, like most mothers in literature, pours water on her daughter's rebelliousness, her boyishness, her lack of decorum. Mammy tries to get Scarlett to have a large meal before she goes to the Wilkes's barbeque because "ladies eat like birds." Mammy shares Mother's ideas, telling Scarlett that a woman who shows appetite, a woman who might eat at the barbeque, acts like a "nigger." She also says, later in the novel, that the ease with which Scarlett gave birth to her child is "just like one of the darkies." Scarlett is being raised to become a fading flower of southern white womanhood. This is someone who trembles in the hurricane wind of real life, of "strong" language, of violations of the code of femininity. Outwardly at least, the fading flower is passive, helpless and deceitful. She is the idea of the Lady raised to the highest degree. Although rhetoric directs us to admire her, she does not fare well as a character in fiction, particularly not where black women stand in contrast to her.

Scarlett's mother comes off better than most white ladies in this literature. She has verve and energy, she is not obsessed with herself, she likes her daughter. Usually, the white mother is the "bad" mother, the withholder, the one without warmth for her daughter. In *Uncle Tom's Cabin*, Little Eva comes home to a couch-ridden, complaining mother, but she, too, has, as a buffer against this rejection, her mammy:

> This woman did not tell her that she made her head ache, but, on the contrary, she hugged her, and laughed, and cried, till her sanity was a thing to be doubted of; and when released from her, Eva flew from one to the another, shaking hands and kissing, in a way that Miss Ophelia afterwards declared fairly turned her stomach.

Although Black Mammy and White Mother have the same job in relation to the white daughter, her reaction to them is different. These are the white girl's stories. Dark and light mothers are seen through her eyes and the dark appears to be much better. Instead of the man in the middle as narrator, we have a young white girl and the terms of the comparison she makes are oddly like his. The dark is flesh, warmth, earthy, while the light is disembodied, desexualized and distant. This triangle, with dark and light on either side, has as its apex the white female narrator, and as its context, not sacred and profane love, but good and bad mothering.

Mammy is the mother from whom a girl can get nurturance but over whom she still has power. Mammy is female flesh that it is possible to touch. Dark flesh is always available to light. From a light woman to a dark, touching is possible, connection is possible. Touch is, too, a gesture of domination and a violation of taboo. In *Uncle Tom's Cabin*, Miss Ophelia is a northern white lady, revolted, as women of her class were meant to be, by physical contact altogether and by contact between black and white flesh on top of that. She shrinks from black Topsy. But Little Eva, the white girl who is a saint, incarnation of everything good, a reproach to the adults around her, manages what neither her mother nor Miss Ophelia can muster. One of the most dramatic moments of the novel occurs when Eva reaches out and touches Topsy.

But Topsy is a child. The flesh of black female characters in literature more often belongs to Mammy, to the dark mother, whose strong, solid, plentiful and available flesh stands in contrast to the bleached, delicate and inhuman flesh of white women. She is not only the ancient Mother-Goddess, the nurturer, giver of life, but the goddess tamed, deprived of her power. The white girl can tell Mammy what to do. Mammy obeys and becomes the "good" Mother. She is invariable and constant. She has no life of her own. In her thick selflessness, she is "something of stability," Scarlett thinks, as she makes her way from a devastated Atlanta to a devastated Tara, "something of the old life that was unchanging."

To Lillian Hellman, her black nurse was "the first and most certain love of my life...was, for me, as for so many other white southern children, the one and certain anchor so needed for the young years, so forgotten after that." Berenice, the cook in *The Member of the Wedding*, is the same flesh, the same thick, secure, mothering flesh. Frankie sits on her lap:

She could feel Berenice's soft big ninnas against
her back, and her soft wide stomach, her warm solid legs.

Breasts. Laps. Legs. Hands. "Incubated in the mystic
pungence of Negro mammies," Zelda Fitzgerald wrote, "the
family hatched into girls." Hatchers. Chickens laying golden
eggs, golden girls with blue eyes. But "mystic" because
somehow the connection is too close, the intimacy and the
passion too impossible to assimilate as a girl moves into adult life,
into culture, into marriage. A man can carry the same childhood
shadow into the world, but there will be an avenue for its
expression. He will crave "dark meat," he will have a white
woman in the house and a black woman in the cabin, he will rape
with impunity. And "pungent." The smell. Us and them. They
smell different from us. While Melanie Wilkes, in *Gone With the
Wind*, lies in excruciating labor giving birth to her child, in
unbearable heat, with flies all over the room and the smell of
Melanie's birth in the air, the smell of Scarlett's sweat, her panic,
her effort, Miss O'Hara still has time to observe that Prissy, in
the corner of the room, has a terrible odor.

The white girl's love and passion for the black woman is
impossible to assimilate, must be rejected. Mammy is, therefore
and after all, made not real. In *Gone With the Wind*, Mammy is
not a person but a collection of fragments. She is a cubist
assemblage, this part, that part, the bosom and the lap, a pair of
arms, a pair of hands. She is rooted to earth, lumbering,
shuffling, puffing. She is an animal. Scarlett observes that
Mammy has "the shrewd eyes of an elephant" or "the
uncomprehending sadness of a monkey's face." Mammy sees
"with the directness of the savage and the child."

Push her away. Dehumanize her. Deny the connection. The
white woman's point of view is ambivalent, a pull toward and
away from the black woman at the same time. In novels where
white girls love their black mammys, they also undercut their
devotion by dehumanizing the black woman. Good feelings on

the part of light toward dark occur in the context of the power that light has over dark. A woman has power to oppress her slaves, but not to free them. White women defy the law to teach black people how to read. Little Eva teaches her mammy. The Grimke sisters taught actual women. Scarlett saves Tara, saves Mammy. White women help Eliza every step of the way in *Uncle Tom's Cabin*, from the woman in a public house who gets her a ferry to the wife of a senator who provides her with clothes for herself and her child. The bonds of motherhood are stronger than the divisions of race, stronger than the law, but it is the white woman who feels these things, is in a position to offer help, which becomes patronage.

To embody the crosscurrents within the context of slavery—the slow spinning out of patronage, devotion, violence, superstition—is the scene in *Gone With the Wind* where Scarlett, now wife, mother, owner of her own business, after the war, is stopped by a Yankee woman on the street in Atlanta and asked how to get a nurse. Scarlett says to stand at the gate and ask "every darky woman who passes——" and she is interrupted by the indignant Yankee:

> "Do you think I'd trust my babies to a black nigger? I want a good Irish girl."

> "I'm afraid you'll find no Irish servants in Atlanta," answered Scarlett, coolness in her voice. "Personally I've never seen a white servant and I shouldn't care to have one in my house."

The white woman says:

> "I wouldn't trust them any farther than I could see them and as for letting them handle my babies..."

And Scarlett thinks of the "kind, gnarled hands of Mammy" of "black hands, how dear and comforting they could be, how unerringly they know how to soothe, to pat, to fondle." It crosses Scarlett's mind that she would like to kill these Yankee women, these "insolent, ignorant, arrogant conquerors."

In white women's literature, black women, if they are present at all, are usually very young or very old. So many mammys. Such affection for the Topsys. All this is distance. "Grandma," "Mammy," "Auntie"—the language of relationship, of family, is made farcical by the actual situation of slavery out of which it comes. It is a code for servitude. The older black woman is meant to take care of the younger white woman—as, in fact, she was. It is the illusion of female care without responsibility. One need not be grateful. One need not respond in kind. One need not love. All that is required—of a good Christian woman—is that she take care of her slaves, not beat them. All that is required is that she give them cast-off clothes and decent enough food. Not respect. Not humanity. Not freedom.

When black women are very young or very old, the white woman is comfortable and the men around her are comfortable. Nothing threatening there. No question—here comes the great danger—seeing the dark and the light as in any way alike. There is no parallel plane. To think of similarity is out of the question.

It is exactly out of the question.

Only now is the question being raised.

If the black woman is very young or very old, she is not a woman. So it goes. This was the accusation made by Sojourner Truth in the nineteenth century addressing a women's rights convention. They were debating votes for women. They spoke of chivalry and how women were meant to be treated, how it was right that they be treated, all the lifting in and out of carriages and that sort of thing. And Sojourner Truth dared to say, being very black: "Ain't I a Woman?"

When the black woman begins to speak in literature, breaking the imposed silence, she is not smiling. She is angry and her anger is directed at white women. Unlike Tituba, who groveled for mercy from the white community, the black woman sees white people—and white women—from a different point of view. The parts become whole, the lap, breast, anchor, sheltering tree of white literature becomes a person, with words and a voice and a different story to tell.

Sometimes, the black man tells the black woman's story. In "Cora Unashamed" by Langston Hughes, Cora Jenkins is a black woman working for a white family. Cora's daughter dies, and she transfers her feelings to Jessie, the white daughter of the house, who surely needs them because the household is, as Hughes says, "careless":

> Nowhere in Melton, not with anyone, did Jessie feel so comfortable as with Cora in the kitchen. She knew her mother looked down on her as a stupid girl. And with her father there was no bond. He was always too busy buying and selling to bother with the kids.

Cora is, like the conventional mammy, "a calm and sheltering tree for Jessie to run to in her troubles," but along comes a trouble that Cora cannot shelter. Jessie gets pregnant by a boy of the "wrong" class—a Greek boy, foreign and dark. The white women say Jessie is "in trouble" and Cora says, "She ain't in trouble neither. No trouble having a baby if you want. I had one." But Cora's values, Cora's language do not, naturally, prevail and Jessie is taken away by the white women of her family, has an abortion, comes home and dies. Cora attends the funeral, where she breaks all the rules. She refuses to submit to hypocrisy and piety. "They killed you," she screams, addressing the coffin, accusing the white women. She leaves the house "forever."

White women in black literature are not only lifeless, but

antilife. The black woman stands outside the rules. Sexuality and paternity have different meanings for her. She is, here and elsewhere, more caring, more human. Like Topsy, who knows neither her parentage nor her age, black women are by convention ignorant of, contemptuous of, or in rebellion against the rules of white civilization. This carries with it implications of savagery and childishness, but also implications of exhilarating freedom. Ambivalent and conflicting readings of this "outsider" role occupy both the makers of the stories and the hearers.

In Ann Petry's novel *The Street,* Lutie Johnson, a black woman, is trying to get off the street, goes to work for white Mrs. Chandler in Connecticut, works in the kitchen, hears the constant anxiety of white women suspicious of and unnerved by the sexual enticement they assume a young black woman to be. The worst of it, for Lutie, is the painful irony that she is paid to give to a white child what she is then unable to give to her own child. Mrs. Chandler is profligate—has magazines she never opens, books ordered and not read, clothes unworn. This arouses Lutie's contempt, but this is endurable. What is not is the vision she has on her street, after work:

> Most of the women had been marketing, for they carried bulging shopping bags. She noticed how heavily they walked on feet that obviously hurt despite the wide cracked shoes they wore. They've been out all day working in the white folks' kitchens, she thought, then they all come home and cook and clean for their own families half the night.

At home, she adds it up, projecting the fate of her son, Bub, and the son of the Chandlers:

> Add it up. Bub, your kid—flashing smile, strong, straight back, sturdy legs, even white teeth, young, round face, smooth skin—he ends up in reform school

because the women work. Go on, she urged. Go all the way. Finish it. And the little Henry Chandlers go to YalePrincetonHarvard and the Bub Johnsons graduate from reform school into DannermoraSingSing.

When the lap and the breast become a speaking, writing woman, the first thing to be said is anger. "Pristine sadism," as Toni Morrison calls it, or blind rage. The saints come tumbling down. In *The Heart Is a Lonely Hunter,* the black idea of angels is a white girl with yellow hair and a white robe. The terms in which the anger takes shape is often aimed at the idea of perfection. Tear the doll to pieces. Dismember perfection. Become as blanket in your disdain as you experience the white world to be toward you. Turn the tables, as Meridian Hill does in Alice Walker's novel, *Meridian,* saying that

there seemed nothing about white women that was enviable. Perhaps one might covet a length of hair, if it swung long and particularly fine. But that was all. And hair was dead matter that continued—only if oiled— to shine.

Imagine as Maya Angelou did:

As far as I knew, white women were never lonely, except in books. White men adored them, Black men desired them and Black women worked for them.

Add it up. It is not often the mother in the kitchen who will write the novel or the play, but her daughter, and she will, like Alice Walker, pay homage to her mother, and she will, like Toni Morrison, tell us the rest of the story. In *The Bluest Eye,* Morrison turns stereotypes inside out. Pecola and two friends drop in on Pecola's mother, Mrs. Breedlove, who is working in the white folks' kitchen. It is a very white kitchen—like the ideal American television kitchen, shining, humming, smelling good. The girl of the house comes in. Against all the little black girls who are not people, Morrison gives this description, drawing a paper doll for her readers:

> She wore a pink sunback dress and pink fluffy bedroom slippers with two bunny ears pointed up from the tips. Her hair was corn yellow and bound in a thick ribbon. When she saw us, fear danced across her face for a second. She looked anxiously around the kitchen.

She calls for "Polly," and the first-name convention applied to her mother infuriates Pecola. Imperiously, the little girl calls again, "Polly, come here," and a deep-dish berry cobbler perched on a counter is pulled to the floor, burning Pecola's legs, causing "Polly" to knock her daughter to the floor, yank and slap her. Her words are "like rotten pieces of apple" and she is torn between attending to "my floor . . . my floor" and stroking "the little pink and yellow girl," for whom her words, unlike rotten apples, are honey.

The little white girl is a nightmare come to life. She is the doll given the narrator earlier in the story. "All the world had agreed that a blue-eyed, yellow-haired, pink-skinned doll was what every girl child treasured." The doll gets dismembered and feelings about it are transferred to white girls, those feelings then transformed in order to get on in the world:

> The best hiding place was love. Thus the conversion from pristine sadism to fabricated hatred, to fraudulent love. It was a small step to Shirley Temple. I learned much later to worship her, just as I learned to delight in cleanliness, knowing, even as I learned, that the change was adjustment without improvement.

At last we meet, the black girl and myself as a girl, in common experience, on common ground, with a common enemy.

Shirley Temple. Blue eyes. Good hair. Pert noses. The Sweetheart of Sigma Chi. Miss America. And the voices that say this is what it means to be pretty and this is what is good and this is a mirror of all your deficiency and only this will do. This is the heroine in the picture show. This is the face on the magazine cover. You must get a man, the swimming pool and the big car. This is what is required.

Fantasies of what it would mean to have blue eyes and blonde hair are derived from humiliation and self-hate. If only I looked "right." If only I looked "white." These are specifically female fantasies of passive power, the power to get as opposed to the power to do. The distorted idea of Cinderella—to walk into the room and turn everyone to stone. The dark girl covered with cinders; the white girl adored. Shirley Temple, who can command. The crooked finger, commanding. The imperiousness, the ability to get people, men especially, to bring you the world on a silver platter. And the attendant self-mutilation, the rituals of girlish life, the pathetic dream that one will wake up in the morning blonde and blue-eyed. Bleaching, Straightening. Heavy aluminum hair curlers. Metallic bobby pins. Straitjacket girdles and other forms of binding the body.

Hair. The endless focus on hair, which, unlike skin, can be managed, changed, arranged, altered. The long blonde tresses of Rapunzel reach down from the window, inspiring awe and envy. To have such hair. The power of such hair. No one darkens her hair, except to cover gray, but many lighten it, down to the caricature of peroxide—the ladies in Miami Beach and their peroxide hair. And the straighteners, from actual irons and ironing boards, common in college life in the 1950s, to the treatments, the pomades and preparations, the chemical, mechanical effort to make hair, at least, pass.

The early sixties. This is one of the most political moments of my life. My black friend Barbara hands me her hair-straightening equipment.

We are in graduate school together, studying Shakespeare. The black movement is gathering force, touching Barbara, touching her friends. The first outward manifestation of what is going on in her mind and heart is a change in clothing, the alteration of appearance, the dropping of the mask. She wears African clothes instead of Saks Fifth Avenue classics. She lets her hair grow natural. And I, still, somewhere, Anne Frank, still the immigrant, still thinking, in spite of my intellectual life, that the fashion magazines pointed the way to the main chance, took Barbara's hair-straightening equipment and put it to good use.

We had Shakespeare and the desire for good grade hair in common. We were both trying to be "white," but Barbara dropped it long before I did. She had once been to the South—she came from Saint Thomas—and been told to go to the back of the bus. She reacted with incredulity. The whole thing was astonishing to her and she did not identify, but she came to do so. We did not talk about it much in the years of our friendship. It was still the period of "color blindness." We listened to Aretha Franklin, swapped clothes and read Elizabethan sonnets.

Then I lost her.

Then the world divided us.

Then the sixties picked up, picked us up and put us down in different places.

She started going out with a black revolutionary and brought him to dinner at my house, where I lived with a white man.

Another dinner party. Another negotiation. Her man and my man, they began to talk. They had between them a common ground called masculine culture. They could touch on this subject or that—sports, politics, the world—without establishing a personal connection. It was not required. They did not like each other, these men, and at least one of them saw the other as his Enemy, but still, they talked.

Her man thought of me as the Enemy, too. I knew that he had told her to rid herself of her white friends, and whether she agreed with him or not, she was about to do so. This was our farewell dinner. I did not know what she was caught up in or how she felt, in what ways her choices made themselves known to her. I played Aretha Franklin records. We did not have the kind of common cultural ground between us that the men had. Without our intimacy, there was little to talk about. I felt paralyzed, unable to name or stop what was happening. She left with him, became more involved in politics, had a child, got a job to support him, and that is all I know of her. I stopped straightening my hair soon after that, but I still have her hot comb in my closet.

America is a shiksa nestling under your arm whispering love love love love.

That is the world according to Portnoy, via Philip Roth. Not for me, it isn't.

Delightful or perplexing though it might be, the experience of having a shiksa in that attitude would send me straightaway and face-to-face with certain kinds of exile. She is not my salvation, nor my ticket to anywhere. She has always been, in literature, but especially in the writing of the men of my tribe, the prize, the valued one, the woman with whom I am meant to compare myself and in whose image I am meant to redo myself. Or was. She came into my life by way of Roth and Saul Bellow. She is onscreen as Grace Kelly, Cybill Shepherd, and Farrah Fawcett. Black people called her Miss Ann. Jews call her The Shiksa. Although the actual world holds within its material boundaries many women of light skin and Christian birth and little change in their pockets, The Shiksa is usually rich. Or her father is.

I am meant to hate her. Everything in literature sets me against her. Folklore and film, high and low culture, Philip Roth and Woody Allen—all, in combination, are serpents on this subject and their hiss goes like this: not only is she good and you bad, but she is a different creature, nothing like you. She has power. You do not, cannot, will not. She is the Holy Grail. Jewish men desire her, wish to attain her, partake of her, acquire her, bathe in her holy light, cleanse and purify themselves in her arms, her bed—if they can win her. But I—I am set forever apart from her.

In *Anti-Semite and Jew,* Sartre has this to say about Jewish women:

> There is in the words "a beautiful Jewess" a very special sexual signification.... This phrase carries an aura of rape and massacre. The "beautiful Jewess" is she whom the Cossacks under the czars dragged by her hair through the streets of her burning village. And the special works which are given over to accounts of flagellation reserve a place of honor for the Jewess.

I look at my grandmother's face. I see exhaustion, self-deprecation and shame. She will not speak of where she has come from, just as Mary McCarthy's Jewish grandmother, described in

Memories of a Catholic Girlhood, waves questions aside: "'All those old things, Mary,' she would say to me half-grumpily. 'Why do you keep asking me all those old things?'" The old things are painful. These people have come here to forget. Exile and pollution. The Jew in history and literature, in the eyes of the anti-Semite and often in the eyes of the Jew, who has taken in the mirror of himself, is a wanderer and the carrier of pollution. The man, wandering, takes on an exceptional role, often becomes prophet or seer because of his situation as "outsider." Attend his words; mark his vision. In *The Heart is a Lonely Hunter,* "Singer is not like other men." He has "the knowledge of one who belongs to a race that is oppressed." Being cast out carries, for men, status, surrounds them with a certain "mystique." But the Jewish woman is not granted such knowledge, status or mystique. She is granted the look of having been raped and dragged through the streets of the village.

And pollution. If the Jew, as Sartre says, carries the taint, is pollution itself, then this is doubled for the Jewish woman, for woman of any ethnicity is seen as polluted, stained, menstrual. She is shut away in a menstrual hut. She is not allowed out of doors in a state of pregnancy. Her childbirthing takes place, like breast-feeding, like everything that is a reminder of the existence of her body, where it cannot be seen or spoken of.

An internalized sense of pollution leads to compulsive cleaning by stock Jewish female characters in serious and popular literature. The woman scrubs, empties ashtrays—it has become cliché. It is not only the frenzied activity of a woman with no outlet, not only a desire to please the man who values her qualities as housekeeper—but a heartbreaking attempt to claw away the idea of pollution. The essence of Jewish female ritual is the *mikva*—the purification of the menstruating female.

I ask my grandmother about the *mikva*. She says let's not talk about it.

In *The Merchant of Venice,* there are two young women, Jessica, the Jew, Shylock's daughter, and Portia, the Gentile, the woman who belongs in the world enough to have mastered its most intricate aspects, especially the art of rhetoric that enables her to confound the Jew and win for her own lover Shylock's famous ducats. About Jessica we see very little, except that she is loved by a Christian and will do anything to marry him. She has no mother—no mother is mentioned—she is the daughter of her father, like so many other women in literature, and this adds to her exile, her uprootedness, somehow cast out of the line of human generation, as dark Topsy was. Jessica, because her lover is friend to Portia's lover, goes to Portia's house to await the outcome of the "plot," Portia's humiliation of Shylock. The women are in the same room, occupy the same space for several scenes in the play, but nothing passes between them. All we hear of Jessica is her desire, addressed to Lorenzo, to "become a Christian and thy loving wife."

Jessica wants to lighten up. She will assure herself a place in the cosmos by her conversion and avoid the insult she has seen heaped on her father, avoid his defensiveness and belligerence, eliminate the stigma. I know this. Jessica will not talk about it. Portia takes no notice. The daughter of the Jewish merchant and the daughter of the nobleman alone in a room have in common their desire to marry the men they love. That is enough.

Elsewhere, the stereotypes of dark and light become the cliches of Jewish and Christian women. From Rebecca in *Ivanhoe* to Miriam in *The Marble Faun* to Durrell's Justine to Thomas Wolfe's "fertile, yolky, fruitful" females, the Jewish woman is the forbidden fruit for the Christian male author. She is the exile par excellence and the Christian attitude toward her is a heightened example of the dark/light tradition. Ambivalence is intensified, she is appealing and forbidden and confounding, for the question of "discovery" is added to the equation, since one can never be quite sure. The profound sexual attraction between white male citizen and female "exotic" plays out most fully with respect to the Jewess. So, too, does the desire to control, contain, to be the light overcoming the darkness—which accounts for the persistent rape of Jewish women in literature and the emphasis on their degradation that Sartre points out as recurrent in pornography.

If the Jew represents exile, by history and tradition, the Jewish woman represents double exile. She most heartily does not belong at the white man's table, although she might visit his bed. The Jewish man may wander, but exile, in the woman, results not in movement, since women do not move, but in profound alienation and victimization. The Jewess in Christian literature is exile turned in on itself, a woman yearning for home and roots who can only find it in the arms of a man, conscious of her victimization, reacting not with anger nor prophecy, as men do, but docility, humiliation and submission. She is extremely in need of being "saved."

Jewish men abuse the Jewish woman on the page, make her the smothering mother, make her "otherness" a source of embarrassment, an umbilical cord that binds them backward, as they see it, keeps them from being born into mainstream American life:

> I doted on the short up-turned gentile nose and imagined myself the singular victim of nature in having a mother with a nose that was a social misfortune.

So the Jewish woman may take the blame for the anxiety and deficiency of Jewish men, be constantly reprimanded by the example of the Gentile woman and told myths about her.

The pattern of ambivalence for the male author takes the form of a story constructed around sexual choice—the blonde or the dark, the Gentile or the Jew, turning her into wife or mistress as symbols of his connection to either one, going between them, torn. Sexual competition becomes the only form of relationship and in this historical pattern it is not actually relationship, not interaction, not one-on-one, but detached mythologizing.

Hemingway turned the blonde Christian woman into a destroyer of men, giving her all the attributes of the dark lady. Anita Loos worked the same scheme of things: *Gentlemen Prefer Blondes . . . But Gentlemen Marry Brunettes*. American literature is full of bad blondes, but to play changes on the stereotypes is still to retain the idea of immutable opposition, to keep dark/light, Jewish/Christian women at opposite ends of the cosmos.

We have no plot in which, as Jewish or Christian women, to set our experience of and feelings about one another. When women come to write the story, we often have followed the same footsteps, worked the same patterns. George Eliot's *Daniel Deronda* has a man in the middle—the title character—and Gwendolyn Harleth on one side, a beautiful woman who *belongs,* is obsessed with herself, marries for the security that money represents, and Mirah Lapidoth on the other side, a waif whom Deronda drags from the river as she is about to kill herself, a supplicant, apologetic exile. Gwendolyn is displaced, unhappy, emotionally adrift, but Mirah is forlorn and dependent. Each in her own way wants Deronda to save her and in the end he chooses Mirah because he has discovered that he, too, is a Jew.

Gwendolyn, like many of Jane Austen's characters, is one of those women whose life begins when a man walks into the drawing room. Left alone in the company of women, Eliot says, she "had a sense of empty benches." And Eliot tells us why:

> Mrs. Vulcany once remarked that Miss Harleth was too fond of the gentlemen; but we know that she was not in the least fond of them—she was only fond of their homage—and women did not give her homage.

She is not only fond of that homage but, true to type as a light lady, imagines that she is entitled to it. She has been brought up with that sense of entitlement and her culture sits beside tradition in encouraging her to feel so. The light is entitled to a place, to homage, to happiness. Blondes have more fun. The dark, on the other hand, is entitled to nothing, must struggle, must overcome. When Mirah is dragged from the river, she "confesses" to Daniel that she is a "Jewess" and asks:

> "Do you despise me for it?" she said presently in low
> tones, which had a sadness that pierced like a cry from
> a small dumb creature in fear.

The dark addresses the light. Lacking entitlement, the dark can only say:

> "I want nothing; I can wait; because I hope and believe
> and am grateful—oh, so grateful! You have not
> thought evil of me—you have not despised me."

Because the plot hinges of separateness, there is little interaction between Gwendolyn and Mirah, yet there is some. Gwendolyn comes to investigate whether or not Mirah might be a rival. She, contemptuous and patronizing, for Mirah is entirely deferential and self-effacing, dismisses her. Mirah thinks Gwendolyn a duchess, admires her. Although they have a man in common, they have nothing in common.

Laurie Colwin does a shade of the same thing in *Happy All the Time,* where Misty, a Jewish woman married to a Christian, relatively at home in his world, with his friends, yet sometimes prey to what her friends describe as the look of "the only Jew at the dinner table," encounters a latter-day Gwendolyn Harleth, named, appropriately, Gem. Gem is what we call on my street "horsey" and is, to Misty, the kind of woman her husband, Vincent, belongs with:

> Gem stood for a part of Vincent that was not second nature to Misty—the part that was sporty and larky and on cheerful terms with the world, the part that had grown up sailing and fishing. Suppose Vincent got tired of someone who was not second nature to him?

Her jealousy is based on mythology and the real Gem turns out to be a scatterbrain who gets seasick on the fishing trip that Misty, in self-pity, has withdrawn from and let Vincent go off on. Everything ends well. The man tells his woman what the "other" woman is like and the woman is relieved.

Honor says that Jewish women are more intelligent and erotic, looks with longing at the ways she perceives Jewish women able to integrate, she says, being attractive women and being brilliant. This she says was prevented, made more difficult among her people. Nancy looks to the little-girlness of her Fairfield background, the repression in WASP women, sees Jewish women freer of it.

There is envy in this talk.

I look at Honor and Nancy and when I do not see *them,* I see simply "the *Wasp* Woman" at home in the world, the culture. I see privilege, removal of the need to struggle, an absence of self-hate and the presence of assuredness.

We clash, coming to each other with our mythologies and the different meanings of our actual experience. Honor sees the house of her grandmother, the large house with its gardens and its servants, struck. Bulldozers churn up the gardens; the house is made into condominiums. She sees the crumbling of her grandmother's house and life, her own past, her connection to solidity, torn apart. Resisting sympathy, not understanding the terms, I become Anne Frank, wiped out in concentration camps. The granddaughter of an immigrant who has no standing heritage to lose, no house to be torn down, no disappeared ease, only the silver candlesticks of my grandmother's wedding to concretize heritage. I cannot understand her pain; she cannot understand my lack of understanding.

There is envy in my distance.

My aunt says that when a Jewish man went out with a Christian woman, he did so "for only one thing." This is the contempt of the Jewish women in the ghetto who watched their men run after *shiksas*; this contempt is born of fear and vulnerability. In it we have all the contradictions of my own adolescence. I tell her this is a reversal of historical archetypes. She is amazed.

Is there nothing to be said except whether a woman's legs are open or closed? Has she nothing about her except her womb?

Here is something. There is no man here. I come to the chicken soup. My heritage, full of people who felt themselves in constant danger, devolved, exactly as the clichés of culture and the stand-up comics say, on chicken soup. To be ill elicited such fluttering and attending from the women of the family, far more than to win a Phi Beta Kappa key, far better than anything. Sickness was not a thing to turn your back on. Women responded. Chicken soup. Here is one kind of entitlement. And so, having shed little of this, I am taken with a cold and it does not occur to Nancy, for example, to bring chicken soup. I not only wish she would, but, in a tantrum, expect her to. She, on the other hand, grew up with and is imbued with the ethos of stiff upper lips and, when ill, does not call out for chicken soup. Stiff upper lips never acknowledge the need for help. A sense of community willing to spring to one's aid, particularly female community and, granted, only certain kinds of aid, stands behind my experience. It becomes, in the places I have come from, a religion; complaint replaces action; the intense sharing among females is a circle of chairs devoted to victimization. Where Nancy comes from, women drink alone behind closed doors. We have only begun to know these things about each other. The poles have only begun to cross.

Denying that distinctions between black and white are chemical means stepping outside civilization. Departing from the fixity of Genesis and patterns of plot in romance and cowboy movies means beginning to imagine a different vision for which there is little common language. Say that neither darkness nor lightness carries with it anything of essence, that the attributes dark and light women have collected through history do not, in fact, describe the way people are or the way the world is. A new possibility arises, a new way of seeing this old dichotomy. Imagine the idea of construction. The dark/light distinction has been made, not given. Thinking of it as a constructed alienation allows you to look at the nuts and bolts, make an analysis, see how it works. If the oppositions of dark and light are made and not given, constructed and not chemical or theological, they can be seen differently and changed.

Tillie Olsen does this in a story called "O Yes." White Carol and black Parialee are Topsy and Eva grown to teen-agers, set down in modern American life. They have had "synchronized understanding" between them, but it has begun to fall away. Estrangement sets in. Understanding what kind and how it has happened is the process of the story.

Carol goes to Parialee's baptismal ceremony at church, where she is overcome. Stamping. Moaning. Stomping. Screams. Shrieks. Humming waves—and Carol faints, or "is drowned under the sluice of the slow singing and the sway." This is her own baptism. The power of darkness. Carol tries to control it and herself, but the power is overwhelmingly attractive and inspires fear and terror in her. Alva, Parialee's mother, explains: "You not used to people letting go that way. . . . You not used to hearing what people keeps inside." Everyone older than Carol—Alva, Carol's mother, Helen, her father, her older sister—they all try to think, to understand what happens, to explain to Carol what they cannot explain to themselves. The older sister calls it "sorting." Girls with good reps from girls with bad reps. Rich girls from poor girls. Black girls from white girls. It happens. Parialee and Carol are sorted. It is high school; teachers and kids, says Carol, "don't like Parry when they don't even know what she's like. Just because . . ."

The unfinished sentence. A story full of the unfinished sentence. Who can explain? It happens. Life goes this way. "Why is it like this?" We are in the mind of Carol's mother. "And why do I have to care?"

It is not chemical, it is made. Sorted. This girl from that girl. Olsen conveys the stifled understanding of how things are made, how understanding pops up and retreats, becomes simply "how the world is," cannot be expressed. The girls are going their separate ways. They have put aside their dolls. This is the grown-up world. This is how it is. And there is the pain of being sorted, which is Carol's pain, the erosion of her friendship. The pain of seeing it happen, knowing what it is, is the mother's pain, who watches and knows and finds it hard to speak.

They loved each other.
They were lost to each other.
Why is it like this?
Why do I have to care?

Another story. In Cynthia Ozick's "The Suitcase," a Christian wife and a Jewish mistress are at a gallery opening.

The father of the man whose opening it is attends. When he speaks, when he looks and when he thinks, he separates the women, he smacks his lips over the idea of the Jewish mistress, thinks about the son's bed. He sees things in the old way: Genevieve, the Jewish woman, as sensuous; Catherine, the Christian wife, as frigid:

> Catherine, though socially and financially Somebody, was surely—at sex—a Nobody. Her little waist was undoubtedly charming, her stretched-forward neck (perhaps she was near-sighted and didn't realize it?) was fragrant with hygiene. Her whole body was exceptionally mannerly, even the puppet-motion of her immaculate thighs under her white dress.

We are back in the world of Whitebread. But this is the father's perception. Behind it, something else is happening. The wife passes by with her arm "slung through the arm of Gotfried's mistress." The women have a connection. The father goes on, describing the Jewish woman:

> A superior woman. . . . A superior race. I've always thought that. Imaginative. They say Corbusier is a secret Jew, descended from Marranos. A beautiful complexion, beautiful eyelashes. These women have compulsions. When they turn up a blonde type you can almost take them for our own.

And the undercurrent between the women goes on, their connection. It is not the Christian wife who says these things. An emergency appears—the wife has to lend the mistress money, is concerned:

> Can you still make the twelve o'clock plane, Gen?— because look, if you can't you can easily stay overnight with us, why don't you, that nice room's all ready.

They are not at opposite ends of the cosmos.

The narrator observes that when Catherine says something, "It sounded exactly like a phrase of Genevieve's."

Women writers have begun to deny the idea of chemistry and look to the idea of construction, to examine the nuts and bolts. What sets us at opposite corners of the cosmos? Shall we accept the idea of chemistry and become the wizards of our own laboratories? Shall we try different compounds? Shall we pour Genesis into a beaker and spill it back and forth at our own discretion, time it to the beats of our own hearts? Or might we become Alice, all of us, Alice at the point of coming to consciousness, looking around at Wonderland, laughing and saying you are nothing but a pack of cards? The Medusa laughs. The Mona Lisa smiles.

I am sitting at a table in an empty room at the moment between daylight and darkness, having come to the end of the journey. I survey the books on my table, which have become companions along the way, and I touch the talismans there that have done the same. The pearl and onyx hairbrush and mirror left to me by my grandmother. I comb. I comb. My hair changes from a mass of snakes like Medusa's to the locks of a princess in a fairy tale to Topsy's pigtails. I rub Priscilla's tigereye ring on my left hand, my aunt's gold chain around my neck.

I summon no genie, but the spirit of Virginia Woolf, as Woolf called up the spirit of Shakespeare's imagined sister. "It is half a century later," I tell her, "and I am not surprised, as you were, to read how one woman liked another in a novel. There are many Chloes liking many Olivias in the books on my table. Our world is larger, our stories more complex. "Cinderella" does not stand for the whole of experience or the only possibility. We are not all like Gwendolyn Harleth in the company of other women with a sense of empty benches.

The benches fill. Nancy sits down to read these pages. Ellen organizes the footnotes. Blanche discusses history while Honor and Inez point to unsolved mysteries. Elizabeth writes in a coffee shop and Priscilla is thinking over a meal. Ilyse, now two years old, is told that this book is for her, that she might know more of what the whole of human experience has been and can be. We pull the benches up to a table set for tea. I pour. Cinderella smiles. Scarlett laughs and Colette leans on her elbow with something very important to say.

NOTES

The notes that follow cite sources for quotations in the text and describe the intellectual background for my thinking on the subject. Each section begins with a bibliographical essay followed by sources of quotations, in order of their appearance in the chapter. Page numbers on the left indicate where the quotation appears in the text.

INTRODUCTION
Two Women Are Alone in a Room

2 Virginia Woolf, *A Room of One's Own* (New York: Harcourt, Brace and World, Harbinger Books, 1957), pp. 86–87.

4 Amanda Haight, *Anna Akhmatova: A Poetic Pilgrimage* (New York: Oxford University Press, 1976), pp. 108–9.

8 Jane Austen, *Pride and Prejudice* (New York: W. W. Norton & Co., 1966), p. 234.

9 Charlotte Brontë, *Jane Eyre* (Middlesex: Penguin Books, 1966), pp. 204–5. George Eliot, *Daniel Deronda* (Middlesex: Penguin Books, 1967), p. 150.
   On links between women writers, influences and affinities both literary and historical, the groundbreaking books on the subject are Elaine Showalter, *A Literature of Their Own* (Princeton: Princeton University Press, 1977), and Ellen Moers, *Literary Women* (New York: Doubleday & Co., 1976).

10 Janet Flanner, *Paris Was Yesterday* (New York: Viking Press, 1972), p. 177.

11 Virginia Woolf, *Mrs. Dalloway* (New York: Harcourt, Brace and World, Harvest/HBJ, 1953), p. 50.

12 Colette, *The Other One (La Seconde)*, trans. Elizabeth Tait and Roger Senhouse (New York: Signet, 1960), pp. 140–41.

14 Carson McCullers, *The Member of the Wedding* (New York: Bantam Books, 1977), p. 113.

1

CINDERELLA
Saturday Afternoon at the Movies

I have used the most available texts of both Perrault's and the Grimm's versions of the story. Perrault's "Cinderella or the Little Glass Slipper" is in *The Blue Fairy Book,* edited by Andrew Lang (New York: Airmont Publishing Company, 1969). There is a graceful translation, along with a nice foreword, in *The Fairy Tales of Charles Perrault,* trans. Angela Carter (New York: Avon Books, 1979). My edition of *Grimm's Fairy Tales* was published by Grosset & Dunlap in 1976.

The sources for the Eastern origins of Cinderella are the compendium made by Marian R. Cox, *Cinderella: Three Hundred and Forty-five Variants* (London: David Nutt, 1893); Arthur Waley's article, "Chinese Cinderella Story," in *Folklore* 58 (1947); and a monograph by Nai Tung Ting, *The Cinderella Cycle in China and Indo-China* (Helsinki: Academia Scietarum Fennica, 1974). Howard Levy has written the only book-length study of foot-binding, *Chinese Foot-Binding: The History of a Curious Erotic Custom* (New York: W. Rawls, 1966), and Andrea Dworkin wrote a powerful interpretation of the custom in *Woman Hating: A Radical Look at Sexuality* (New York: E. P. Dutton, 1976). William A. Rossi has a section on "Oriental Pedoerotomania," in *The Sex Life of the Foot and Shoe* (New York: Ballantine Books, 1978), pp. 32–51.

The literature of interpretation of fairy tales is vast, particularly among Jungians. I would urge anyone interested in pursuing this subject to read the work of Marie-Louise von Franz, especially *The Feminine in Fairy Tales* (Zurich: Spring Publications, 1972). The connection between Cinderella's hearth and the Roman goddess Vesta is made by Harold Bayley in *The Lost Language of Symbolism,* vol. I (London: Williams and Norgate, 1912), written rather long ago but one of the few commentaries that refrain from discoursing on "femininity," which many others feel compelled to do.

The obvious source of some of the information about "Cinderella" is Bruno Bettelheim, *The Uses of Enchantment: The Meaning and Importance of Fairy Tales* (New York: Random House, Vintage Books, 1977). My interpretations of that information, equally obviously, differ from his. I would urge attention to actual social arrangements in the societies out of which these stories came—that having a stepmother, for example, would have been common in a world where many women died young in childbirth and husbands remarried many times. Bettelheim sees no specifically "female" elements in the story. ("Sibling" means, in his book, either brothers or brothers and sisters, not simply sisters.) His "relative lack of interest in women's development" was pointed out by Janet Horowitz Murray, *New Boston Review* III, no. 3 (December 1977): 18. For the kind of discussion a resolute Freudian would disdain, see Marcia Lieberman, "Some Day My Prince Will Come: Female Acculturation Through the Fairy Tale," *College English* (December 1972): 383–95.

18 Anne Sexton, "Cinderella," in *Transformations* (Boston: Houghton Mifflin Company, 1971), p. 55.

Jacob and Wilhelm Grimm, "Cinderella," in *Folk-Lore and Fable,* vol. XVII of *The Harvard Classics,* ed. Charles W. Eliot (New York: P. F. Collier & Son [n.d.]), p. 103.

2
MOTHERS AND DAUGHTERS
Blood, Blood and Love

We come to a terrain that has begun to be mapped.

It would have been impossible to see the material in this chapter without three extraordinary books: Adrienne Rich's *Of Woman Born* (New York: W. W. Norton & Co., 1976); Nancy Chodorow's *The Reproduction of Mothering* (Berkeley: University of California Press, 1978); and Dorothy Dinnerstein's *The Mermaid and the Minotaur* (New York: Harper & Row, 1976). To understand more about who becomes the storyteller and who doesn't, see also Tillie Olsen, *Silences* (New York: Delacorte Press, 1978).

Mothers and daughters now appear with more frequency than before in popular literature and magazines as a subject for inquiry among scholars—particularly biographers—and as material for serious fiction, drama and poetry. Among the many novels that focus on mother–daughter relationships written in our time are E. M. Broner, *Her Mothers* (New York: Holt, Rinehart and Winston, 1975); Rosellen Brown, *The Autobiography of My Mother* (New York: Doubleday & Co., 1976); Lisa Alther, *Kinflicks* (New York: Alfred A. Knopf, 1976); and Margaret Drabble, *Jerusalem the Golden* (New York: Popular Library, 1977). Two interesting plays on the subject are Jane Bowles' "In the Summer House," in *My Sister's Hand in Mine: The Collected Works of Jane Bowles* (New York: Ecco Press, 1978), about two generations of mothers and daughters, and Honor Moore's "Mourning Pictures," in *The New Women's Theatre* (New York: Random House, Vintage Books, 1977), on the theme of a mother's death, a theme that is becoming archetypal for women writers. There are many more literary works about mothers and daughters, some in print, some in the typewriter.

In literary criticism, there is Jane Lilienfeld, "Deceptiveness of Beauty: Mother Love and Mother Hate in *To the Lighthouse,*" *Twentieth Century Literature* 23 (October 1977): 345–76, and Judith Kegan Gardiner, "A Wake for Mother: The Maternal Deathbed in Women's Fiction," *Feminist Studies* 4, no. II (June 1978): 146–65. That entire issue of *Feminist Studies* is devoted to motherhood. The recent publication of *The Lost Tradition: Mothers and Daughters in Literature,* ed. Cathy N. Davison and E. M. Broner (New York: Frederick Ungar Publishing Co., 1980), will, hopefully, further discussion on the subject, for the book covers a great deal of ground and is immensely provocative.

40 *Sister of the Road: The Autobiography of Box-Car Bertha,* as told to Dr. Ben L. Reitman (New York: Harper Colophon Books, 1975), pp. 28–29.

44 Virginia Woolf, "A Sketch of the Past," in *Moments of Being,* ed. Jeanne Schulkind (New York: Harcourt Brace Jovanovich, 1976), p. 87.

45 Sylvia Plath, *Letters Home,* ed. Aurelia Schober Plath (New York: Harper & Row, 1975):

"Both my babies..." p. 12.
"At the end..." p. 13.
"The children..." p. 25.

Liv Ullmann, *Changing* (New York: Alfred A. Knopf, 1976), p. 124.
The first thing Ullmann says in this book is that when she was born, the nurse whispered "apologetically" to her mother, "I'm afraid it's a girl. Would you prefer to inform your husband yourself?"

46 Tillie Olsen, "I Stand Here Ironing," in *Tell Me a Riddle* (New York: Delta Books, 1961), p. 12.

50 There is no solid biography of Mary Lamb. The facts of her life in this chapter are drawn from Ernest Ross, *The Ordeal of Bridget Elia: A Chronicle of the Lambs* (Tulsa: University of Oklahoma Press, 1940), and Katharine Anthony, *The Lambs: A Story of Pre-Victorian England* (New York: Alfred A. Knopf, 1945). The Anthony is more vivid, more sympathetic. The best modern scholarship on the Lambs appears in the three-volume edition of *The Letters of Charles and Mary Lamb,* ed. Edwin W. Marrs, Jr. (Ithaca: Cornell University Press, 1975–78), which includes Charles' description of the murder of his mother, of Mary's subsequent mental states, along with her letters to her lifelong friend, Sarah Stoddart, whose own life was eventually spent nursing an ailing mother.

Quoted in Anthony, *The Lambs: A Story of Pre-Victorian England,* p. 40.

53 R. D. Laing and A. Esterton, *Sanity, Madness and the Family* (Middlesex: Penguin Books, 1964), p. 41. Laing, who develops his idea of "social intelligibility" so clearly in this book, does not describe the recurrence of mother-daughter violence in the cases he studies and therefore does not apply the "social intelligibility" concept to it, that is, does not analyze mother-daughter relations, as he does so many other aspects of family life, politically.

54 Toni Morrison, *Sula* (New York: Bantam Books, 1975), p. 65.

55 Morrison, *Sula,* p. 67.

57 Robert and Jane Coles, *Women of Crisis* (New York: Delacorte Press, 1978), p. 30.

58 Nancy Cunard, "Black Man and White Ladyship" (1931), reprinted in *Nancy Cunard: Brave Poet, Indomitable Rebel,* ed. Hugh Ford (Philadelphia: Chilton Book Company, 1968), pp. 103–9.

59 Woolf's "Angel in the House" appears in her essay, "Professions for Women," in *The Death of the Moth and Other Essays* (New York: Harcourt Brace Jovanovich, Harvest/HBJ, 1974), p. 237. The remark about her obsession with her mother—and the termination of that obsession with the writing of *To the Lighthouse*—is in "Sketch of the Past," in *Moments of Being,* p. 80.

Virginia Woolf, "Sketch of the Past," in *Moments of Being,* p. 87.

60 Plath, *Letters Home:*
"My ever-growing wish..."; "It never occurred to me..." p. 5.
"I yielded..." p. 10.

61 Plath, *Letters Home:*
"During the first year..." p. 13.
"My husband outlined..." p. 12.
"All the schoolboys..." p. 230.

62 Nancy Hunter Steiner, *A Closer Look at Ariel* (New York: Fawcett Books, Popular Library, 1973), pp. 99, 100, 102.

65 "I did not learn..." I have taken Colette's words from the collection compiled by Robert Phelps, *Earthly Paradise* (New York: Farrar, Straus & Giroux, 1966) *(En Pays connu,* p. 32).

"Madame Thomazeau is a harpy..." and "I never thought..." Phelps, *Earthly Paradise (Sido,* pp. 33, 12).

66 "If the newspapers..." and "No half-grown males..." Phelps, *Earthly Paradise (Sido,* pp. 10, 35).

68 "I am the daughter..." Phelps, *Earthly Paradise (Naissance du Jour,* p. 23).

70 *Letter to a Child Never Born,* trans. John Shepley (New York: Simon & Schuster, 1976), pp. 15–16.

3

SISTERS
Sometimes I Feel Like a Sisterless Child

Three sets of actual sisters form the nucleus of this chapter: Angelina and Sarah Grimké; Charlotte, Anne and Emily Brontë; Virginia Stephen Woolf and Vanessa Stephen Bell. There are, of course, many more sister relationships in history, particularly among women writers, that would have been interesting to look at, among them Jane Austen and her sister Cassandra. The problem is, here as elsewhere, obliterated information. Much has been destroyed. Cassandra Austen burned her sister's letters. There is, usually, only one side of the story to work with, as in the case of Virginia Woolf, where the diaries, letters and her writing allow some interpretation of how Woolf saw her relationship with her sister, but little record of Vanessa Bell's side of it. One-sidedness aside, these are the general sources for the biographical information in the chapter.

Although there is information about the Grimkés scattered through most histories of the abolition and women's rights movements and in the biographies of other women whose lives crossed theirs, the single substantial work is Gerda Lerner's *The Grimké Sisters from South Carolina* (New York: Schocken Books, 1971). I am grateful to Gerda Lerner for her work in women's history and for providing the text of Sarah Grimké's dream. For a discussion of relationships between black and white women in the nineteenth century, including the Grimké sisters' relationship with Sarah Douglass, a black woman active in the abolition movement, see Lerner's article, "Black and White Women in Interaction and Confrontation," *Prospects: An Annual of American Cultural Studies II* (1976): 193–208.

Original sources for the Brontë sisters' lives are the early edition of their letters—Clement Shorter, *The Brontës: Life and Letters*, 2 vols. (New York: Haskell House Publishers, 1969)—and Mrs. Gaskell's classic, which is itself a study in female relationships, *The Life of Charlotte Brontë,* vol. VII of *The Life and Works of Charlotte Brontë and Her Sisters* (London: Smith, Elder & Company, 1900). There is a modern edition of the Brontë letters, mostly Charlotte's, excellently edited and introduced by Muriel Spark: *The Brontë Letters* (London: Macmillan & Co., 1966). Among the books on the Brontës' life and work written in our own time, I have found the following especially helpful: Margot Peters, *Unquiet Soul: A Biography of Charlotte Brontë* (New York: Doubleday & Co., 1975); Winifred Gérin, *Anne Brontë* (London: Allen Lane, 1978); *Charlotte Brontë* (Oxford: Clarendon Press, 1968); and *Emily Brontë* (Oxford: Clarendon Press, 1971); and Helene Moglen, *Charlotte Brontë: The Self Conceived* (New York: W. W. Norton & Co., 1976). Of all the articles about the Brontës, two shed light on the sister relationship. Edward Chitham's "Almost Like Twins," *Brontë Society Transactions* 16, no. 5 (1975): 365–73, is about Emily and Anne. Margaret Drabble spoke interestingly about the Brontës and, not incidentally, about literary sisters, which includes herself, in "The Writer as Recluse: The Theme of Solitude in the Works of the Brontës," *Brontë Society Transactions* 14, no. 4 (1974): 259–69. It would be interesting to analyze Drabble's relationship with her writer-sister A. S. Byatt and the appearance of sisters in the novels of each of them.

Virginia Woolf's diaries, letters and hitherto unpublished autobiographical writing are now in print. They provide the best source for Virginia's relationship with Vanessa. I have used the two published volumes of *The Diary of Virginia Woolf,* ed. Anne Olivier Bell (New York: Harcourt Brace Jovanovich, 1977, 1978), and five volumes of *The Letters of Virginia Woolf,* ed. Nigel Nicolson and Joanne Trautmann (New York: Harcourt Brace Jovanovich, 1975–79), as well as *Moments of Being,* ed. Jeanne Schulkind (New York: Harcourt Brace Jovanovich, 1976), and several biographies: Quentin Bell, *Virginia Woolf: A Biography* (London: Hogarth Press, 1972); Roger Poole, *The Unknown Virginia Woolf* (Cambridge: Cambridge University Press, 1978); and Phyllis Rose, *Woman of Letters* (New York: Oxford University Press, 1978). There is relevant material in S. P. Rosenbaum, *The Bloomsbury Group: A Collection of Memoirs, Commentary and Criticism* (Toronto: University of Toronto Press, 1975).

74 Brontë, quoted in Shorter, *Life and Letters,* vol. I, p. 315.

Woolf, *The Letters of Virginia Woolf,* vol. II, p. 109.

Stein, *Everybody's Autobiography* (London: Heineman, 1938), p. 115.

77 Gaskell, *The Life and Works of Charlotte Brontë and Her Sisters,* p. 97.

81 Marie-Louise von Franz, *The Feminine in Fairy Tales,* rev. ed. (Zurich: Spring Books, 1976), p. 85.

85 The dream is recorded in Sarah Grimké's diary, a portion of which appears in Lerner, *The Grimké Sisters from South Carolina,* pp. 63–64.

Lerner, *The Grimké Sisters,* p. 78.

89 Katherine Mansfield, "The Daughters of the Late Colonel," in *The Garden Party and Other Stories* (Middlesex: Penguin Books, 1951), p. 118. The story is often anthologized.

90 "Camp Cataract," in *My Sister's Hand in Mine: The Collected Works of Jane Bowles* (New York: Ecco Press, 1978), p. 360.

91 Bowles, "Camp Cataract," pp. 363, 396.

93 Woolf, "A Sketch of the Past," in *Moments of Being,* pp. 92, 98.

94 Woolf, in *Moments of Being,* p. 98.

95 "I like Nessa very much..." *Letters of Virginia Woolf,* vol. I, p. 53.

"While I had lain in bed..." Woolf, in *Moments of Being,* p. 162.

97 In *The Bloomsbury Group,* ed. S. P. Rosenbaum. The essay is on pp. 169–73; the quotation here is on p. 171.

100 The quotations are from Woolf's letters to Violet Dickinson in January 1907. *Letters of Virginia Woolf,* vol. I, pp. 275–76.

101 Shorter, *Life and Letters,* vol. II, p. 15.

102 Jane Austen, "The Three Sisters," in *Love and Friendship and Other Early Works* (London: Women's Press, 1978), p. 104.

103 Letters between Virginia Woolf and Clive Bell written at this time are in *Letters of Virginia Woolf,* vol. I:
"Kiss my old Tawny..." p. 357.
"Whisper into your wife's ear..." p. 362.
"Why don't you come to lunch..." p. 334.

104 Clive Bell's letter about *The Voyage Out* is published as an appendix in Quentin Bell's biography of Woolf, vol. I, p. 209.

4
FRIENDS
Perpendicularity

In this chapter, too, the diaries and letters of Virginia Woolf have been not merely useful but indispensable. Without the actual evidence, the myth that Woolf did not get along with Mansfield would live on; likewise, without the new information on Mansfield in print. For the discussion of Woolf, I have relied on the primary sources in diaries and letters already mentioned and on the work of several Woolf scholars who began some time ago to investigate Woolf's relationships with women and to see these as essential to her development. I am grateful to Ellen Hawkes for her help in seeing the subject this way and for her inspiration about understanding Woolf altogether. Her essay, "The Magical Garden of Women: Virginia Woolf's Literary Sisters and Women Friends," appears in the forthcoming *New Feminist Essays on Virginia Woolf,* ed. Jane Marcus (London: Macmillan, 1980). Her article "The Virgin in the Bell Biography," *Twentieth Century Literature* 20, no. 2 (April 1974): 96–113, is essential reading on the subject, as is the work of Jane Marcus, particularly "Art and Anger," *Feminist Studies* 4, no. 1 (February 1978): 69–98. This essay is about Woolf's friendship with yet another relatively "unknown" (to us) woman, Elizabeth Robins.

Mansfield's life has been treated with a great deal of coyness for a long time. John Middleton Murry omitted many of her letters when he made his collection, considering them "too painful" for publication. Antony Alpers, whose biography of Mansfield was for many years the most substantial one in print, has recently revised that book, admitting how heavily censored the first edition was, adding information that makes my speculations in this chapter possible. (Antony Alpers, *Katherine Mansfield: A Biography* [New York: Alfred A. Knopf, 1953], and *The Life of Katherine Mansfield* [New York: Viking Press, 1980].) Fifteen letters from Mansfield to Woolf were published in the *Adam International Review,* nos. 370–75 (1972–73). Ida Constance Baker, Mansfield's longtime intimate friend, wrote a memoir under her pseudonym: *Katherine Mansfield: The Memories of L.M.* (London: Michael Joseph, 1971). Mansfield's reviews of Woolf's novels appear in *Novels and Novelists,* ed. John Middleton Murry (New York: Alfred A. Knopf, 1930). Many scholars have written about the literary relationship between the fiction of Woolf and Mansfield. One of the most interesting of these is Ann L. McLaughlin, "The Same Job: The Shared Writing Aims of Katherine Mansfield and Virginia Woolf," *Modern Fiction Studies* 24, no. 3 (Autumn 1978): 369–82.

On relationships among American women in the nineteenth-century struggle for women's rights, there is some very good work, beginning with Alice Rossi's analysis, "A Feminist Friendship: Elizabeth Cady Stanton and Susan B. Anthony," in *The Feminist Papers,* ed. Alice B. Rossi (New York: Columbia University Press, 1973; Bantam Books, 1974), pp. 378–96. Stanton's own writing provides a gold mine on the subject: *Eighty Years and More: Reminiscences, 1815–1897* (New York: Schocken Books, 1971) and the second volume of her collected papers, letters and diary, edited by Theodore Stanton and Harriet Stanton Blatch (New York: Arno Press, 1969). Naturally, the lives of all the women in this period who were activists cross and intersect and the biographies of each of them give hints of their relationships with each other. Katharine Anthony's *Susan B. Anthony: Her Personal History and Her Era* (New York: Doubleday & Co., 1954) gives a good account of the Stanton-Anthony friendship. On Lucy Stone and Antoinette Brown, there is less material in print. (Elinor Rice Hays, *Morning Star: A Biography of Lucy Stone* [New York: Harcourt, Brace and World, 1961]; Alice Stone Blackwell, *Lucy Stone: Pioneer of Women's Rights* [Boston: Little, Brown, 1930].) The standard histories of the period are good beginnings and there is a wealth of material in the Schlesinger Archives at Radcliffe College, particularly on the Blackwell family.

Two "classic" essays on nineteenth-century women's friendships, both with theoretical frameworks that take them beyond any particular period and provoke me to look at the subject more broadly are Carroll Smith-Rosenberg, "The Female World of Love and Ritual: Relations Between Women in Nineteenth-Century America," *Signs* 1, no. 1: 1–29, and Nancy Cott, "Sisterhood," in *The Bonds of Womanhood: "Woman's Sphere" in New England, 1780–1835* (New Haven: Yale University Press paperback, 1977), pp. 177–96. Useful and interesting in similar ways is the current scholarship about female "networks," a process of uncovering connections between women and the support offered by such connections in the past.

12 *Sappho,* trans. Mary Bernard (Berkeley: University of California Press, 1958), p. 85.

Stanton to Anthony: see Alice Rossi, ed. *The Feminist Papers* (New York: Bantam Books, 1974), p. 389.

Mansfield to Woolf: *The Letters of Katherine Mansfield,* ed. John Middleton Murry (New York: Alfred A. Knopf, 1936), p. 68.

Toni Morrison, *Sula* (New York: Bantam Books, 1975), p. 149.

117 Sir Francis Bacon, "On Friendship," *Essays, Advancement of Learning, New Atlantis, and Other Pieces* (New York: Odyssey Press, 1937), p. 78. The entire essay is on pp. 75–82.

118 Ralph Waldo Emerson, "Friendship," *Essays* (New York: Thomas Y. Crowell, 1951), pp. 137–56.

120 *Sappho,* p. 17.

122 Jeremy Taylor, *A Discourse of Friendship* (1657), intro. William H. Powers (Cedar Rapids, Iowa, 1913). The passages about possible friendship with women are on pp. 72–73.

123 Katherine Philips' poems were originally published in 1667. Selections can be found in *The World Split Open,* ed. Louise Bernikow (New York: Vintage Books, 1974).

124 *Letters from Orinda to Poliarchus,* 2d ed. (London: Bernard Lintot, 1729), p. 39.

126 Leonard Woolf observed the most exclusive masculinity at Garsington. "The only distinguished women whom I ever saw at Garsington were Margot [Asquith], Katherine Mansfield and Virginia; but there were always a galaxy of male stars, from ancient red giants like Yeats to new white dwarfs from Balliol" (*Beginning Again* [New York: Harcourt, Brace and World, 1963], p. 202). Leonard Woolf's comment, in this same volume of his autobiography, about Mansfield and Middleton Murry is worth noting: "There was an atmosphere about them then of what I can only describe as the literary underworld, what our ancestors called Grub Street" (p. 203).

Woolf wrote to Lytton Strachey in July 1916: "Katherine Mansfield has dogged my steps for three years—I'm always on the point of meeting her, or of reading her stories, and I have never managed to do either." Trautmann and Nicolson note that "Lytton had just met her at Garsington, where she spoke enthusiastically of *The Voyage Out* and told him that she wanted to meet Virginia." *The Letters of Virginia Woolf,* ed. Nigel Nicolson and Joanne Trautmann (New York: Harcourt Brace Jovanovich, 1975–79), vol. II, p. 107.

127 The information about Mansfield's "crushes" is documented in the revised biography by Antony Alpers. Mansfield's remarks about Wilde are quoted on p. 91: "In New Zealand Wilde acted so strongly and terribly upon me that I was constantly subject to exactly the same fits of madness as those which caused his ruin and his mental decay."

130 "My God, I love..." *Adam International Review,* p. 19.

131 Roger Poole analyzes Woolf's situation about and attitude toward "childless-ness" in *The Unknown Virginia Woolf.*

132 "The poems *look* delightful..." *Adam International Review,* p. 19.

133 "I think what an abrupt precipice..." and "I find it much easier..." *The Diary of Virginia Woolf,* ed. Anne Olivier Bell, vol. I (New York: Harcourt Brace Jovanovich, 1975–79), p. 265.

135 Gertrude Stein, *The Making of Americans* (New York: Harcourt, Brace and World, 1962), p. 282.

136 "We have the same job..." August 1917. Mansfield adds: "Don't let THEM ever persuade you that I spend any of my precious time swapping hats or committing adultery." *The Letters of Katherine Mansfield,* pp. 71–72.

"Smells like a civet cat..." This is an entry in Woolf's diary, dated 11 October 1917: "We could both wish that one's first impression of KM was not that she stinks like a—well civet cat that had taken to street walking. In truth, I'm a little shocked by her commonness at first sight; lines so hard & cheap. However, when this diminishes she is so intelligent and inscrutable that she repays friendship..." *Diary of Virginia Woolf,* vol. I, p. 58.

137 "If you do come..." *The Letters of Katherine Mansfield,* p. 164.

Mansfield wrote to Ottoline Morrell on July 21, 1918, that she had just heard of her mother's death and on July 25 wrote again thanking Ottoline for her condolences. On August 14, she responded to Dorothy Brett's letter of sympathy. The letter to Virginia Woolf on this subject was written in July.

138 "She's done for." Woolf wrote this in her diary, August 1918, vol. I, p. 179. She went on to write of no longer having "faith" in Mansfield and of her "callousness." The entry ends: "I'm relieved now that they didn't come. Or is it absurd to read all this criticism of her personally into a story?"

139 Woolf's diary entry is in vol. II, p. 226.

142 Stanton's remarks to Anthony and Stone are quoted in Katharine Anthony's biography, p. 121.

Antoinette Brown to Lucy Stone: "My heart has just been called back..." is from a letter written in 1848 in the Schlesinger Archives. "If Florence were either settled..." is from the same source, written in 1878. This is one of the more interesting and least documented relationships among the women of the period. Brown and Stone married into the Blackwell family; Elizabeth Blackwell was the first woman doctor and Brown and Stone each married one of her brothers. When Lucy Stone was planning her wedding to Henry Blackwell, she wanted Brown to perform the ceremony and wrote to her:

"We want to harden your heart enough to help in so cruel an operation as putting Lucy Stone to death." Hays, p. 125. Alice Rossi wrote about Brown and Stone in her chapter on "The Blackwell Clan," in *The Feminist Papers*.

145 Stevie Smith, *The Holiday* (London: Virago Press, 1979), p. 28.

146 Simone de Beauvoir, *Memoirs of a Dutiful Daughter,* trans. James Kirkup (1959 [in English]; New York: Harper & Row, 1974), pp. 112, 113, 119.

Morrison, *Sula,* pp. 44, 85.

148 Lillian Hellman, "Julia," *Pentimento* (Boston: Little, Brown, 1973), pp. 101–47. It is interesting that Hellman's Julia is very much like De Beauvoir's Zaza, both admired by their friends for "boyishness" and audacity.

149 On Anne Hutchinson and Mary Ðyer, there is a good amount of information in *Notable American Women 1607–1950* (Cambridge: Harvard University Press, Belknap Press, 1971), pp. 536–37; in Emery Battis, *Saints and Sectaries* (Chapel Hill: University of North Carolina Press, 1962)—the church scene is described on p. 247—and in Lyle Koehler, "The Case of the American Jezebels: Anne Hutchinson and Female Agitation During the Years of Antinomian Turmoil," *The William and Mary Quarterly,* 3d series, vol. 31 (1974): 55–78.

5
LOVERS
Paris in the Twenties

Many of the women in this chapter have been written about, but literary histories of the period do not usually focus on connections between them, ignoring the significance of a lesbian literature and culture. Janet Flanner's *Paris Was Yesterday* is an exception, including as it does portraits of the women written about here.

On the literature of women loving women, there are significant general books: Jeanette Foster, *Sex Variant Women in Literature* (London: Frederic Muller, 1958); Delores Klaich, *Woman + Woman: Attitudes Toward Lesbianism* (New York: Simon & Schuster, 1974); and Jane Rule, *Lesbian Images* (New York: Doubleday & Co., 1975). Research into the lesbian past is a phenomenon of recent scholarship in history and literature. For understanding the issues involved, all of Adrienne Rich's writing is crucial, especially the poems in *The Dream of a Common Language* (New York: W. W. Norton & Co., 1978), and the essays in *On Lies, Secrets and Silence: Selected Prose 1966–1978* (New York: W. W. Norton & Co., 1979). A landmark essay is the paper delivered by Bertha Harris at the Modern Language Association forum on "The Homosexual in Literature" in 1974, a revision of which appeared as

"Notes toward Defining the Nature of Lesbian Literature," *Heresies* 1, no. 3 (Fall 1977): 5–8. As this book was being completed, a brilliant article appeared, surveying the literature discussed here and more, including references to the essential creative and critical work on the subject: Blanche Cook, "Women Alone Stir My Imagination: Lesbianism and the Cultural Tradition," *Signs* 4, no. 4 (Summer 1979): 718–39.

Natalie Barney has been the subject of two recent biographies by men, and both contain useful information, although it is to be expected that the work women are now doing on her life and writing will see the material in different ways: George Wickes, *The Amazon of Letters: The Life and Loves of Natalie Barney* (New York: G. P. Putnam's Sons, 1976), and Jean Chalon, *Portrait of a Seductress: The World of Natalie Barney,* trans. Carol Barko (New York: Crown Publishers, 1979). There is a collection of tributes to Barney and excerpts from her writing in *Adam International Review* 29 (1962).

Yale University Press has been publishing Gertrude Stein's lesser-known work. Janet Flanner wrote a foreword to *Two: Gertrude Stein and Her Brother and Other Early Portraits* (New Haven, 1951), and Natalie Barney did the same for *As Fine as Melanctha* (New York: Arno Press, 1954). Stein's biography was written by Janet Hobhouse: *Everybody Who Was Anybody: A Biography of Gertrude Stein* (New York: G. P. Putnam's Sons, 1975), and one of Alice Toklas by Linda Simon: *The Biography of Alice Toklas* (New York: Doubleday & Co., 1977). Additional source material is in Richard Bridgman, *Gertrude Stein in Pieces* (New York: Oxford University Press, 1970); Samuel Steward, *Dear Sammy: Letters from Gertrude Stein and Alice B. Toklas* (Boston: Houghton Mifflin Company, 1977); Edward Burns edited Toklas's letters: *Staying On Alone* (New York: Liveright, 1973). Among the useful articles on Stein's work in the context of this chapter are "Cynthia Secor, Alice and Gertrude," *Female Studies VI: Closer to the Ground: Women's Classes, Criticism, Programs* (Old Westbury, New York: Feminist Press, 1972), pp. 150–51; Catherine Stimpson, "The Mind, the Body and Gertrude Stein," *Critical Inquiry* (Spring 1977): 489–506; Lynn Z. Bloom, "Gertrude Is Alice Is Everybody: Innovation and Point of View in Gertrude Stein's Autobiographies," *Twentieth Century Literature* (Spring 1978): 81–93; Elizabeth Fifer, "Is Flesh Advisable? The Interior Theater of Gertrude Stein," *Signs* 4, no. 3 (Spring 1979): 472-83.

For information about Romaine Brooks, there is Meryle Secrest's *Between Me and Life: A Biography of Romaine Brooks* (New York: Doubleday & Co., 1974). On Radclyffe Hall, a hateful biography exists, written by the director of her publishing house, Loval Dickinson, *Radclyffe Hall at the Well of Loneliness: A Sapphic Chronicle* (New York: Charles Scribner's Sons, 1975). He considers his subject "pathological" and thinks that women who love women are minor-league men. The biography written by Lady Una Troubridge, who spent most of her life with Hall, has recently been reissued: *The Life of Radclyffe Hall* (New York: Arno Press, 1975).

Colette's portrait of Renée Vivien is in *The Pure and the Impure,* trans. Herma Briffault (New York: Farrar, Straus & Giroux, 1966), pp. 79–98. *The Pure and the Impure* is a collection of Colette's writing about sexuality and includes glimpses of the Parisian lesbian culture. "Night Without Sleep" (*"La Nuit Blanche"*), about herself and "Missy," was first published in *Les Vrilles de la Vigne* (1908) and appears in *Earthly Paradise* (New York: Farrar, Straus & Giroux, 1966), pp. 164–68. The picture of Missy in *The Pure and the Impure* is quite different.

H.D. never wrote an autobiography, but there are indications of her relationship with Bryher in her *Tribute to Freud* (New York: McGraw-Hill, 1974). Bryher's autobiographical works are *The Heart to Artemis* (New York: Harcourt, Brace and World, 1962) and *The Day of Mars, 1940–1946* (New York: Harcourt Brace Jovanovich, 1972). Barbara Guest is at work on a biography of H.D. that ought to make up for the extraordinary oblivion into which the poet and the work have fallen.

Virginia Woolf remains the best source of information about her relationship with Vita Sackville-West, along with the observations of Sackville-West's son and publication of her diary in Nigel Nicolson's *Portrait of a Marriage* (New York: Atheneum, 1973; Bantam Books, 1974). The second volume of Woolf's diary covers this period, and the letters written to Sackville-West and others are in the third volume of her letters. Joanne Trautmann has an interesting article, "The Jessamy Brides: The Friendship of Virginia Woolf and Vita Sackville-West." *Pennsylvania State University Studies,* no. 36 (1973).

156 Stein, *The Making of Americans* (New York: Harcourt Brace and World, 1962), p. 396

Barney, quoted in *Adam International Review*, p. 63
Woolf, *The Letters of Virginia Woolf,* ed. Nigel Nicolson and Joanne Trautmann (New York: Harcourt Brace Jovanovich, 1975–79), vol. III, p. 352.

Colette, *"La Nuit Blanche,"* *Earthly Paradise,* pp. 167–68.

160 Virginia Woolf, *Orlando: A Biography* (1928; New York: Harcourt Brace Jovanovich, Harvest/HBJ, 1956), pp. 193–94.

163 Colette, in *Earthly Paradise,* p. 164.

165 Bryher, *The Heart to Artemis,* pp. 186–87.

166 Preface to Stein's *As Fine as Melanctha* (New Haven: Yale University Press, 1954), p. vii. Barney says, also, that Stein was "still envying her knights errant: Thornton Wilder, Scott Fitzgerald, Hemingway, Carl van Vechten, Bernard Fay, Max White, etc., for being initiated and able to spin, undazed, around her circles."

167 Sigmund Freud, "The Psychogenesis of a Case of Homosexuality in a Woman" (1920), *Collected Papers,* vol. II (New York: Basic Books, 1959), pp. 202–31. In this essay Freud takes great pains to distinguish between "gender identity" and "object choice." That he does so has been lost on many of his critics and on his followers, especially Helene Deutsch. See her "Homosexuality in Women," *International Journal of Psycho-Analysis* XIV (1933): 34–57.

Bryher, *The Heart to Artemis,* p. 201.

169 "an apparition..." *The Diary of Virginia Woolf,* ed. Anne Olivier Bell (New York: Harcourt Brace Jovanovich, 1975–79), vol. II, p. 255.

"Could you come..." *Letters of Virginia Woolf,* vol. III, p. 128.

170 "Stag like or race horse like..." and "All these ancestors..." *Diary of Virginia Woolf,* vol. II, p. 306.

171 *Letters of Virginia Woolf,* vol. III, p. 155. The letter is written to Jacques Ravenal. "Much preferring my own sex..." is also written to him, a month later. *Letters,* vol. II, p. 164.

172 "Yet she could not resist..." Woolf, *Mrs. Dalloway* (New York: Harcourt, Brace and World, Harvest/HBJ, 1953), pp. 46–47.

"It was a sudden revelation..." Woolf, *Mrs. Dalloway,* p. 47.

173 "The strange thing..." Woolf, *Mrs. Dalloway,* p. 50.

174 "Why do I think of you..." *Letters of Virginia Woolf,* vol. III, p. 352.

"I'd like three days..." *Letters of Virginia Woolf,* vol. III, p. 390.

"I like your energy..." *Letters of Virginia Woolf,* vol. III, p. 412.

"If I saw you..." *Letters of Virginia Woolf,* vol. III, p. 443.

"I feel like a moth..." *Letters of Virginia Woolf,* vol. III, p. 469.

175 "What clothes..." *Letters of Virginia Woolf,* vol. III, p. 531.

The conversation with Strachey is reported in a letter to Vita, *Letters of Virginia Woolf,* vol. III, p. 352.

177 Letters to Quentin Bell and Ottoline Morrell, *Letters of Virginia Woolf,* vol. III, p. 556.

180 *The Autobiography of William Carlos Williams* (1948; New York: New Directions, 1967), p. 229.

For E. M. Forster's part in the protest and details about the Bloomsbury reaction, see P. N. Furbank, *E. M. Forster: A Life,* vol. II (London: Secker and Warburg, 1977–78), pp. 153–55.

183 "I hold the conviction..." quoted in Nicolson's *Portrait of a Marriage* (New York: Bantam Books, 1974), p. 110.

185 Colette, from "My Friend Valentine," in *The Other Woman: A Short Novel and Stories* (New York: Signet, 1975), p. 125.

186 Virginia Woolf, "Slater's Pins Have No Points," in *A Haunted House and Other Short Stories* (New York: Harcourt, Brace and World, Harvest/HBJ, 1972), p. 111. In a letter written in 1927, Woolf notes: "Sixty pounds just received from America for my little Sapphist story of which the Editor has not seen the point, though he's been looking for it in the Adirondacks." *Letters,* vol. III, p. 431.

187 Colette, in *Earthly Paradise,* pp. 167–68.

188 Gertrude Stein, *Everybody's Autobiography* (New York: Random House, 1973), quoted in Linda Simon, *The Biography of Alice Toklas* (New York: Doubleday & Co., 1977), p. 209.

189 Virginia Woolf, *Three Guineas* (New York: Harcourt, Brace and World, 1966), p. 53.

6
CONFLICT
Off with Her Head

Antonia Fraser's biography *Mary, Queen of Scots* (New York: Delacorte Press, 1969) is a reliable source of information, as is J. E. Neale's *Queen Elizabeth I,* reprint ed. (London: Jonathan Cape, 1971). Edith Sitwell wrote a bizarre book about the Queens: *The Queens and the Hive* (London: Macmillan & Co., 1962; Penguin Books, 1966). Elizabeth Tudor's letters were edited by G. B. Harrison (London: Cassell, 1968), and Mary Stuart's by Agnes Strickland (London: Henry Colburn, 1948). Some letters are reprinted in *Letters of Queen Elizabeth and King James of Scotland* (London: Camden Society, 1849), pp. 42–49.

194 Plutarch, quoted in Jane Harrison, *Prolegomena to the Study of Greek Religion* (New York: Arno Press, 1975), p. 136.

Euripides, *Andromache,* act 2, lines 174–75.

Charlotte Brontë, *Villette* (New York: E. P. Dutton, Everyman's Library, 1957), p. 407.

201 Strickland, *Letters of Mary, Queen of Scots,* p. 70.

202 Strickland, *Letters of Mary, Queen of Scots,* p. 149.

203 Elizabeth's poem is in *The World Split Open,* ed. Louise Bernikow (New York: Vintage Books, 1974), pp. 51–52.

205 Jane Harrison, *Prolegomena to the Study of Greek Religion.* See especially the chapter "The Making of a Goddess," pp. 257–321.

206 These are Ovid's versions in the *Metamorphoses.*

208 Charlotte Brontë's letters to M. Heger are quoted in Margot Peters, *Unquiet Soul: A Biography of Charlotte Brontë* (New York: Doubleday & Co., 1975), pp. 150–54, 167–69.

210 Brontë, *Villette,* p. 407.

211 Brontë, *Villette,* pp. 64, 104.

213 This is a translation by L. R. Lind, in *Ten Greek Plays* (Cambridge, Mass.: Riverside Press, 1957), lines 26–32.

214 *Andromache,* lines 116–17, 899–904, 384–86.

215 Colette, *The Other One,* trans. Elizabeth Tait and Roger Senhouse (New York: Signet, 1960):
    "All the virgin strength..." p. 114.
    "This old Clara..." p. 112.

216 Colette, *The Other One,* p. 127.
    Colette, *The Other One,* p. 141.

218 Djuna Barnes, *Nightwood* (New York: New Directions, 1961), p. 143.

221 Jane Austen, *Persuasion* (New York: New American Library, 1964), p. 31.

222 Austen, *Persuasion,* p. 152.

223 Austen, *Persuasion,* p. 232.

7

THE LIGHT AND THE DARK
White Women Are Never Lonely
Black Women Always Smile

Leslie Fiedler wrote provocatively about the Fair Maiden and the Dark Lady as a literary theme in *Love and Death in the American Novel,* rev. ed. (New York: Stein & Day, 1966). His point of view, the subject of his book, is what these figures mean to men. He is brilliant on the subject, as he is on the homoerotic content of relations between white men and black men in American novels. In *The Jew in the American Novel* (Herzl Institute Pamphlet no. 10, New York, 1959), Fiedler raises many of the issues discussed in this chapter, again, as is his intention, from the point of view of male writers.

Relations between black women and white women are, as I say, little discussed from a female point of view. One of the only essays on the subject in print is Adrienne Rich's "Disloyal to Civilization: Feminism, Racism, Gynephobia," originally published in *Chrysalis* magazine and reprinted in *On Lies, Secrets and Silence* (New York: W. W. Norton & Co., 1979), pp. 275–310.

In her study of Canadian literature, *Survival: A Thematic Guide to Canadian Literature* (Toronto: Anansi, 1971), Margaret Atwood discusses a pattern similar to the one discussed here, translated into slightly different cultural terms, in her chapter "Ice Women vs. Earth Mothers," pp. 195–212.

Two other relevant articles are Constance Fulmer's "Contrasting Pairs of Heroines in George Eliot's Fiction," *Studies in the Novel* 6 (Fall 1974): 288–94, and Livia E. Bitton's "The Jewess as a Fictional Sex Symbol," *Bucknell Review* 21, no. 1 (Spring 1973): 63–83.

226 Zelda Fitzgerald, *Save Me the Waltz* (Carbondale: Southern Illinois University Press, 1967), p. 85.

Thomas Wolfe, *The Web and the Rock,* quoted in Bitton's article, "The Jewess as a Fictional Sex Symbol," p. 85.

Alice Walker, *Meridian* (New York: Pocket Books, 1977), p. 107.

230 *Antony and Cleopatra,* act 1, sc. 2, lines 138–45.

232 George Eliot, *Daniel Deronda* (Middlesex: Penguin Books, 1966), p. 171.

234 Virginia Woolf, *A Room of One's Own* (New York: Harcourt, Brace and World, Harbinger Books, 1957), p. 50.

235 Isabelle Eberhardt, *The Oblivion Seekers,* trans. Paul Bowles (San Francisco: City Lights Books, 1975), p. 68.

236 *The Journals of Dorothy Wordsworth,* ed. E. de Selincourt, vol. II (Reprint ed., Hamden: Archon Books, 1970), pp. 9–10.

Margaret Fuller, quoted in Belle Gale Chevigny, *The Woman and the Myth: Margaret Fuller's Life and Writings* (New York: Feminist Press, 1976), p. 436.

244 Harriet Beecher Stowe, *Uncle Tom's Cabin* (New York: Signet, 1966), p. 181.

245 Lillian Hellman, *An Unfinished Woman* (Boston: Little, Brown, 1969), p. 14.

243 Carson McCullers, *The Member of the Wedding* (New York: Bantam Books, 1977), p. 113.

Fitzgerald, *Save Me the Waltz,* p. 5.

247 Margaret Mitchell, *Gone With the Wind* (New York: Macmillan Co., 1936), p. 671.

249 "Cora Unashamed," from *The Ways of White Folks,* in *The Langston Hughes Reader* (New York: George Braziller, 1958), p. 7.

250 Ann Petry, *The Street* (Boston: Houghton Mifflin, 1964), p. 33.

Petry, *The Street,* pp. 388-89.

251 Walker, *Meridian,* p. 109.

Maya Angelou, *Swingin' and Singin' and Gettin' Merry Like Christmas* (New York: Random House, 1976), p. 6.

252 Toni Morrison, *The Bluest Eye* (New York: Pocket Books, 1972), pp. 86, 22.

256 Jean Paul Sartre, *Anti-Semite and Jew,* trans. George J. Becker (New York: Schocken Books, 1965), pp. 48–49.

259 "I doted on the short..." from Edward Dahlberg's autobiography, *Because I Was Flesh* (New York: New Directions, 1964), quoted in the excellent *The Jewish Woman in America* by Charlotte Baum, Paula Hyman, Sonya Michel (New York: Dial Press, 1976), p. 225.

260 "Mrs. Vulcany..." Eliot, *Daniel Deronda,* p. 150.

261 "Do you despise me..." Eliot, *Daniel Deronda,* p. 234.

"I want nothing..." Eliot, *Daniel Deronda,* p. 251.

262 Laurie Colwin, *Happy All the Time* (New York: Alfred A. Knopf, 1978; Pocket Books, 1979), p. 210.

264 Tillie Olsen, "O Yes," in *Tell Me a Riddle* (New York: Delta Books, 1961), 39–62.

266 Cynthia Ozick, "The Suitcase," in *The Pagan Rabbi and Other Stories* (New York: Schocken Books, 1976), pp. 103–27:

"Though socially and financially..." p. 108.

INDEX